Maximizir
Your Mini Farm

Maximizing Your Mini Farm

Self-Sufficiency on ¼ Acre

Brett L. Markham

Skyhorse Publishing

Skyhorse Publishing books may be purchased in bulk at special discounts for sales promotion, corporate gifts, fund-raising, or educational purposes. Special editions can also be created to specifications. For details, contact the Special Sales Department, Skyhorse Publishing, 307 West 36th Street, 11th Floor, New York, NY 10018 or info@skyhorsepublishing.com.

Skyhorse® and Skyhorse Publishing® are registered trademarks of Skyhorse Publishing, Inc.®, a Delaware corporation.

Visit our website at www.skyhorsepublishing.com.

10 9 8 7 6 5

Library of Congress Cataloging-in-Publication Data is available on file.

ISBN: 978-1-61608-610-7

Printed in China

Acknowledgments and Dedication

It all starts with the people who read *Mini Farming: Self-Sufficiency on ¼ Acre*. Some folks who read it sent me questions asking for clarification of information I had included in the book. Others sent me questions about the specifics of growing particular crops. Some readers asked if I had any ideas for improving efficiency further, and still others asked if I had considered writing about topics such as making wine. Taken in aggregate, all of this input led me to the conclusion I needed to write another book, and I started preparing an outline that detailed what I would like to include.

Meanwhile, a lot of people read the book – more people than I had imagined given that the subject matter seems somewhat off the beaten path. So many people bought and read the book that my editor asked if I would be interested in writing another!

I once saw a sign in a man's office that stated: "Luck is what happens when preparation meets opportunity." My readers had already inspired the preparation, Jennifer McCartney at Skyhorse Publishing provided the opportunity, and this book was born.

Both preparation and opportunity were needed, so I gratefully acknowledge the support of both my readers and my publisher without whom this book would not exist.

But there is another element to preparation that I would like to acknowledge: three teachers.

Being a gifted child isn't all its cracked up to be, especially if instead of being well-off like Doogie Howser, your family belongs to that class commonly called "the working poor" in a rural area of Southwestern Virginia. Even though our country prides itself on equality of opportunity, the reality is that the opportunities for enrichment that exist for the children of doctors and lawyers are far greater than for the children of men who weld or drive trucks. There is often even a mindset among teachers whose expectations follow along socio-economic stereotypes rather than looking at the child individually and seeing what is really there.

My academic life really started in fifth grade with the advocacy of Miss Gwen Johnson who pulled out all the stops to get me the widest exposure possible. She made sure I had trips to major historic sites for cultural enrichment, was properly challenged, and had unlimited access to all the books my heart could desire on any subject. She made sure I had membership in the Science Explorers of Roanoke Valley and numerous other opportunities for enrichment. Miss Johnson, who I forgive for breaking my heart by becoming Mrs. Canaday, did more for me in less than a year than all of my prior education combined.

Mrs. Yola Lambert is a teacher of enormous accomplishment. She came from Barbados to teach Latin to English-speaking students in the Shenandoah Valley. She taught me Latin for four years and made special accommodations for my education when I was the only student taking Latin IV. Though I didn't realize it at the time, her instruction in things like the subjunctive tense, translating Cicero's orations against Catiline and the Aeneid of Virgil enhanced all of my other education and my understanding of language generally. When she introduced me to the Junior Classical League, she introduced me to all manner of ideas in realms as diverse as culture and engineering that continue to enhance my knowledge and life.

Ms. Sheila Brockmeyer went out of her way to advocate for me in high school, and she secured my access to self-directed and free-form study of everything under the sun that interested me at my own pace. Under her sponsorship I was able to study topics not officially offered as classes, including religions, philosophy and even relativity. Although it isn't always obvious, I still pull from that knowledge base today. In addition, even though she was a single mother whose time was precious, she served as our debate coach and dedicated many of her weekends to a debate team that helped me refine my logic skills and ability to research a variety of topics.

So this book is lovingly and thankfully dedicated to three teachers who advocated on my behalf and whose subsequent influence in my life, albeit indirect, has been positive and pervasive: Mrs. Gwen Canaday, Mrs. Yola Lambert and Ms. Sheila Brockmeyer.

Contents

Foreword

Whenever you visit a small town in New England, you will inevitably encounter buildings with storefronts on the first floor and apartments on the second floor. At one time, the first floor was the shop of a black-smith, seamstress, pharmacist or attorney while the second floor was living space. If you look in the backyard, you might still see evidence of extensive gardens. The home was not just a home—it was also a center of production for essentials needed by both the family and neighbors. In other words, the home paid for itself because it had been turned into an income-producing asset.

This was also the case with farmers. If you drive a little farther out of town, you'll find homes that were obviously farms at one time, with barns attached to the dwelling through a covered breezeway. The home and the farm were extensions of each other in the countryside, just like the smithy and the home were extensions of each other in town.

Over time, as we have shifted from each person owning his or her own means of production to being employees who supply only labor, our approach to our dwellings has changed. In purely economic terms, the average suburban house is an expense more than anything else.

Though at certain times the value of property has appreciated, this is far from a guaranteed outcome, as the millions of Americans who now owe the bank more than their house is worth can attest.

All of our economic production occurs someplace else and a portion of that outside production is used to pay for the house. The house is now used as a place to sleep and watch TV, or maybe invite some friends over for a barbecue. On average, it is owned (though I use that term very loosely) for five years before being turned over to someone else as a place to sleep. Economically, it is more akin to an expensive hotel than the homes of our not-so-distant ancestors.

When I first explained to a friend why it is important to reverse that trend by mini-farming, he stated that because he had a good-paying job, it was more economically efficient for him to buy his cucumbers at the supermarket for a dollar than to waste his valuable time growing them. There are a lot of errors in his reasoning.

The first error is that the cucumbers you can buy at the supermarket for a dollar have been impregnated with a systemic neonicotinoid insecticide to cope with cucumber beetles. The idea of insecticides that become part of the flesh of a crop is even scarier than the insecticides you are able to wash off. If he wants a cucumber free of insecticides like that, he's going to have to spend five dollars, not just one dollar. When you start including tomatoes, zucchini and Swiss chard in that equation—that is, if you want to eat foods that have superior nutrition and fewer pesticides—it's going to cost a pretty penny.

The second error is the false assumption that he would be exchanging time at his valuable job for time spent growing cucumbers. The average adult American spends four and a half hours daily watching television.[1] The time he would be using to grow cucumbers wouldn't take time away from his job, but would rather take away time from television. No doubt, a great deal of television content is fascinating, entertaining and enlightening, but time spent in front of the television also correlates highly to weight gain[2] and other health problems.[3] Time that is taken from television to be spent on mini-farming is likely a very healthy choice that would pay long-term dividends in good health. If he got his kids involved, it would even reduce their risk of developing ADHD.[4]

But his most important error, in my opinion, is his reliance on his job. Though there are some people whose jobs are truly secure, that is by far the exception rather than the rule. And even in secure jobs, wages have been failing to keep pace with inflation for a decade.

When I first put my fingers to the keyboard to write *Mini Farming: Self Sufficiency on ¼ Acre*, it was the spring of 2006. Gas cost $2.20/ gallon in my area. As I write this in the summer of 2011, gas is $3.87/gallon. That's an increase of 76 percent. The price of home heating oil has increased by a like amount in the past five years. In March of 2006, the Dow Jones Industrial Average was at 11,279, and after five years it is at 11,444, so no aggregate value has been gained in the market.

---

1 Fredericksen, C. (2010), "Time Spent Watching TV Still Tops Internet," *The E Marketer*, December 15, 2010.

2 Rosen, D. (2009), "Watching TV Leads to Obesity," *Psychology Today*, August 13, 2009.

3 *The Telegraph*, June 9, 2009, "TV Before Bed Cause Chronic Health Problems, Study Claims."

4 Christakis, Dimitri A., Zimmerman, Frederick J., DiGiuseppe, Davie L. and McCarty, Carolyn A. (2004) "Early Televison Exposure and Subsequent Attentional Problems in Children." *Pediatrics* 113 (2004):708-713.

Official unemployment numbers exceed 9 percent. That number only represents people actively collecting unemployment benefits, and doesn't account for people whose benefits have run out or who have taken jobs at a lower rate of pay. Meanwhile, for those who remain employed, wages have remained stagnant for the past decade or have even lost ground both for high school and college graduates.[5] So the increase in gas prices (and all of the items including supermarket foods that rely on fuel for transportation) are not being absorbed by higher wages.

Meanwhile, changes in the U.S. job market have made chronic job insecurity a way of life, so much so that studies have shown the incredible levels of stress engendered by the lack of security are a stronger predictor of poor health than even hypertension or smoking.[6]

And speaking of health, the U.S. Department of Agriculture has revised its dietary guidelines, but cost is a primary consideration in food choice for 49 million Americans.[7] A University of Washington study ascertained that junk foods cost, on average, $1.76 per 1,000 calories whereas healthy foods cost $18.16 per 1,000 calories.[8] Eating healthy is, in fact, more expensive.

Self-sufficiency has become even more important for Americans than it was five years ago. Self-sufficiency allows you to take control of some necessity of your life, and by doing so, puts you in control of your own destiny. When you are in control of your own destiny, the stress of the economy becomes less important.

When you boil everything down, mini-farming helps you take control of two necessities of life: food and shelter. It's pretty obvious how it helps you take control of your food supply, but it is less obvious how it lets you take control of your shelter. Mini-farming helps you take control of your home by turning it into a center of production rather than a center of consumption.

This book is a sequel to *Mini Farming: Self Sufficiency on ¼ Acre.* At the time I wrote *Mini Farming*, I wasn't anticipating writing anything further on the subject. But over time, I had more information that I wanted to share. Taken individually, none of these tidbits of knowledge may seem particularly important, but in aggregate this information can help you shorten the experience curve dramatically so you get maximum production with minimal problems right from the start.

Examples include the underlying principles of pruning an indeterminate tomato or how to grow squash on a trellis for maximum productivity per unit area.

In addition, in the intervening time, I made a couple of simple inventions that will help you plant more quickly or water your chickens in winter. None of it is really profound in my opinion, but I think it is eminently useful to help people get more done in less time.

I also wanted to convey more skills that could be helpful for gift-giving or starting a small business. I have been a successful fermenter for many years, so I have included chapters on making your own wine, vinegar and cheese.

Just as I did in *Mini-Farming*, rather than simply telling the reader to "do this" or "do that," I explain the underlying ideas, research and prin-

5 Sanchez, R. (2010), "Will Middle Class America Ever See a Real Raise Again?" *ABC News*, August 6, 2010.
6 *Science Daily*, August 9, 2009, "Job Insecurity Leads to Health Problems in U.S. Workers."
7 Rubin, R. (2011), Associated Press, "Fresh Food Choices can Feel Like Luxury in Lean Times."
8 Parker-Pope, T. (2007), *New York Times*, "A High Price for Healthy Food," Dec. 5, 2007.

ciples behind my conclusions. By conveying an understanding of the fundamentals, I hope to lay the groundwork that allows improvisation on the part of the reader.

As previously stated, this book is a *sequel*. It builds on the knowledge already contained in its predecessor, so I have not repeated the detailed information on composting, soil fertility, seed starting, double-digging, or canning. Rather, in this book, I assume you already have that knowledge. *Mini Farming* weighs in at 2.6 pounds. It simply isn't practical to tack another 2.6 pounds onto that and expect people to be able to carry much less read the result. So this book can be considered a continuation of the first, as the two books are intended to be used together.

Though I have presented economic arguments in favor of mini-farming, there are other compelling factors that are just as important. Too often today we view ourselves and each other in purely economic terms. We are *homo economicus*. If it can't be quantified, packaged and sold at a dollar price, its value isn't even considered. But when we look back on our lives, our regrets do not revolve around material things such as the car we didn't buy or the overtime we didn't work. Instead, our regrets revolve around the time we didn't spend with loved ones, the things we didn't do with them, and the things we didn't say and wish we could.

The value of mini-farming and of making the home a center of production rather than consumption is that it allows for more time, and better quality time, to be spent with kith and kin. It allows for greater self-sufficiency and hence less stress about jobs. It allows for the enjoyment of food so superior it can't be purchased at any price, and the health that flows from both the food and the physical activities involved in its production. The time family spends together actively blanching broccoli is time that can be spent interactively, rather than merely being in proximity with each other while watching a television. Mini-farming allows for a more abundant and more satisfying life. Mini-farming is an intergenerational activity as timeless as the earth and soil we hold in our hands, linking our generations together in an unbroken chain from the beginning of time to the limitless possibilities of the future.

Brett L. Markham
New Ipswich, NH
2011

PART I
Getting the Most out of Your Vegetables

Soil and Fertility

1

In *Mini Farming: Self Sufficiency on ¼ Acre*, I spent several chapters discussing soil and fertility in depth. The reason is because proper soil management and fertility practices are the foundation upon which everything else is built to make mini-farming an economically viable enterprise rather than merely a hobby. Optimum soil leads to reduced problems with pests and diseases, supports higher yields with greater density, creates more nutritious food and allows you to spend less money and effort on getting more food.

In this chapter, I am going to summarize what you need to know, plus add a bit more information. This summary should be enough to get you started, though it doesn't substitute for the in-depth knowledge in *Mini Farming: Self Sufficiency on ¼ Acre.*

Raised Beds

I recommend planting in raised beds for a number of important reasons. Raised beds that have been double-dug and enriched with finished compost retain water while properly draining so that oxygen levels in the soil are optimal, nutrients are bound in a living symbiotic matrix for release to plants as needed and soil temperatures allow for early working. Furthermore, the close spacing of plants in a raised bed increases yields over use of row gardening while growing closely enough together to shade out weeds.

Beds are also useful for practicing crop rotation on a small scale. Every crop has slightly different requirements and places slightly different demands on the soil as well as enhancing it in different ways. Probably the single most dangerous thing that can be done, in terms of pests and disease, is growing the same crop in the same place year after year. By doing this, diseases and pests build up until they are ultimately beyond control. Rotating crops between beds substantially reduces pest and disease problems.

In general, beds should be placed near each other, but with enough space for walking between them. The space between the beds can be sod/grass, crushed stones, bark mulch or practically anything else. Usually, sod/grass is not a problem, and that is what is between my beds. However, these can serve as a reservoir for diseases such as botrytis and a breeding ground for wireworms while providing easy access to slugs, so if disease problems are experienced or wireworms start doing serious damage, using (untreated) bark mulch or straw between the beds to suppress grasses may be wise. Also, if any grass isn't mowed regularly, it can grow over into a bed. Next thing you know you'll be pulling grass out of your beds by the handful.

Composting

Composting is the key to preserving and enhancing the fertility of the soil. The law of conservation of matter says that matter cannot be created or destroyed. Without getting into the physics of matter/energy systems, in practical terms this means that the elements in a plant came from the soil,

and unless those elements are put back into the soil, a mini farmer will find it necessary to purchase outside inputs such as fertilizer. Thus, if the foliage of a tomato plant has taken phosphorus from the soil, and that plant is simply discarded, the phosphorus will need to be replenished from an outside source. But if instead that plant is composted, the phosphorus can then be returned to the soil via the compost and thereby reduce the need for an outside source of phosphorus.

Compost is a complex and literally living substance made from the aerobic decomposition of organic matter. Other than volatile elements such as nitrogen, all of the essential elements added to the pile as part of the composted materials are retained. But, in addition, the process of composting breaks down poisons, destroys both human and plant pathogens, generates a wide array of beneficial soil organisms that help plants get the most from the nutrients in the soil and even produces antibiotics for combating diseases.

Composting, therefore, is absolutely crucial from an economic perspective because of the way it reduces the need for fertilizers; it also serves to passively prevent a whole host of pest and disease problems. The importance of composting cannot be over-emphasized. You should be adding at least four cubic feet of finished compost to every 4'x8' bed annually.

pH

pH is a measure of how acidic or alkaline the soil is. It is important because plants generally have a certain range of pH preference for optimal growth and because the pH of the soil actively affects which microorganisms will thrive in the environment and how readily the nutrients contained in the soil can be used by plants. The pH is measured on a scale from 0 to 14. Zero (0) is highly acidic, like battery acid; 14 is highly basic like lye, and 7 is neutral.

Many sources list a pH preference range for each plant, but these sources often differ in the details. For example, one source will list the preferred pH for tomatoes as 5.8 to 6.5, whereas another will list it as 6 to 7. The simple fact is that you don't need to be that detailed, as with only a very few exceptions, plants grown for food in gardens will grow well with a pH ranging from 6 to 7. True, a cucumber can grow at a pH as high as 8, but it will also grow at 6.5.

Because pH corrections can take months to show results and because the constant rotation of beds between crops makes it impractical to customize the pH of a bed to a given crop, it makes sense to test each bed individually, and correct the beds to a uniform pH of between 6 and 6.5. The exceptions are that the beds used for potatoes should have the pH lower than this, and the beds used for brassicas (such as cabbage and broccoli) should have extra lime added to the holes where the transplants are placed. These practices will be specifically covered in the chapters pertaining to those particular plants.

In most of the country, the soil pH is too low and needs to be raised to be within an optimal range. Correcting pH using lime can be problematic in that it takes several months to act. Though the gardening year should start in the fall, along with any soil corrections so the lime has time to react with the soil; the reality of life is that the decision to start a garden is generally made in the late winter or early spring. Thus, the farmer is stuck trying to correct pH within weeks of planting instead of months.

However, with a bit of creativity and use of alternate materials, both short and long term corrections can be made to pH.

There are many liming materials available for this purpose, but only four I would recommend: powdered lime, pelleted lime, dolomitic lime and wood ashes. Others such as burnt and hydrated lime act more quickly, but are hazardous to handle and easy to over-apply. If you choose to use these latter products, please follow package directions closely.

Pelleted lime is powdered lime that has been mixed with an innocuous water-soluble adhesive for ease of spreading. It acts no more or less quickly than the powdered product, but costs more. Lime can take as long as a year to take full effect, but will remain effective for as long as seven years.

Dolomitic lime contains magnesium in place of some of the calcium. In most soils in the U.S. (excepting clay soils in the Carolinas), its use for up to ¼ of the liming is beneficial to supply needed magnesium with calcium. It is used at the same rate as regular lime, takes as long to act, and lasts as long.

Measured pH	Sandy	Sand/Loam	Loam	Clay and Clay/Loam
4	5.5	11	16	22
5	3	5.5	11	16
6	1.25	3	3	5.5
7	None	None	None	none

Pounds of lime required to adjust the pH of 100 square feet of bed space.

Wood ashes are a long-neglected soil amendment for pH correction. They contain a wide array of macronutrients such as potassium and calcium but also contain elements such as iron, boron and copper. They act more quickly in correcting soil pH, but do not last as long. Wood ashes are applied at twice the rate of lime for an equal pH correction but should not be applied at a rate exceeding five pounds per 100 square feet. So, in effect, wood ashes are always used in conjunction with lime, rather than on their own.

The pH scale is a logarithmic value, similar to a decibel. As such, the amount of lime needed to raise the pH from 4 to 5 is greater than the amount of lime needed to raise the pH from 5 to 6. Furthermore, the effectiveness of lime is strongly influenced by the type of soil. So the accompanying table reflects both of these factors. The numbers represent pounds of powdered limestone per 100 square feet. For wood ashes, double that number, but never exceed five pounds per 100 square feet in a given year. Wood ashes can seldom be used exclusively as a pH modifier. Rather, they are best used when mixed with lime.

One further note about lime. A lot of sources say you shouldn't apply fertilizer at the same time as lime because the lime will react with the fertilizer and neutralize it. To some extent, this is true. However, lime stays active in the soil for as long at least seven years, so the fertilizer will be affected anyway. As long as both are thoroughly incorporated into the soil, don't worry. In addition, these concerns largely pertain to inorganic fertilizers such as ammonium nitrate. When the fertilizers are organic, and constituted of such compounds as blood meal or alfalfa meal, the adverse effect of the lime is considerably reduced.

Though excessively alkaline (e.g. a pH higher than 6.5) soils are rare in the United States, they exist in a few places such as the Black Belt prairie region of Alabama or can be accidentally created through excessive liming.

Correcting an excessively alkaline soil can be done using a variety of substances, including elemental sulfur (known as flowers of sulfur), ammonium sulfate, sulfur coated urea and ammonium nitrate. These latter methods are seen to be best practices in industrial agriculture, but they are excessively concentrated and can hurt the soil biology, so aren't recommended for a mini farm aiming at sustainability.

Some authorities also recommend aluminum sulfate, but the levels of aluminum, if the pH ends up changing, can be taken up by the plant and can become toxic to both plants and animals. So I recommend either straight flowers of sulfur (if growing organically) or ammonium sulfate (if you don't mind synthetic fertilizers). In practice, the amount of ammonium sulfate required to lower soil pH a given amount is 6.9 times as much as sulfur, so you'll likely use sulfur for cost reasons.

Sulfur works by combining with water in the soil to create a weak acid. This acid reacts with alkalies in the soil to form water-soluble salts

Measured pH	Sand	Loam	Clay
8.5	4.6	5.7	6.9
8	2.8	3.4	4.6
7.5	1.1	1.8	2.3
7	0.2	0.4	0.7

Pounds of sulfur needed to adjust the pH of 100 square feet of bed space.

that are leached from the soil and carried away by rains. Because it creates an acid directly, it is easy to overdo sulfur, so it should be measured and added carefully, then thoroughly incorporated into the soil. It takes about two months to reach full effectiveness, but results should start to manifest in as little as two weeks.

Ammonium sulfate works by virtue of the ammonium cation combining with atmospheric oxygen to create two nitrite anions (negatively charged ions), two molecules of water, and four hydrogen cations (positively charged ions). These hydrogen cations are the basis for acidity, and they will then acidify the soil.

So, how do you measure your pH? You can use a soil-testing kit or a pH meter. The cost of pH meters for home use has dropped considerably in recent years, with accurate units selling for as little as $13. Simply follow the directions that come with your individual meter for measuring each bed.

Macronutrients

Macronutrients are generally defined as being nitrogen, potassium and phosphorus, as these are the elements that are required in greatest quantity by plants. To these, I also add calcium, magnesium, sulfur, carbon, hydrogen and oxygen. These latter three are supplied by water and the atmosphere so they won't be further considered here except to note that proper aeration of soils allows beneficial bacteria access to oxygen. Furthermore, avoid walking on beds to prevent the soil from being compacted. Raised beds in general, due to being higher than their surroundings, usually don't have a problem with becoming waterlogged, which helps keep water from forcing out the oxygen that these beneficial microorganisms need.

Most soils in the U.S. are acidic and require lime for optimum growing. Adding lime also adds sufficient calcium automatically. Furthermore, those few soils in the U.S. that are alkaline are usually made so from the high natural limestone content of the soil. So, in general, calcium levels should be fine.

The major problem you will see that involves calcium is blossom end rot. Blossom end rot is caused by uneven uptake of calcium, usually due to extreme variations in rainfall. Usually this can be avoided through properly thorough watering. There are also some commercial preparations on the market that contain a readily absorbed calcium salt called calcium chloride that are effective.

In general, if you are using dolomitic lime for at least a portion of your lime needs, your soil will not be deficient in magnesium. However, the soil chemistry of competing cations such as magnesium and potassium is complex, and a plant could end up deficient even though there is sufficient elemental magnesium in the soil. Magnesium can become unavailable if potassium is present in a severe excess, or if the organic matter that forms the biological colloid that makes magnesium available to the plant is present in insufficient amounts.

A clear symptom of magnesium deficiency is often observable in seedlings that have been held too long in nutrient-poor starting mixes before being transplanted: interveinal chlorosis (the green turns yellowish between the veins) of older/lower leaves, often combined with curling leaf edges that have turned reddish brown or purple. If this symptom manifests, the deficiency can be corrected in the short term by adding Epsom salt (magnesium sulfate) at a rate of eight ounces per 100 square feet. This form of magnesium is easily absorbed by plants. However, the deficiency should be addressed in the long term by adding sufficient levels of compost to the soil, and using dolomitic lime.

Sulfur is an important constituent of amino acids—the core building blocks of DNA and life itself. As such, the primary source of sulfur in the soil is organic matter. Soils rich in organic matter through composting hold onto sulfur so it can't be leached out and convert it to the sulfate form needed by plants a little at a time as needed. However, even the most meticulous composting won't replenish all the sulfur lost because what we eat is seldom composted. So sulfur, in some form, should be added annually.

Elemental sulfur is not a good choice for this task unless it is already being used to alter the pH of the soil. In its elemental form, particularly in soils that aren't rich in organic matter, it isn't available to plants as a nutrient. Sulfur is best added in the form of either garden gypsum (calcium sulfate) or epsom salt (magnesium sulfate). It can be added at the rate of five ounces per 100 square feet every year for either product.

Phosphorus is a constituent of the enzymes essential for energy production within cells. The primary source of phosphorus in soil is from plant and animal wastes, in which it exists in an organic form not immediately accessible to plants. The phosphorus is converted as needed to an inorganic phosphate form that is usable by plants via microorganisms in the soil. This is, overall, the best method of maintaining soil levels of phosphorus because most of the phosphorus is held in reserve until needed and can't be leached out of the soil by rain.

The process of microorganisms converting phosphorus into a usable form is temperature dependent, and it is not at all unusual for spring transplants to suffer from deficiency because of this, even though there is adequate phosphorus in the soil. This is a condition that is better prevented than corrected, and can be done by simply using a good liquid fish fertilizer at the time of transplant and every week thereafter until soil temperatures are consistently above 55 degrees.

You should also test your beds for phosphorus. Numerous test kits are available, and they all work fine when used according to the directions in the kit. If your soil is deficient, you should add phosphorus in the form of bone meal in preference to rock phosphate. Bone meal is broken down slowly in the soil, so you should test your soil and add it at least five weeks prior to planting. The amount you'll need to add depends on the results of your soil test, and the instructions will be in the testing kit.

The reason why rock phosphate should be avoided is because it is high in radioactive substances that can be taken up by plants. In fact, one of the primary dangers of smoking is the radioactivity of the smoke, which is a result of tobacco being fertilized with rock phosphate. Tobacco is part of the same family of plants as peppers, eggplant, tomatoes, potatoes and many other garden edibles. So if you don't want to be eating radioactive substances, rock phosphate is best avoided.

Potassium is abundant in most soils, though usually in forms not readily available to plants. These unavailable forms are converted by the microbial life in the soil into forms that plants can use as the plants require it. Though potassium is required for life, its deficiency is not as readily noted as other essential nutrients. Plants are smaller and less hardy than they would otherwise be, but this might not be evident unless compared side-by-side to the same plant grown

⊗ Both the Rapitest and LaMotte testing kits will provide pH, nitrogen, phosphorus and potassium levels and recommendations.

in non-deficient soil. Therefore, use a test kit to determine if there is any deficiency.

Conscientious composting practices that return crop wastes to the soil are the primary source of potassium in a mini farm. This is, however, inadequate as the potassium removed in crops that are consumed or sold can't be returned in this fashion, so a certain amount of potassium will need to be supplied.

Nearly all plant materials contain usable levels of potassium, so occasionally supplementing your compost supply with an outside supply of compost will help maintain your levels of potassium. Alfalfa meal, usually used as a source of nitrogen, also contains potassium. Wood ashes, discussed earlier as a way of lowering pH, also contain substantial amounts of potassium along with other minerals. Greensand, a mineral originally formed on the ocean floor, is also a source of potassium along with micronutrients. The same applies to kelp, seaweed and fish meal. Depending on the results of soil testing, these materials can be used in any combination to supply potassium that is removed from the soil by crops.

Nitrogen is a primary constituent of amino acids and the DNA within plant cells. Though we live in an atmosphere that is roughly 78 percent nitrogen, this form of nitrogen is inert and not useful to plants. In nature, the nitrogen is converted into a usable form through a bacterial process known as nitrogen *fixation*, that is usually done through rhizobium bacteria that live in symbiosis with the roots of legumes. This is why cover cropping is so important (as explained in *Mini Farming: Self Sufficiency on ¼ Acre*). A proper cycle of cover cropping and crop rotation can reduce the need and cost of outside sources of nitrogen.

Deficiencies in nitrogen show themselves quickly in the loss of green color, starting with the oldest or lowest leaves on the plant. Because the rate at which nitrogen in the soil can be made available to plants is affected by temperature, this deficiency is most often seen early in the season when soil temperatures are below 60 degrees. There may be enough nitrogen in the soil, but the bacteria can't keep up with the demand of the crops. It is better to prevent this problem than correct it, and early plantings should be supplemented with a liquid fish fertilizer until well established and soil temperatures are sufficient to support natural nitrogen conversion.

Just as with most other nutrients, composting should be your first source of maintaining soil fertility. But because you can't compost crops that you eat or sell, and because nitrogen losses in composting can be as high as 50 percent, you will need to add nitrogen as it is removed by crops. Good crop rotation with legumes and legume cover crops can help as well; sometimes this is enough. But often nitrogen needs to be added, and a soil test can tell you how much you need.

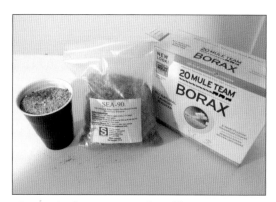

⊘ Wood ashes, sea minerals and borax are sources of micronutrients for your beds.

Sources of nitrogen include compost from an outside source, various fish, feather, alfalfa, cottonseed, blood and bone meals, well-rotted manure from chickens and other animals, etc. I like using diverse sources in order to also include as many other micronutrients as possible. Because we keep chickens, the chicken manure added to our compost pile dramatically reduces our overall need for outside sources of nitrogen, but to an extent this comes at the cost of feed for the chickens. In terms of dollar cost, however, this works in our favor as the eggs are more valuable than the feed, so the manure is free.

Micronutrients

A large array of minerals have been identified as being essential for human health, and more are being discovered all the time. So far, the following are known to be needed: potassium, chlorine, sodium, calcium, phosphorus, magnesium, zinc, iron, manganese, copper, iodine, selenium, molybdenum, sulfur, cobalt, nickel, chromium, fluorine, boron and strontium.

These can only be acquired through the food we eat. We can get them through plants, or through animals that have eaten plants. But ultimately, they have to enter plants through the soil. Thus, defi-

cient soils, even if the plants seem perfectly healthy, ultimately lead to problems with human health.

Because industrial farming doesn't have human health as its goal; farm management practices have led to a long-term decline in the mineral content of foods. A number of studies have shown that in just a thirty-year period, the content of vitamins and minerals in foods have declined by anywhere from 6 percent to 81 percent.[1,2]

There are a number of elements needed by plants that are needed in small quantities, and are thus described as micronutrients. Overall, due to over-farming, these are deficient in agricultural soils because they were never restored as they were depleted. Only a handful of plant micronutrients are officially recognized: boron, chlorine, copper, iron, manganese, molybdenum and zinc. That is because severe deficiencies of these elements usually give clear adverse symptoms in plants.

However, as plants are the start of our food chain and humans require far more than just these seven minerals, soil deficiency in any mineral needed for human health should be avoided as its disappearance from plants means we don't get enough in our diet.

Composting to maintain the fertility of the soil and retain these elements is important. To a degree, as described in *Mini Farming*, these elements can also be added in small quantities to your beds. This is easy to do with elements such as calcium or iron that can be easily obtained, but more difficult with fluorine or strontium. And even if these are available, you may be missing something we haven't learned about yet.

1   Bergner, Paul (1997), *Healing Power of Minerals, Special Nutrients, and Trace Elements* (The Healing Power), ISBN-13: 978-0761510215.
2   Marie-Mayer, Anne (1997), "Historical Changes in the Mineral Content of Fruits and Vegetables."

The easiest way to make sure the soil has all of the trace elements needed is the periodic addition of ocean minerals. Over the ages, rain and erosion have moved a great many minerals that would ordinarily be on land in abundance into the sea. Over-farming without replenishment has exacerbated this problem. Though I am able to go to the seashore and collect kelp from the beach for my own compost, this is seldom practical for most people. What I recommend as a solution for the most robust and nutritionally complete plants possible is the periodic addition of a small quantity of ocean minerals.

In essence, seawater contains, in varying amounts, every known element save those made artificially in nuclear reactors. In 1976, Dr. Maynard Murray published a book entitled *Sea Energy Agriculture* in which he highlighted the results of numerous studies he had made from the 1930s through 1950s on the addition of ocean minerals to agricultural land. Though his book was published some time ago, I have discovered that in growing beds side by side, those treated with sea minerals do, in fact, produce obviously healthier plants.

The big problem with using ocean water directly is obvious: you can't grow plants in salt water because it kills them. In fact, one of the practices of ancient warfare was to sow your enemies' fields with salt so they wouldn't be fertile. Fortunately, only a small quantity is required, and when package directions are followed not only is there no harm, but plants become more healthy and more resistant to insects and diseases. It is also fortunate that on a mini farm, the amount of sea minerals required is tiny, so even a ten-pound bag of sea minerals from various sources will literally last for years. (I use five pounds annually.) There are a number of companies offering sea minerals such as GroPal, Sea Agri, Sea Minerals from Arkansas and others. The key is that each offering is a bit different, so be sure to scale the package directions appropriately.

The one micronutrient that I don't believe sea minerals provide in sufficient quantity is boron. You'll see boron deficiency in hollow stems for broccoli and hollow or grey centers of potatoes. The amount of boron required is tiny, and can be derived from borax. Use extreme caution because borax in higher concentrations is an effective herbicide that will leave your beds sterile for years if it is dumped on them indiscriminately. Sufficient borax can be added with one tsp dissolved in one gallon of water and used to lightly sprinkle over a single 4' x 8' bed before a regular watering. Once a year is plenty.

Conclusion

Healthy plants require healthy soil. Use of composting practices will help reduce the need for outside inputs plus provide optimum soil health for suppression of diseases. Raised beds allow for more aerated soil, higher levels of production, and the use of less fertilizer overall. Ideally, the process of amending beds for pH range and nutrient deficiencies will start in the fall; at a bare minimum start as soon as the soil can be worked in the spring. Cover cropping and crop rotation fill out the mix to create the most healthy soil possible, thus making whatever crops you grow more productive. I have only given basic information in this chapter, so for more in-depth knowledge of bed construction, double-digging, composting and soil fertility practices such as biochar, please see *Mini Farming: Self Sufficiency on ¼ Acre*, in which several chapters are devoted to covering these subjects in depth.

2

Asparagus

No, asparagus is not poisonous! Well, the berries made by the female plant are poisonous, but the rest of the plant isn't. And the compounds that make urine smell ... different ... to the 22 percent of the population who are able detect it are perfectly safe. In addition, it is a nutritional goldmine, rich in folic acid, antioxidants, minerals, and even vitamins E and C. No wonder it was cultivated by the ancient Greeks, Egyptians and Romans.

The asparagus in stores is sold by the pound, so sometimes it is sold when old and the stems have turned woody (so it weighs more). In terms of usable portions, it is quite expensive. Organic asparagus, even frozen, sells for $7/lb at my local supermarket. If there were ever a compelling argument for growing your own asparagus, the price and quality of what can be found at the supermarket should be enough.

Though it takes a few years to get established, asparagus is easy to grow and can be eaten fresh, frozen, dried for use in soups, and even canned using a pickling method so that it will keep for years. Once you have a bed of asparagus started, if you properly care for it, it will last twenty to thirty years.

Selecting the Right Variety

Asparagus is one of the few dioecious species of plants grown in gardens, meaning that a plant is either entirely male or entirely female, rather than combining both male and female attributes within the same flower or plant as is seen with tomatoes. All asparagus variants grow just fine anywhere in the country, so they should be selected based on your own tastes. Popular open-pollinated varieties include Mary Washington, Argenteuil (also known as Precoce D'Argenteuil) and Conover's Colossal. Though there are hybrid male-only varieties available as crowns (i.e., bare-root plants), I'd encourage growing one of the open-pollinated varieties from seed because of the ease of seed-saving so that if anything ever happens to your bed, you can re-create it instead of relying on a company that may have gone out of business.

Starting Asparagus

Asparagus is easy to start from seed. Start it indoors six weeks before last frost, and plant it out when you plant out your tomatoes. Because some of the seeds are male and some are female—and only the male plants produce substantive shoots—start twice as many plants as you think you'll need. Transplant them in two rows in your bed, six inches apart. The next year, cull all the female plants but the two strongest, leaving these so that you can produce seed. Then cull the weakest of the male plants until you have plants every 12" to 18" in each of the two rows in the bed.

Planting Asparagus

Asparagus can be grown from either seed or bare-root plants known as "crowns." The primary difference is that crowns are an already-established plant, and will produce useful shoots a year earlier than growing from seed. Whether growing from seed or crowns, you should keep in mind this is a pretty permanent planting, and the bed should be prepared accordingly.

The single most important aspect of an asparagus bed is drainage. Wet feet, that is, waterlogged roots, are the death of asparagus. Raised beds are an important tool in this regard, but make sure the raised bed isn't located in an area of the yard that gets flooded. The second most important consideration is soil pH; asparagus prefers a soil as close to neutral as possible. Thus, because of the long time frames needed for lime to work, an asparagus bed should be prepared and pH correctives added in the fall prior to the transplanting of crowns or seedlings in the spring. The third most important consideration is light; asparagus needs at least six hours of direct sunlight daily. Fourth, beds should be four feet wide, and 1.5' long for each plant; so when growing six plants, you'll need a bed 4' wide and 8' long. (Make sure the long side faces south for greatest sun!)

Finally, the bed should have plenty of reserve fertility. This is accomplished by double-digging as described in *Mini Farming*; incorporating properly aged compost into the bottom of the trenches, working even more compost—a good 4"-6"—into the top of the bed. This can all be done in advance. Then, a month or so before planting, add trace minerals and then use organic sources to correct any deficiencies in major nutrients. The use of organic sources is especially

Asparagus growing ❯❯ through the straw mulch used to suppress weeds.

important with asparagus because you can't just till more stuff into the bed later (remember: asparagus takes three years to produce, and the plants last as long as twenty years). Anything added later will just be mixed with compost as a top dressing. The annual spring top-dressing should be five cubic feet of compost per 4'x8' bed. You should mix 3 lbs of wood ash, 1 lb of lime, 2 lbs of bone meal, 2 lbs of alfalfa meal and 1lb of blood meal into the compost before application, and then cover with a 2" matting of clean straw.

There is one other very important thing you need to know about asparagus: it loves arsenic, sucking it up like a vacuum cleaner, and will give it to you. Arsenic is not a problem unless your bed is in an old apple orchard that was treated with arsenic as an insecticide, but the one thing you absolutely must avoid is pressure-treated wood that has been treated with arsenic compounds anywhere near your bed. All you have

to do to keep your asparagus safe is keep pressure treated wood away, and don't try to grow it where arsenic was used heavily in the past. This is absolutely no joke—it is entirely possible for someone who disregards this advice to munch an asparagus stalk and then quite literally flop over dead.

Weeds

Because an asparagus planting is long-term, weed problems can accumulate and quickly overwhelm the plants. Furthermore, because the crowns that produce the shoots tend to grow upward, weed control via hoe can inadvertently damage them. The standard protocol for dealing with weeds in asparagus beds is to use flame weeding, mulching or other (non-herbicidal) means to keep weeds away from the bed. Grasses are especially invasive, so don't let any get close enough for the seeds to fall into the bed. Apply 2"-4" of compost yearly to the bed, and cover that with 2" of clean straw to smother weeds. Pull any weeds that still manage to grow by hand before they produce seed.

Diseases

Asparagus is vulnerable to a number of root-rot diseases, but these are highly unlikely to manifest in an asparagus bed situated as described earlier. It can also be affected by botrytis mold spread from grasses, but proper weed control as earlier described will prevent this. There are also some viral diseases that can kill off asparagus. These are believed to be spread by aphids, but are extremely rare in home-grown beds as opposed to commercial situations where acres upon acres of asparagus are grown. All you have to do is create a well-drained raised bed, control weeds and control aphids when/if they appear, and you'll have no disease problems.

Pests

Asparagus aphids are very rarely an issue because a wide array of natural predators such as ladybugs keep them in check. If you find a large population of aphids (they will hide under the bracts of the leaves), they can be effectively controlled with two applications of insecticidal soap a week apart.

Asparagus beetles are more of a threat. These are usually metallic blue or black and a quarter of an inch long, though some orange species exist. The adult asparagus beetle does little direct damage, it is the offspring that are a problem. The eggs appearing like black specks hatch into green

to gray worm-like larvae as much as ½" long that eat voraciously. The defoliation weakens the plants.

Primary control of asparagus beetles is to cut down all asparagus foliage at the end of the season when it has turned yellow/brown and add it to the compost pile. This denies the beetles a place for offspring to overwinter. During the season, just vigorously shaking the foliage will dislodge the larvae, and because they will be unable to climb back up the stalk, they will dehydrate and die in the soil.

Harvest

If grown from transplanted seedlings, allow asparagus to grow without harvesting anything for two years. This will allow the foliage to store energy in the crowns that will enhance their ability to survive over the winter. If grown from transplanted crowns, allow them to grow without harvest for the first year. Then, the first year you harvest, only harvest the stalks that appear for one week. In subsequent years over the next twenty or thirty years, you can harvest stalks for a full six weeks as they appear in spring. Then let the rest of the stalks grow out into full plants to replenish the crowns.

Harvest of asparagus isn't all at once. You'll see a stalk here and a stalk there. The stalks should be cut with a sharp non-serrated knife just below ground level when they are no more than 8" tall. (Much bigger and they get woody.) Put an inch of water in the bottom of a wide-mouth canning jar, and put the stalks in the water in your refrigerator until you have enough of them to cook or preserve. They'll keep just fine for a couple of weeks this way.

» Save asparagus spears upright in water in the refrigerator until ready for use.

Saving Seed

Collect the ripe red berries from the female plants, bring them inside, and let them dry out on a paper plate. Next, crush the berries and winnow out the seeds. Keep the berries out of reach of children as the attractive red berries are poisonous, and as few as seven of them might send someone to the hospital.

Preservation and Preparation

Asparagus can be kept fresh in the refrigerator for a couple of weeks if the bottom ends are in water, or it can be blanched and then dehydrated or frozen. Pickling works extremely well with asparagus. Even though it is technically feasible, I don't recommend pressure canning because the resultant mush is vile in my opinion. For fresh eating, asparagus can be eaten raw, steamed or stir-fried with excellent results. Frozen packages can be cooked in the package in the microwave if vented to prevent explosions.

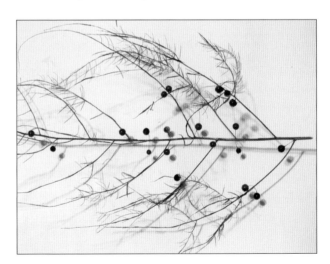

» Asparagus berries are easy to collect for seed-saving, but don't let children have them.

Pickled Asparagus

Ingredients:

60 asparagus spears
½ cup coarse salt
1 gallon cold water
3 ⅓ cups distilled white vinegar
1 ⅓ cup sugar
2 teaspoons coarse salt
2 teaspoons mustard seed
1 tbsp dill seed
1 yellow onion, sliced into rings
4 cloves of garlic

Procedure

1. Clean the asparagus, cut 1" off the bottom and then cut the spears 3½" long so they will fit upright in the canning jars while leaving 1" to the top. Put the cut spears in a large bowl, add ½ cup of coarse canning salt (sea salt is fine too), and then cover with water for two hours. After the two hours, drain and then rinse the asparagus, and pat it dry.
2. Clean and sterilize four wide-mouth pint canning jars and lids.
3. Combine the vinegar, sugar, 2 teaspoons of salt, dill seed, mustard seed and onion in a saucepan over medium heat. Bring to a slow boil, then turn down to a simmer.
4. Pack the asparagus spears upright and tightly in the jars. Add a clove of garlic to each jar, then pour in the pickling liquid to within ¼" of the rim.
5. Adjust the two piece lids and process in a boiling water canner for 10 minutes

These can be enjoyed fresh from the jar, as a garnish, or as a tasty addition to salads.

Asparagus

Ingredients:

20 fresh asparagus spears
1 lemon
1½ Tbsp butter
2 cloves garlic

Procedure:

1. Wash and dry asparagus spears, cutting off the bottom one inch. Cut the lemon in half, setting aside one half for later. Mince the garlic cloves. Preheat the butter in the pan over low-medium heat.
2. Add the garlic to the butter and stir-fry until slightly browned.
3. Add the asparagus, and stir-fry until tender.
4. Squeeze the juice from ½ of the lemon over the asparagus in the pan
5. Cut the remaining half lemon into thin slices.
6. Serve the asparagus with the lemon slices as garnish.

Delicious!

⊗ Asparagus fresh from the garden makes this simple dish a culinary delight!

3

Beans

Beans are one of the most versatile vegetables grown in the garden. They can be used to replenish nitrogen in the soil, eaten raw, and made into everything from soups and stews to tofu. They are also one of the most evocative in terms of cultural imagery, with the cowboy carrying his supply of dried beans on a lonely trek, and even odes composed in honor of the ... music ... we often make after eating them.

The variety of beans available crosses species and is truly amazing, with literally hundreds of varieties available from traditional cultures and more modern breeding. There are seed companies that offer over a hundred varieties! But despite this diversity made possible by dedicated seed savers, the reality is that most beans available in the supermarket are from only a handful of varieties, and fully 85 percent of the soy crop in this country has been subject to artificial genetic modification to breed traits such as herbicide resistance.

Furthermore, beans are very commonly over-cropped and adding insult to injury, supplies of dried beans are sometimes several years old. Unless you know a farmer and can get them fresh, the best way to have a decent bean is to grow it yourself. Luckily, they are among the easiest to grow of all garden crops.

Variety Selection

Beans can be divided into categories in various ways, but for most mini farmers they can be categorized in terms of growing habit (bush beans versus pole beans) or culinary use (green beans versus dry beans). But they can also be divided even further to include Lima beans, cow peas (aka "black-eyed peas"), yard-long beans and more. As they grow well anywhere in the country, the biggest concern is the farmer's personal taste.

When beans are grown fresh and compared, you soon discover a tremendous difference in flavors and textures that is not evident in supermarket fare. A green bean is definitely not just a green bean! There is a big difference in flavor between the Blue Lake and Old Homestead varieties. You may even find that, like in my family, different family members prefer the taste of different varieties. What I encourage you to do is grow more than one variety each year, and keep trying out new varieties while continuing to grow favorites you've discovered along the way. A mix of green and dried varieties is best for menu diversity throughout the year.

Rather than tell you exactly what to grow, instead I'll list some of the varieties that I've grown and enjoyed in each category as a starting point for your own investigation.

Blue Lake, Green Pole: There are many variants of this, some of which offer a wide array of disease resistance. Blue Lake pole beans used to be the dominant bean grown for commercial processing, and it definitely holds up well to canning and freezing. Blue Lake is very mildly flavored and thus ideal for picky eaters who might not otherwise like green beans.

Kentucky Wonder, Green Pole: This is a a very productive pole bean that will produce 8" long beans as long as you keep it harvested. It seems to never stop! Kentucky Wonder is also very versatile in that, if you allow the beans to mature into a dried bean instead of harvesting while green, they make an excellent dry bean for baking and soups. It is also a good freezing bean with a very distinctive flavor.

Top Crop, Green Bush: If you want to put a lot of beans away, you'll find the production impressive. The plants grow up to 2' tall, and start producing beans about fifty days from planting.

Jacob's Cattle, Dry Bush: This is my favorite dry bean. Not only is it tasty, but it is productive and grows really well on the outside edges of the corn patch. It is easy to harvest and a very attractive white bean with purple splotches.

Black Turtle, Dry Bush: In my wife's opinion, the best choice for bean soup recipes. It has an assertive but excellent flavor and very good cooking qualities. It isn't as productive as some varieties, but more than makes up for that with it's flavor.

Henderson's, Bush Lima: Lima beans are a little tricky in terms of timing the harvest. You want to catch them when they are big, but before they start to mature. Henderson's has a very defined "Lima bean" flavor with a hint of butter. Shelled out, they steam nicely.

Soil Preparation

Beans don't grow well in acidic soil, so the bed where you plan to grow beans should be corrected to a pH of between 6 and 6.5 well in advance of planting. Enrich the soil with compost, and make especially sure of sufficient potassium and phosphorus. If the soil is a bit low in nitrogen, that's okay as long as you use a bacterial inoculant when planting as the beans will make their own nitrogen.

Planting Beans

Beans can be planted anytime after the last expected frost date for your area by planting the seed 1" deep directly in the soil. If average soil temperatures are under 60 degrees, though; germination will be poor. Though beans can be productive over a period of several weeks, they eventually stop producing, so for a longer harvest you should plant beans in two phases, with the first phase being about a week after the last expected frost date when soil temperatures are above 60 degrees, and the second phase being three weeks later. In most of the United States, this is sufficient to give yields until fall. If you live in an area with a growing season of 120 days or longer, you can also plant a third phase in another three weeks.

Beans will generally grow fine with or without any inoculant; however, in order to maximize their utility in a crop rotation based on their ability to fix atmospheric nitrogen into the soil, an inoculant should be used. This will also increase yields.

A little bit of inoculant goes a long way. What I do is put the bean seeds I will be planting in a jar, mist them with a bit of water, add a couple of teaspoons of inoculant and gently swish them around until they all have some inoculant on them. Then I plant them about 1" deep.

With bush beans, I plant them 5" apart in all directions. With pole beans, I plant them 5" apart in one row 6" away from the frame on the North side of the bed. Pole beans can grow as much as 9' tall, which can be pretty inconvenient

for harvesting. You can either make your trellis so it slants away from the bed and put a 6' support on the top of the leaning trellis, or prune the bean vines as they reach the top of a conventional trellis. Either way will work.

Weeds, Pests and Diseases

Weeds are seldom a problem with bush beans grown in beds because the beans sprout and grow quickly and the leaf cover they provide effectively shades out weed competition. All you need to do is keep any grass growing around the bed trimmed, and make sure the bed is prepared and weed-free prior to planting.

The two major pests you'll likely see in beans are bean beetles and Japanese beetles. Japanese beetles start as grubs in your lawn (or that of your neighbors). If you have a lot of property so there is a good buffer with your neighbors, treating your entire lawn and beds with milky spore disease can be a good preventative after the disease has become established in a couple of years. Japanese beetle traps are pretty controversial as a pest control measure, because some studies show that they attract more beetles than they trap and will likely bring in beetles from the neighbors. They work well for me, though, when placed downwind of the garden at least 100' away.

Japanese beetles attract each other. So one way to keep them controlled is to simply pick them off by hand into a small bucket of soapy water. (The soap lowers the surface tension of the water so the beetles sink and drown rather than floating on top where they will climb up the sides of the bucket and fly back onto your beans.) If you keep them picked off daily once they are noticed, you'll

⊘ The dense foliage of closely spaced beans shades out weeds.

likely prevent the problem all together. They can also be controlled by organic sprays such as pyrethrin and rotenone used according to package directions, but this is a last resort as such sprays are expensive.

Adult bean beetles overwinter in the debris from the prior year's bean crop. So cleaning out your bed at the end of the season and composting the plants is an important preventative. Bean beetles look like slightly larger than average lady bugs with a bronze cast. They lay masses of yellow eggs on the undersides of the leaves which hatch into spiny yellow grubs about ¼" long. Both the adults and the grubs eat everything but the veins in the leaves of the bean plants, and they eat voraciously. Except in the cases of large-scale monocropping, bean beetles can be controlled by cleaning up the prior year's plants, smashing any egg masses or grubs found under the leaves, and flicking the adults into a bucket of soapy water. In the extremely rare cases where they can't be controlled by these measures, the grubs can be controlled with insecticidal soap or light horticultural oil (be sure to get under the leaves) and the adults can be controlled with neem oil preparations. The most effective control I have found for potato beetles is an organic bacterial poison called spinosad used according to label directions.

Disease is seldom a problem with beans in a properly managed mini-farm environment because crop rotation and debris removal control most likely diseases. If you have a problem with sclerotina (which looks like a white mold), switching to pole beans will likely solve the problem.

Harvest

Dry beans need to stay on the bush or vine until they are tan/brown, dry and brittle. Once they have reached that stage, pick them into a bag, then break open the pods and allow the beans to settle to the bottom. Discard the large debris and pour the beans into a large bowl. You'll notice a lot of smaller debris, but this is easily discarded through a process known as winnowing.

It takes a bit of practice to get the hang of winnowing, but the idea is simple. The beans are heavier than the debris, so if the beans mixed with debris are poured into another bowl from a height while the wind (either natural or artificial via a fan) is blowing, the debris will be blown away and the debris-free beans will be alone in the second bowl. I have found this works best using a fan on medium speed a couple of feet away, and pouring from a distance no greater than three feet. Using this method, you only have to pour from one bowl into the other a couple of times to have perfectly clean beans.

Once the dry beans have been winnowed, set them aside in an uncovered bowl for a few weeks for the moisture to dissipate, giving them a stir with your hand once in a while. Then store them in an airtight container in a cool, dark place.

Green or "snap" beans are best harvested as soon as they are large enough to use. If you keep

⊗ Black turtle beans in a bowl after winnowing.

the plants picked clean and don't allow the beans to start maturing, the plants will keep generating flowers and beans for a few weeks. Incidentally, plants grown like this that are not allowed to set seed fix the most nitrogen into the soil. Harvest the beans in the afternoon when the plants aren't damp to avoid spreading diseases, and store them in a bag in the refrigerator for up to a week until you have enough beans to eat or preserve.

Seed Saving

In the case of dry beans, simply using the ones you have stored for food is sufficient if you intend to use them the next year. Otherwise, you'll want to dehydrate them a bit using the techniques described in *Mini Farming*. To save seed from green or snap beans, treat them like dry beans. Allow at least twenty plants to grow to mature their pods into the dry-bean stage (making sure that is the only variety of beans you are growing at the time!), and then winnow like dry beans.

Preparation and Preservation

Green beans can be kept in a plastic bag in the refrigerator for up to a week. After that, they can be pickled, canned, or blanched and then frozen or dehydrated. They are best steam-blanched for four minutes, cooled in ice water for another four minutes, and then frozen. But that is simply my own preference, and many people like green beans that have been pickled as dilly beans, preserved via pressure canning or reconstituted from dried form into stews and casseroles.

Old Fashioned Green Beans

Ingredients:

1 lb fresh green beans with the ends removed and cut into 1" pieces
1 small onion
3 tsp butter
¼ cup of water
½ tsp salt
dash of pepper
1 chicken bouillon cube (use good stuff, not the bouillon that is mostly MSG or salt.)

Procedure:

Cut the onion into slices and sauté in the butter until soft. Stir in the beans, then add the water, salt, pepper and bouillon. Crush the bouillon with a fork or spoon until it is dissolved. Cover and cook until the beans are crisp-tender.

Beets and Chard

Beets and chard (also known as Swiss chard) are variations of the same *beta vulgaris* species commonly descended from a sea beet that grows wild around the Mediterranean. Though beets are grown for their roots and chard for their leafy greens, the greens of both are edible. Beets, beet greens and chard are an absolute nutritional powerhouse. The roots contain glycine betaine, a compound shown to reduce homocysteine levels in the blood. Homocysteine levels are predictive of coronary artery disease, peripheral vascular diseases and stroke, so beets are definitely a case where cleaning your plate is a good idea!

In addition to this, beets supply minerals such as manganese, magnesium and iron, as well as B vitamins such as niacin, pantothenic acid, pyridoxine and folates. Beet greens and chard are also an excellent source of vitamin K, which plays a role not just in blood clotting, but also in bone formation and limiting damage to brain tissues. They also contain vitamin C, beta carotene, zeaxanthin, lutein and a host of other important antioxidants.

That's all well and good but . . . are they tasty? Absolutely! And, even better, they are among the easiest crops to grow on your mini farm.

Variety Selection

Given properly prepared soil, beets and chard can be grown practically anywhere in America that plants will grow. I've never tried a variety of either that wasn't delicious, though you'll find over time that certain varieties may grow a little better or taste a little better in your specific location. I'll give you a list of my favorite varieties, and I think you'll find them well-suited, but please don't limit yourself to just my suggestions.

Beets: Bull's Blood, Early Wonder, Cylindra, Detroit Dark Red

Chard: Ruby Red, Rainbow (a/k/a 5 color silverbeet), Fordhook Giant

Soil Preparation

Beets and chard grow best in deeply dug, rock-free soils rich in organic matter that have a pH between 6.5 and 7.5. The beds should be fertilized normally, though adding a teaspoon of borax (mixed with something like bone meal or wood ashes for even distribution) per thirty-two-square-foot bed is a good idea because beets are sensitive to boron deficiency. One major problem with germination of beets and chard is that soil can crust over the seeds, leading to plants being trapped underneath the crust. This will cause uneven stands with different rates of maturity. To solve this problem, make sure there is plenty of well-finished compost in the soil.

Starting and Planting

Beets and chard can be grown as both spring and fall crops. During the heat of the summer when temperatures climb above 80 degrees and stay there, they'll become bitter and tough. Chard can be harvested at practically any stage, but beets aren't usually ready for harvest before 50-60 days. On the other hand, chard and beets don't germinate well at soil temperatures below 50 degrees. In my area, the best time to plant is a month before last frost. This is late enough that the soil is sufficiently warm, but early enough that the beets are at harvesting size before the summer heat makes them tough.

Beets and chard can be succession planted, but in my experience this works best in the fall because the cooler weather during the later development of the beets keeps them sweeter, whereas a second spring crop of beets can be hit-or-miss depending upon the summer weather. For fall planting, plant your first crop about seven weeks before first frost and your second crop about four weeks before first frost.

It is entirely possible to transplant beets and chard that are grown inside first as seedlings. Though this is seldom done on a commercial scale because of the care required to avoid damaging the taproot and the tightness of the timing; on the scale of a mini farm, transplanting can improve production by allowing the grouping of more uniformly sized seedlings, thereby preventing plants that sprouted earlier from shading out those that sprouted later. Simply start the seeds inside in soil blocks two weeks before the seeds would usually be sown outside.

Whether using seeds or transplants, space your planting at 3" in all directions for beets and 4" in all directions for chard. During the spring planting, plant them about ½" deep and keep the planted area evenly moist until germination. If a crust forms, use a standard kitchen fork to lightly break up the crust no more than ⅛" deep.

⊗ You can fit a lot of beets into a bed when planting at 3″ intervals.

Because the seeds often contain seeds for multiple plants, about a week after germination you'll want to go back and thin out the extras. Save the thinned plants—roots and all—for a delicious salad green.

Weeds, Pests and Diseases

Because the plants are spaced so closely together, once they start growing they will shade out most weed competition (provided the bed was weed-free at the start). What few weeds remain should be carefully pulled by hand.

Beets and chard seldom have pest or disease issues that are economically important on the scale of a mini farm, though in commercial monocropping with inadequate rotation quite a few pests and diseases are problematic. Cleaning up debris at the end of the prior season, rotating crops between beds, mowing the lawn and keeping grasses and weeds out of the beds are usually sufficient measures to avoid problems.

Leaf miners and other beet-specific pests spread from nearby weeds that are botanically related, such as lamb's quarters, and the more generalized pests such as leaf-hoppers and carrion beetles migrate from tall grasses nearby. The diseases either accumulate in the soil from growing a crop in the same place year after year, or are transmitted by pests. So 95 percent of the time, just doing basic mini farm maintenance will prevent any problems. Those few that remain, if they become economically threatening, can be controlled with organic sprays such as neem or pyrethrin/rotenone used according to label directions.

Harvest

Chard and beet greens can be harvested as soon as they appear, but should be allowed to grow to at least a couple of inches before picking. Don't harvest more than a couple of leaves from beets intended to produce roots, as doing so would reduce the yield. With chard, harvest the outside leaves first as they get large enough, and then the next layer of leaves will continue to grow. Keep harvesting like that in succession and the chard will produce for three weeks or more. As the beet greens or chard are harvested, you can store them in a plastic bag in the refrigerator for up to a week until you have enough to prepare or preserve.

Though it varies somewhat with the variety of beet, in general, beets should be harvested when they are no larger than 2" in diameter. If you wait longer than that to harvest (and especially if you

⊗ New beets can be planted for fall as soon as the spring crop is harvested for maximum productivity.

wait until the heat of summer is intense), they tend to get woody. When harvest time comes, grab the leaf stalks just above the root and pull the beets out of the ground. Cut off the leaf stalks two inches above the root and set aside the leaves for eating, and then hose all the dirt off the beets outside. Let them dry for a bit, and then prepare or preserve as desired.

Seed Saving

Beets and chard are biennials, meaning they produce seed in their second year of growth. (Some varieties of chard will produce seed in their first year.) South of Maryland, you can mulch the plants with 6" of straw at the end of the season and they'll produce seed in the second year. North of Maryland, you'll need to cut off the tops, store the roots indoors overwinter and then put the roots out again in the spring. They will produce a flower stalk four feet long.

Beet pollen is very mobile, so if you are saving seed, make sure you have only one variety of beet or chard in flower in your garden. Beets and chard are also subject to inbreeding depression,

so you should have at least twenty plants in the flowering and seed-setting population.

To harvest the seeds, cut the stalk when most of the seed pods have turned brown and hang inside upside down for two or three weeks. Then, use your hands to strip the pods from the stalk into a bag, break up the pods so the seeds fall to the bottom of the bag, and discard the larger debris. You can separate the seeds from the smaller debris using the winnowing method described in the chapter on beans. Then, dry the seeds using a desiccant such as dried silica gel for a couple of weeks, and store in an airtight container in a cool, dark place.

Preparation and Preservation

Beet greens and chard can be stored in a plastic grocery bag in the refrigerator for up to a week prior to fresh use or preservation. Both beet greens and Swiss chard contain oxalic acid. Though the oxalic acid is not present in sufficient quantities to be problematic for most people, if anyone in your family is prone to kidney stones you can prepare them in such a way as to reduce the amount of oxalic acid. Cook the greens by boiling them in

⊗ Chard and Beet Greens are easily preserved by freezing.

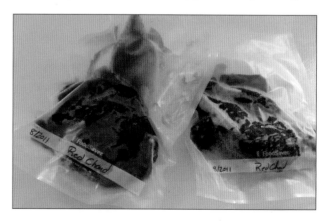

a couple of inches of water until wilted, and then discard the water and eat the greens.

Greens are best preserved by blanching for two and half to three minutes, cooling in ice water for four minutes, drying and then vacuum sealing for the deep freeze. Unfortunately, they don't stand up well to pressure canning and they don't reconstitute well from dehydrating. Even so, I dehydrate many greens so that I can later reduce them to powder in the food processor and blend that powder into spaghetti sauce and soups for an added nutritional boost.

If not properly prepared, beets literally taste like the soil in which they were grown. The outer layer of the beet, known as the "skin" needs to be removed. Once the skins have been removed, the beets can be sliced, rinsed lightly, and then used in your recipes. This can be done by peeling the beets with a peeler, or by roasting and/or boiling the whole beets until tender and then slipping the skin off after plunging them into cold water. This latter method is best as it gets the entire layer that absorbed the flavor of the soil. When boiling beets this way, leave about an inch of the stalk at the top and don't remove the root at the bottom. The loose dirt should be removed prior to boiling, and this can be accomplished using a high-pressure stream of water from a garden hose outside or by washing them off thoroughly in the kitchen sink and using a vegetable brush if needed.

Beets can be stored whole for as long as three months by cutting off the tops, leaving only ½" of stem, and layering the beets in damp sand or peat moss in a container with a tight-fitting lid. The container should be stored in a cool place—preferably just slightly above freezing. Though beets can be frozen, the results aren't impressive. Pressure canning them reduces them to an indistinct mush. The best long-term storage methods for beets are dehydrating and pickling.

Once the skins have been removed from the beets, they can be sliced uniformly, steam blanched for four minutes and then dehydrated until hard. Beets dehydrated this way will reconstitute just fine for soups and stews.

Pickled Beets

Ingredients:

6-8 lbs of beets with the skins removed, sliced uniformly

1 lb onions, skins removed and sliced thinly

1 thinly sliced lemon (rind and all, remove seeds)

4 cups of vinegar (either white or cider vinegar, 5 percent acidity)

2 cups of water

2 cups of sugar

1½ tsp pickling salt

1 Tbsp ground cinnamon

½ tsp ground cloves

1 tsp ground allspice

Procedure:

Cook beets and remove skins. Slice uniformly. Slice the onions and the lemon, and combine with the sliced beets. Prepare a syrup with the remaining ingredients and bring just barely to a boil. Add the sliced beets, onions and lemon to the syrup, bring to a simmer and hold at a simmer for 15 minutes. Pack the vegetables into hot sterilized jars and then pour in syrup leaving ¼" head space. Adjust the two-piece caps and process in a boiling water canner for 10 minutes. Yield: 8—10 pints of pickled beets.

Cabbage, Broccoli and Cauliflower

Broccoli made the news during the administration of President George H. W. Bush because he said he didn't like it. But since that time, broccoli, cabbage and cauliflower have made the news dozens of times in a more positive sense, indicating that the elder statesman might want to re-examine his palate and plate. These delectable delicacies have been in the news quite often for their cancer-fighting benefits.

Cabbage, broccoli, cauliflower and other plants in this family all produce sulforaphane, a potent anti-cancer compound. Along with this, they are rich in fiber, vitamins, minerals, anti-oxidants and more. But the primary reasons they are featured in more meals at my house than any other vegetables is they are not only delicious, but easy to preserve in an appetizing state and incorporate into meal planning.

Variety Selection

Most varieties of cabbage, broccoli and cauliflower will grow just fine in most parts of the country if grown during the right time of year. However, because they are a cool-season crop that is frost-hardy, they tend to do better in the north. As long as the maturation date is no more than sixty days longer than the growing season (and most mature much more quickly), that variety can be grown in your area.

My favorite varieties of cabbage are Early Jersey Wakefield and Golden Acre. Both are early maturing and form a compact head with excellent sweet flavor. My favorite varieties of broccoli are Atlantic and Waltham 29. Both of these varieties produce a lot of side shoots once the main head is cut and have a classic broccoli taste. I usually plant Atlantic in the spring and Waltham 29 in the fall. I've had best results in my area with the Early Snowball variety of cauliflower. Cauliflower is vulnerable to earwigs, and we have a lot of them! A quick-growing cauliflower gives the best odds of a harvest with minimal insect damage.

The foregoing are simply my current preferences and will necessarily reflect my own tastes as well as climate and soil. These are excellent varieties for starting your exploration, but you shouldn't limit yourself.

Broccoli produces side shoots after the main head has been cut.

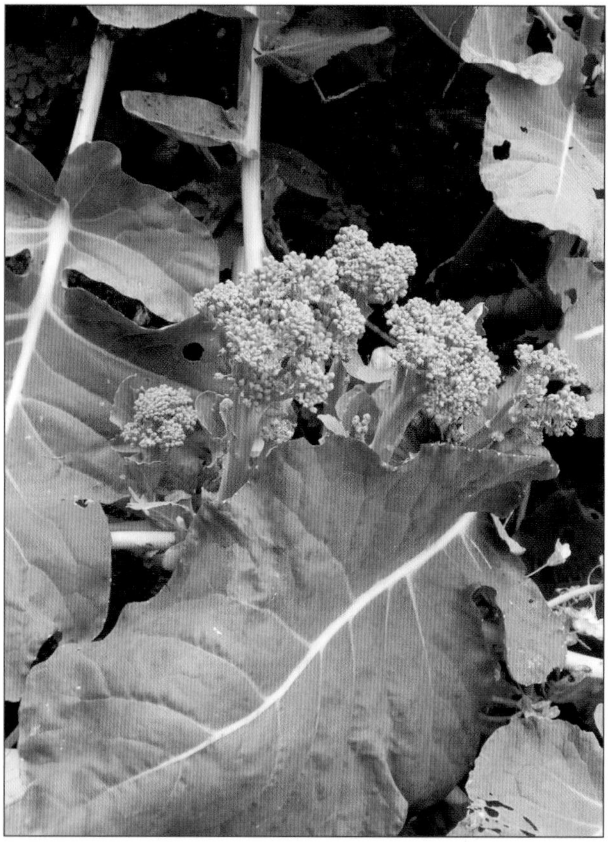

Soil Preparation

Soil pH should be adjusted to 6.5, and the soil should be generously amended with compost and as-needed for sufficient levels of all nutrients. Broccoli in particular is sensitive to boron deficiency, so pay close attention to micronutrient supplementation. The bed should be weed-free prior to planting.

Starting

For spring crops, start cabbage, broccoli and cauliflower indoors eight weeks before last frost, and plant outside three weeks before last frost. Broccoli and cauliflower can be planted out a bit later if desired without harm, but if you delay transplanting the cabbage it might not produce as large a head as it would otherwise produce.

Insufficient boron causes hollow stalks in broccoli.

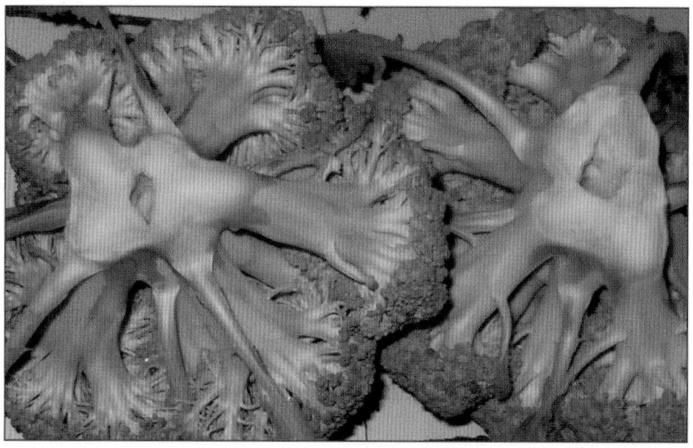

Broccoli grows well closely spaced. »

For fall crops, the timing of planting is a bit more complicated, but easily understood. Mark the date of first fall frost on your calendar, and then mark the date thirty days after. Now, count backwards the number of days to maturity for that variety, count back another ten days to make up for diminishing sunlight, and mark that day on your calendar. That is the day you put your transplants in the ground. Now, count backwards five weeks from that date and mark that date on your calendar. This is the day you start the seedlings inside for your fall planting.

So, given my first fall frost of September 6 and Atlantic broccoli maturing in 62 days, my projected date of harvest is October 6th. The transplants should be put into the beds 62+10 days beforehand, on July 26. The seedlings should be started indoors five weeks before that date, on June 21.

This technique, incidentally, is suitable for any frost-hardy crop grown in fall such as kale, kohlrabi and mustard greens.

Planting

Broccoli, cabbage and cauliflower get pretty big, but they can nevertheless be spaced closely in the beds. Doing so helps to shade out weed competition. In fact, it is very rare for me to have more than a couple of weeds in a bed of these vegetables. So space the plants every 12"-18".

This will allow you to fit as many as thirty-two plants in a single 4'x8' bed.

Early in the season, the availability of nitrogen in the soil is not reliable because the soil temperature may be too cool for microorganisms to work. Because cabbage, broccoli and cauliflower are heavy feeders, you may see signs of nitrogen deficiency almost immediately in the form of older leaves turning yellow. This is easily prevented by watering spring transplants heavily every couple of days with fish fertilizer until they are well-established and danger of frost is past.

Weeds, Pests and Diseases

As long as the bed was prepared and weed-free prior to planting, with these large-leaved vegetables planted so closely together, most weeds will be shaded and have difficulty growing. While the plants are small, you can remove weeds between them with careful use of a stirrup hoe; once they are larger you can easily hand-pull any weeds encountered.

As with other crops, the best approach to pests and diseases is prevention through crop rotation and proper sanitation. Especially when growing in raised beds that prevent waterlogged roots and with properly adjusted soil pH, most disease problems simply will not occur.

Cabbage, broccoli and cauliflower are subject to a few likely pests. Chief among them in common are cabbage loopers. These are the small green worm-like larvae of a nondescript moth with mottled gray and brown coloration. The moths lay eggs either singly or in groups of as many as six on the underside of leaves. When the leaves hatch, the green larvae grow quickly as they consume three times their body weight in vegetable matter daily, leaving a slime of fecal matter in their wake. They have a distinctive "looping" style of locomotion.

Since these pests seldom eat the crowns of broccoli or cauliflower and only rarely bore into the heads of cabbage, on the scale of a mini farm their economic impact is usually small and they can be adequately controlled by hand-picking. (I feed mine to the chickens who consider them a rare delicacy!) If, however, infestation becomes a serious risk, they can be controlled with a Bt (bacillus thuringiensis) preparation used according to label directions. Cabbage loopers have a lot of natural enemies, and among them is the nuclear polyhedrosis virus (NPV). If you are observant and you find any whitish cabbage loopers hanging limply from vegetation, they are dying from NPV. If you can collect them in a can, wait a few hours for them to die, and then mash them up into a water-based spray; any cabbage loopers that eat the coated vegetation will die from NPV in about a week.

Cabbage root maggots can be a problem with early plantings, particularly if immature compost has been added to the beds. These are the larvae of a fly that looks similar to an ordinary house fly. The tell-tale symptom is plants that look wilted even though they are thoroughly watered. The easiest prevention is to plant no more than three weeks before last frost and never use immature compost. Diagnosis is easy: when you pull up a stunted and wilted plant, there will be little white grubs all over the roots. This problem is best prevented by later planting and using only well-matured compost; once you have the problem I have found that it can be solved if caught early by drenching the roots of affected plants with a mixture of neem and pyrethrin/rotenone. If the root damage from the maggots wasn't too extensive, the plants will re-establish themselves and thrive.

Earwigs can be a real nuisance, especially with cauliflower, but also to a lesser extent with cabbage. Earwigs are harmless to humans (they can inflict a minor but harmless pinch with their abdominal pincers) but are a nasty-looking brown creature about ¾" long with prominent pincers on their abdomen. They hide in the heads of cauliflower or in the leaves of cabbage and do tremendous damage from the inside-out that may go undetected until harvest. I have found no organic sprays that are truly effective in dealing with earwigs, though non-organic carbaryl/Sevin will work. They can be prevented by surrounding beds with dry gravel, and they can be trapped by placing damp loosely rolled newspaper near problem areas overnight and disposing of the newspaper in the morning.

Clubroot is a disease of cabbage-family crops that has symptoms similar to cabbage root maggot infestation: the plants are wilting in spite of adequate water. This disease cannot thrive at a pH exceeding 6.8, so it can be prevented by mixing a handful of lime into the soil in the hole you make for transplanting.

Other common diseases such as alternaria, black leg, black rot, downy mildew, turnip mosaic virus" and others can be controlled through conscientious composting of plant residues, rotating which beds are planted with cabbage-family plants, keeping weeds far away from beds and not working in the beds during wet weather. If these measures are insufficient, you can pre-treat seeds (which may harbor some of these diseases) by immersing them in water at 122 degrees F for five minutes prior to planting, and downy mildew can be treated by spraying with one tablespoon of baking soda mixed with a gallon of water.

Harvest

There's more art than science in determining when to harvest cabbage. The heads should be harvested when they reach full-size for that variety, but before the heads crack. In general, there's no such thing as harvesting too early— it is better to be safe than sorry.

The harvesting time frame for broccoli is likewise limited. You want the broccoli to reach its full growth, but you don't want the buds to start flowering. (The flowers are, however, perfectly edible.) Cauliflower should be harvested when the curd is still firm, and before it becomes grainy-looking. The key here is your observation skills. As the florets and curd get larger, examine them daily for any signs of florets opening or the curd getting grainy. Harvested heads can be kept in the refrigerator in a plastic bag for up to a week until enough have been accumulated for cooking or preservation.

When harvesting cabbage, broccoli and cauliflower, use a sharp knife and cut at an angle. In the case of both broccoli and cabbage, you will likely get many individual florets growing on the broccoli plant that can be harvested over the next couple of weeks for use in salads, or several mini-cabbages that taste delicious when steamed.

Seed Saving

Cabbage, broccoli, cauliflower and other plants in the same family such as kale and kohlrabi can all interbreed. As their pollination is via wind and insects, maintaining purity requires that only one variety be allowed to flower for seed production at any given time.

To save seed for broccoli, just don't harvest the heads from twenty or more plants in close proximity. Allow them to flower, and soon they will develop seed pods. Once the pods have turned tan/brown, strip them from the plant into a bag,

⊗ A perfect broccoli crown ready for harvest.

break up the pods, remove the larger debris and then winnow out the smaller debris and dehydrate using silica gel.

Both cabbage and cauliflower are biennial, meaning they produce seed in the second year. In the Southern parts of the U.S. where winter temperatures seldom fall below 20 degrees, cabbage and cauliflower can be mulched with hay over the winter, and cleaned off in spring. In parts of the country where the temperature stays lower than that in the winter, you'll need to bring in the plants to overwinter in a cool (35-40 degree) and dark place, such as an unheated basement. To do this, dig up twenty plants from the fall crop, and store them in damp dirt in five gallon buckets. When spring comes, plant them outside again. To help the cabbages form a flower stalk, use a sharp knife to cut an X in the head. Once cabbage and cauliflower have bolted, they are processed just like broccoli.

The high likelihood of cross-breeding among this species makes it difficult to save seeds from more than one variety in any given year, but the seeds stay viable for five years when properly stored, so if you time your seed saving right, you can stay well-supplied with all the seed you need without danger of cross-breeding.

Preparation and Preservation

With the root and outer leaves removed, a head of **cabbage** will keep in the refrigerator for two weeks if wrapped tightly in plastic wrap. **Broccoli** and **cauliflower** will keep for a week in a tied plastic bag until you've accumulated enough for use or preservation. All three freeze just fine when cut into 1½" chunks. For freezing, cut into chunks,

blanch for four minutes, cool in ice water for four minutes, remove excess water, seal, and freeze.

Cabbage (as well as kale, collard and and turnip greens) can be turned into sauerkraut via lactic acid fermentation, and cabbage, broccoli and cauliflower can be successfully pickled in pint jars using vinegar. Broccoli and cauliflower turn to mush when pressure-canned, but cabbage holds up okay. Pack blanched cabbage pieces into pint jars, cover with hot water leaving 1" of head space, and process for forty-five minutes. Cabbage that has been blanched and dehydrated does fine in winter stews, but broccoli and cauliflower don't dehydrate well.

If you discard the stalks of broccoli after cutting off the florets, you should consider using them to make broccoli-slaw instead. To make broccoli-slaw, peel off the outer layer of the stem and then julienne the rest of it. Broccoli-slaw sells in the produce section for as much as $5 for a 12-ounce bag. I like adding broccoli slaw to regular salads.

Baked Cauliflower

Ingredients:

1 large head of cauliflower cut into 1" pieces
¼ cup olive or walnut oil
1 tsp garlic powder
½ tsp salt
¼ tsp ground black pepper

Procedure:

Preheat oven to 450 degrees. Cut up the cauliflower and place in a large bowl. Add the oil and spices, and mix thoroughly until uniformly coated. Put the coated cauliflower in a roasting pan arranged in a single layer. Bake for twenty minutes until crisp on the outside, but fork-tender.

Pickled Cabbage

Ingredients:

- 1 gallon of chopped cabbage
- 2 large onions, diced (optional)
- ½ cup coarse non-iodized salt
- 4 cups sugar
- 4 cups vinegar
- 1 ½ cups water
- 2 Tbsp mixed pickling spices
- 1 spice bag

Procedure:

Combine the cabbage and onion in a large bowl, mix together with the coarse salt, cover with plastic wrap and allow to sit in the refrigerator overnight. In the morning, flood with fresh water to remove the salt, and drain. Combine the sugar, vinegar and water in a large pot, add the spices well tied in the spice bag, and bring to a simmer for 5 minutes. Add the drained cabbage to the pot, stir thoroughly, and bring to a gentle boil for 5 minutes. Remove and discard the spice bag. Pack into sterilized pint jars and process in a boiling water bath canner for 10 minutes.

⊗ Broccoli can be fried, baked, or steamed as in this photo.

6

Carrots and Parsnips

My mother always told me that carrots were good for my eyes. That's certainly true, as the beta carotene they contain is a precursor for important compounds that assist with vision. But carrots also contain appreciable amounts of vitamin K, vitamin C, folate, potassium and manganese. Parsnips are a member of the same botanical family, but being white they lack carotenes. Nevertheless, they make up for that lack with added amounts of vitamin E, twice the folate of carrots, and B vitamins. For some reason, parsnips aren't as popular as carrots, but as they are both calorically and nutritionally dense; if you find them appetizing they merit equal growing space to carrots in a self-sufficiency enterprise.

Variety Selection

There are very few varieties of **parsnips** available, and these include Harris Model, Hollow Crown, All American and Half-Long Guernsey. All are long-season varieties that are planted in the spring and harvested after the first fall frost.

The varieties of carrots available number in the hundreds and encompass an endless array of colors, lengths, widths and tastes. These range from the tiny Thumbelina carrot that is literally no bigger than your thumb all the way through the multi-colored Cosmic Purple carrot. In general, carrots fall into a few broad categories. These include Imperator-type varieties that are long and tapered, Nantes that are cylindrical and high in sugar but don't keep well, Danvers with a high fiber content and good keeping qualities, and Chantenay types that are short and wide, and so better-suited for heavy soils. Even though most carrots you'll find in the supermarket are Imperator type carrots; these are usually among the least tasty varieties. We eat a lot of carrots. The primary varieties that I grow are Saint Valery, Scarlet Nantes and Danvers Half-Long, though I usually plant some purple carrots such as Dragon for variety. The Saint Valery carrots are 12" long and as much as 3" in diameter—real monsters. They store well, have a high germination rate for carrots and therefore tend to be quite productive. Scarlet Nantes carrots are blunt-tipped and about 7" long. They are reddish, sweet and almost core-less. They are a great variety for juicing. Danvers Half-long grow well in tough soils, are about 7" long and are a favorite at markets.

Soil Preparation

Carrots and parsnips require a soil that is deeply dug, cleared of stones, light and with a pH of 6.5-7.5; though they will grow at a pH as low as 6.0. They prefer a soil that is rich in phosphorus, potassium, calcium and micronutrients, but go very easy on the nitrogen. Wood ashes as a form of potassium are well-loved by carrots and parsnips. When preparing the bed, use about half the nitrogen-bearing fertilizer that you would for other crops. Also avoid any form of fresh manures, especially animal manure. Carrots and parsnips will taste just like the manure and your entire crop will be a loss. You should ideally add *fully matured* compost in the fall to beds destined for carrots in the spring, because freshly added or immature compost will inhibit germination as well as causing deformities in the shape of the carrots. The deformed carrots are perfectly safe to eat, but not marketable. Stones will also cause deformities. Again, this isn't a problem in terms of edibility or flavor, but will make the carrots less marketable and more difficult to store.

Planting

Carrots and parsnips are among the slowest germinating crops in the garden; this slow rate of germination can be problematic because weeds will likely sprout first, and there is difficulty in maintaining optimum levels of soil moisture long enough for the seeds to sprout. They also don't like being thinned as they are very fragile when young, and should therefore be planted at optimum spacing from the beginning.

These crops should be planted three weeks before last frost or when soil temperatures are above 50 degrees at a 4" spacing in all directions. Parsnip seeds aren't too difficult to handle, but carrot seeds are small. If you find them difficult to handle, there are several seed companies that sell carrot seeds that have been encapsulated in an innocuous substance that will break down once the seeds have been watered. These encapsulated seeds are the size of a BB and much easier to handle. Alternately, you can have someone with smaller fingers take on the task.

In spring plantings, the seeds should be planted no more than ¼" deep because the lower temperatures will make germination take longer, and the fragile seedlings will have too much difficulty breaking through the soil if they are planted more deeply. For late summer plantings, they can be planted more deeply.

Carrots and parsnips take a long time to germinate, but this is very much temperature dependent. At a soil temperature of 42 degrees, they take 51 days to germinate. At 50 degrees, they take 17 days to germinate, but at a soil temperature of 59 degrees, they require only ten days. Only six days are required at 72 degrees, but germination rates at temperatures higher than that decline. Use of a soil thermometer to time your planting can help a great deal with these vegetables.

After the seeds are planted, you should water twice daily using a fine mist until the seedlings are well established. Once they are established, a weekly deep soaking providing the equivalent of an inch of water is sufficient.

The one growing problem you may encounter with carrots is green shoulders. If they grow up out of the ground, the tops of the carrots will turn green and they will become bitter. If you see carrot tops poking up out of the ground at all, hill them with some dirt and it won't be a problem.

Weeds, Pests and Diseases

Weeds are a real problem with carrots and parsnips because even if the bed is seemingly weed-free at the time of planting, the long period of germination can give weeds a head start. With the seedlings in such a delicate state, weeding at an early point can be too disruptive.

There are a lot of ways to handle this. If you time your planting for a soil temperature of 59 degrees, then germination will take only ten days. Another approach often cited in gardening literature is to soak the seed bed and then lay a board over it to seal in the dampness and deprive potential weeds of light. No doubt this works in some cases, especially with sandy soils, but in my case the soil adheres to the board and when the board is lifted, the seedlings come with it. You can also solarize the bed by giving it a good soaking a couple of months before planting and covering with closely stapled clear plastic until time to plant. This will raise the temperature of the top two inches of the soil high enough that weed seeds will be unable to survive. What I do is go over the bed slowly with a flame weeder just prior to planting, and disturb the soil as little as possible while putting in the seeds. This only kills seeds in the top ¼" of soil, but it works well enough and is quickly accomplished. While I am at it, I use the flame weeder to get all the weeds and grasses growing along the edges of the beds.

Though, theoretically, there are a lot of potential pest and disease problems with carrots; on the scale of a mini farm, if you are practicing crop rotation and cleaning up debris at the end of the season, you really only have two pests of concern: wireworms and carrot flies.

Wireworms are the larvae of click beetles, and are usually a problem when growing in areas that were previously sod, or are abutted by sod. Thus, they are a common problem with mini farms in particular, because raised beds are usually located in areas that were previously used for growing grass. Wireworms burrow into many edible root

⊗ Wireworms are easily identified but not easily controlled.

crops including carrots, parsnips, potatoes and more.

If you surround your bed frames with a mulch that smothers out grasses such as a thick layer of bark or gravel, that will help diminish populations over time. Turning up the soil in the beds a couple of days prior to planting will encourage birds to eat them. Also, when we turn the soil, we scan it for wireworms and other grubs, and feed them to our chickens. You can also bait the wireworms by burying some pieces of cut potato attached to a skewer (for ease in locating) two to four inches under the soil surface. Pull up the skewers twice a week and dispose of the wireworms. If you put the skewers into the beds intended for root crops a week prior to planting and keep them in place until a week after germination, damage from wireworms will be reduced considerably. Figure on one skewer per four square feet of bed space.

Carrot flies are the other likely pest. Carrot flies look like a regular housefly, except they are more streamlined. Often, you won't see them. Once attracted by the smell of the foliage of parsley, carrots, celery, parsnips and related plants, they fly in and lay eggs in the soil at the base of the plant. When the eggs hatch, the grubs burrow into the roots and ruin them. Unfortunately, you won't find the problem until you harvest the roots and start cussing.

An important aspect of preventing carrot flies is to avoid anything that injures or disturbs the foliage. Bruised foliage is a powerful attractant. Luckily, when spaced so closely together, the plants will usually shade out any weeds, so the primary cause of bruised foliage—weeding—can be avoided. If you must weed, do so carefully.

Another trick that works surprisingly well is to attach some wooden stakes to the corners of the bed, and wrap a 2' high section of clear plastic around the bed, stapling it to the stakes and the edges of the bed. Carrot flies seldom fly any higher than 18" from the ground, so the plastic baffles them and they move on to easier pickings.

Finally, carrot flies (and some less common pests such as carrot weevils) don't like wood ashes. If you use wood ashes when you prepare the bed, and water the bed every couple of weeks with a mixture of two tablespoon of wood ashes per gallon of water, they will be deterred.

⊗ Carrots grown in a box with a landscape fabric bottom to outwit wireworms.

Harvest

Carrots and parsnips can be harvested at any stage, however the balance of bitter turpenes and sugars favors the turpenes when harvested early. Parsnips are best left until after the first hard frost, as this sweetens them. Carrots, on the other hand, should be harvested no more than two weeks later than the specified maturity date of that variety, as letting them sit in the ground too long can make them fibrous.

To harvest carrots or parsnips, water thoroughly to make the roots easier to pull; grasp the foliage as close to the root as possible, and pull while giving a slight twist. If the tops break off, you can use a digging fork or hand shovel to dig around the affected roots and lift them out gently. Cut off the tops ¼" above the root and immediately place in the compost pile. Let the roots sit out in the sun for a couple of hours for the dirt to dry, then dust it off with a soft brush. Carrots should be washed immediately prior to use.

Seed Saving

Carrots and parsnips are biennials, meaning they produce seed in their second year. During their first year, they store energy in the root. If allowed to stay in the ground over the winter, they will sprout in the spring, sending up a seed stalk with a beautiful flower called an umbel that is identical to Queen Anne's lace. In fact, Queen Anne's lace is a wild carrot from which our domesticated varieties are derived, and it will interbreed freely with garden carrots.

Because wild carrots are so widely distributed and this family is insect-pollinated, isolation techniques are recommended for saving carrot seed, though they aren't necessary for parsnips. In addition, inbreeding depression can be a problem, so ideally seeds will be saved from a population of at least twenty plants.

⊗ Carrot flowers can be impressively large.

Bag the umbels (using a spun polyester material such as what you can buy as a floating row cover) when they have not yet flowered to keep insects from getting to them. You don't have to bag all of the umbels, just one from each plant that you will be using for seed. Once the umbels have flowered, use a horsehair or camel hair brush to cross-pollinate. The technique is straightforward: every day for two to four weeks once the flowers have formed, remove the bags from as many flowers as you can keep free of insects at one time. Gently rub the brush over the flowers in each umbel, going back and forth so that all flowers of each umbel have been touched. Replace the bags, then remove the bags from another set of umbels and continue until all of the umbels have been processed.

Once the umbels have matured, cut them from the plant and allow them to mature indoors in a cool, dry place for another two weeks. The seeds can be stripped from the umbels by rubbing with your hands and separated from the chafe by winnowing.

Preparation and Preservation

Carrots and parsnips can be stored whole for a few months in moistened peat moss or clean sand. The tops are cut ½" above the root so they don't suck the moisture out of the roots. They can also be blanched for four minutes and then either cooled, dried and frozen or dehydrated. If dried thoroughly, they can be stored in the refrigerator in a sealed bag for a couple of months.

Carrot and Parsnip Pickles

Ingredients:

- 1 pound carrots
- 1 pound parsnips
- 3½ cups vinegar
- 1½ cups sugar
- 2 tsp ground cinnamon
- 1 tsp ground allspice
- 1 tsp sea salt or other non-iodized salt
- ½ tsp ground cloves

Procedure:

Quarter the carrots and parsnips lengthwise and cut into spears 3½" long. Pack into clean pint jars. Combine the remaining ingredients in a saucepan, and bring to a light boil for 5 minutes. Pour this into the jars, completely covering the spears and leaving ½" headspace. Adjust the two-piece lids and process in a boiling water canner for 15 minutes.

Lemon Dill Carrots

Ingredients:

- 1 pound of carrots
- 1 lemon
- 3 Tbsp walnut oil (butter can be substituted)
- ½ tsp dried dill weed

Procedure:

Preheat oven to 350 degrees. Cut the carrots to uniform thickness, coat thoroughly with walnut oil, then add one quarter of the zest of the lemon and all of its juice (making sure to remove any pits) and uniformly cover with dill weed. Spread in a single layer in a covered (it is important that it be covered!) baking dish. Bake for 30 minutes or until fork-tender.

⊗ This dish is enhanced with dill fresh from the garden.

7

Corn

Corn is one of the biggest commercial crops in the country—used to make everything from corn starch baby powder to ethanol for vehicles. Unfortunately, it is also one of the most genetically modified. Depending upon the state in which it is grown, between 79 percent and 95 percent of all corn grown in the United States is genetically engineered.[3]

There is sufficient debate regarding the safety of such crops that the European Union currently bans importing or growing genetically engineered corn for human use. Whether they are safe or not I cannot pretend to know with certainty. Much of the data pertaining to its dangers seems rather alarmist, but the data pertaining to its safety is from biased sources. Perhaps the strangest development in this debate is the adoption of Federal laws that preempt state laws requiring that products containing genetically modified crops be labeled.[4]

Thus, other than the laws that ban the use of genetically modified seeds in USDA Organic produce, there is no way to know whether what you are eating contains genetically engineered organisms.

3 USDA Economic Research Service (2010), Adoption of Genetically Engineered Crops in the U.S.: Corn Varieties.
4 Lasker, Eric (2005), *Federal Preemption and state Anti-"GM" Food Laws.*

As I have mentioned, I find the data pertaining to the safety or harm of genetically engineered corn rather murky. Other than buying expensive organic-labeled products, the only way to assure the corn you eat is free of genetically engineered attributes is to grow it yourself.

Varieties

Corn is a staple of the human diet in many places, and as a result many variations of corn have been created for different uses. Flour corn can be ground into a fine flour. Flint is used to make coarse corn meal. Dent corn is used in animal feeds and industry. Pop corn is used to make (you guessed it) popcorn. But the type of corn most commonly grown by home gardeners is sweet corn.

Of the many varieties of flint corn available, Floriani Red Flint is one of the most productive open-pollinated varieties available. Grain yield is roughly five pounds per 4'x8' bed. Blue Hopi is an heirloom variety with a distinctive blue color and fantastic flavor, though it is slightly less productive at four pounds per 4'x8' bed.

Sweet corn falls into three categories based upon genetics: Normal Sugary (Su), Sugary Enhanced (Se) and Supersweet (Sh2). These genes determine how much sugar is in the kernel and how long the sugar will stay in the kernel before turning to starch. All of the genes that result in sweet corn are recessive traits that spontaneously arose in flint or dent corn. As a result of the recessive quality of these traits, sweet corn should be separated from field corns that may be pollinating at the same time by at least 400 yards. Otherwise, the kernels of the sweet corn won't be sweet.

Su sweet corns are the oldest varieties of sweet corn. Nearly all available open-pollinated varieties of sweet corn have this genetic profile. Examples of popular open-pollinated varieties include Golden Bantam (yellow), Country Gentleman (white), Stowell's Evergreen (white) and Double Standard (bicolor). Common hybrids with Su genes include Early Sunglow (yellow), Silver Queen (white) and Butter and Sugar (bicolor).

Su sweet corn needs to be kept well away from Sh2 sweet corn, but can be grown near Se sweet corn and vice versa. Harvest timing is critical, and it should ideally be processed within thirty minutes of harvest, as the sugar starts turning to starch the second the ear is picked from the stalk. Even so, Su varieties deliver a classic corn taste, and hold up well to being blanched and frozen on the cob.

Se sweet corn has even more sugar than Su corn—so much so that it can keep at high quality for two to four days after harvest if refrigerated. Although some projects for producing open-pollinated Se varieties are underway,[5] all commercially available Se varieties are hybrids. Se corn has excellent taste, but is comparatively delicate so it doesn't stand up well to processing. It is better for fresh eating. Popular Se varieties include Kandy Korn (yellow), Argent (white) and Precious Gem (bicolor).

Sh2 sweet holds its sugar content for as long as ten days after harvest, and is thus ideal for truck-shipping and display in supermarkets. In addition, though more ideal for shipping than eating, the kernels are tougher, and so stand up better to rough handling. All commercially available Sh2

---

5   The Organic Farming Research Foundation has funded a project to create two open pollinated, sugary enhanced sweet corn varieties. Joseph's Garden in Paradise, Utah, is undertaking a similar effort.

varieties are hybrids, and they must be separated from Se and Su types to avoid developing starchy kernels. Popular Sh2 varieties include Challenger (yellow), Aspen (white) and Dazzle (bicolor).

Though there are a staggering number of varieties available, for mini-farming I recommend sticking to Su and Se varieties because they are more tolerant of planting depth and soil temperature variations. For seed-saving, you are limited to open-pollinated varieties that, so far, are entirely Su strains. I recommend Floriani Red Flint or Blue Hopi for corn meal, and Golden Bantam or Stowell's Evergreen for sweet corn. These are beginner recommendations and through experimentation you'll likely find other varieties that you like.

Soil Preparation

Corn is a seriously hungry plant, requiring plenty of food, light and water for optimal production. In addition, it is shallow-rooted, a fact that makes proper soil management all the more critical. Corn prefers a pH of 6.0 to 6.5, and lots of organic matter tilled throughout the top six to eight inches of soil. It is a heavy feeder and in agrigbusiness production is typically treated with high-nitrogen fertilizers three times during the course of the season. However, this is because the artificial fertilizers they use are highly soluble, and they pay little attention to maintaining high enough levels of organic matter in the soil to hold onto those nutrients. A properly prepared bed will not need additional fertilizer to produce great corn.

To prepare a bed for corn, add at least six cubic feet of mature compost per 48 square feet of bed and mix it into the top six to eight inches of soil.

Adjust the pH to somewhere between 6.0 and 6.5 using lime. Add micronutrients in the form of sea mineral solids at the manufacturer's recommended rate. Amend the soil using organic fertilizers based upon a home soil test for nitrogen, phosphorus and potassium. Finally, to provide additional both slow and fast release nitrogen, add ten pounds of alfalfa meal and two pounds of blood meal per forty-eight-square-foot bed, in addition to what you have already added based upon soil test. The compost will work with the nutrients to hold them in the soil so rain won't wash them out, and make them available to the corn as the plant requires. Using this method, I have never needed to add fertilizer during the season.

Starting and Planting

Corn can be temperamental about planting depth, temperature, water levels and more, especially when dealing with hybrid Sh2 varieties. But even Su varieties can suffer from staggered germination, seeds rotting in the ground before they can sprout, and other woes.

Though this solution certainly won't work on the scale of the agri-giant Monsanto, for a mini-farm it works extremely well: instead of planting your seeds in the ground, start them indoors one week before last frost. Then, plant out your corn seedlings at one-foot spacing in all directions one week after last frost. This allows you to skip all these problems and have a nice, uniform stand of corn.

If you don't want to do this, then plant your seeds 1" deep spaced 12" apart one week after last frost, and water daily until they sprout.

Also, if you follow my practice of planting beans with corn (see *Mini Farming*), wait until a week after the corn seedling have emerged before planting the beans. Otherwise, the beans will sprout first and shade out your corn.

Corn is wind-pollinated and strongly outbreeding. Pollination is necessary to produce kernels on the ears. Planting the corn so closely spaced is generally sufficient to yield adequate pollination, but just to be sure, once the pollen-bearing tops have grown, I reach in and gently shake a few corn plants every once in a while to distribute the pollen.

Weeds, Pests and Diseases

In agribusiness production on the scale of hundreds of acres and where harvesting is mechanized, weeds are a serious problem for corn. Mass spraying with herbicides is practiced, and genetically modified corn that is immune to the herbicides is planted. Fortunately, on the scale of a mini farm, weeds can be controlled with little effort. If you clear the bed of weeds before planting, a weekly hand-weeding or use of a stirrup hoe between plants is sufficient.

Though in commercial mono-cropping there are a lot of pest problems, in a properly run mini farm where crop sanitation and rotation are practiced; there are only a couple of notable pests that are easily controlled. Japanese beetles can defoliate the corn and thus reduce productivity. Japanese beetles are a ubiquitous lawn grub. If you have a lot of property so there is a good buffer with your neighbors, treating your entire lawn and beds with milky spore disease can be a good preventative once the disease has become

established in a year or so. Japanese beetle traps (available at hardware stores) can work well, but they must be placed downwind of the garden at least 100' away.

Japanese beetles attract each other. So one way to keep them controlled is to simply pick them by hand into a small bucket of soapy water. If you keep them picked off daily once they are noticed, you'll likely prevent the problem all together. They can also be controlled by sprays such as pyrethrin and rotenone used according to package directions, but this is a last resort as such sprays are expensive.

The other notable pest is corn ear worm. This is the larva of a large but rather nondescript moth. Though it will attack nearly anything edible in the garden, including tomatoes, broccoli and lettuce, it is primarily a risk for corn because the damage it has done is not visible until harvest. Because the moth can't overwinter north of Maryland, it tends to be more consistently damaging in the South, though winds blow it well up into Canada.

The moth lays its speck-sized eggs on corn silk. The hatched eggs produce a tiny worm that crawls down the silk into the ear, and burrows its way in. It grows as it eats and by the time it is done it can be a good three inches long. Often, it will not be immediately detected because its head resembles a kernel of corn and it will have bored through the cob and put its head in place of a corn kernel. It can be a bit unsettling when an ear of boiled corn is chomped, and you pull away with a worm dangling from your mouth! Sometimes the worm simply eats along the outside of the ear. Almost always, it eats some of the silk, which prevents kernels from being pollinated and growing.

Damage from corn ear worm can be substantially reduced with a critically timed application of Bt (bacillus thuringiensis) mixed with corn oil from the supermarket and using liquid lecithin (available at health food stores) as an emulsifier. Mix one heaping tablespoon of liquid lecithin and three level tablespoons of Bt (in this case, Dipel DF) with one quart of corn oil. Mix thoroughly. Apply 0.5 ml of the mixture to each corn tassel. I use a small syringe (without the needle) that I picked up from a veterinary supply company to measure the amount accurately. Apply it to the corn tassel, and distribute it evenly by hand.

The oil can adversely affect pollination but is extremely effective in controlling ear worm damage during the crucial stage. There is a short five to eight day window when it can be applied with minimal impact on pollination and still achieve good control. If you observe your corn carefully, that time period starts 57 days after the start of silk growth, or 34 days after the silk is fully grown.

This sort of observation may not be feasible. But all is not lost! You can also judge when to apply the oil by waiting until the tips of the silk have just barely started to turn brown and wilt. If you peel back the husk from an ear of corn, you'll discover that silk is only attached to less than the top inch of kernels.

This is the optimal method as it provides greatest control with minimum use of materials. However, it might not be practical. Especially if you are raising a substantial amount of corn, the process can quickly become tedious. If this is the case, you can deal with the problem by using a Bt or spinosad preparation according to label directions, and thoroughly spraying the corn once a week using an ordinary garden sprayer starting once the silk has formed. The water-based spray will have no adverse effect on pollination and as long as you don't skip, adequate control will be maintained.

Though corn is vulnerable to about a dozen diseases of commercial importance in large-scale farming, within the format of a mini-farm in which soil fertility is properly maintained, crops are rotated among beds and crop debris is composted, none of them are likely to be an issue at all. Likewise, many of the diseases that manifest in agribusiness production are the result of damage to the corn stalk or ears from machines. As mini-farming methods don't use machines, this won't be a problem. If in spite of good cultural practices you encounter disease problems, switching to a hybrid Su corn for future plantings will likely take care of them.

Though it isn't a pest or disease problem per se; lodging of corn hurts productivity in large-scale production and can certainly be a problem on a mini farm. Lodging is defined as stalk breakage below the corn ear, and it is usually caused by severe winds or weather. Because corn is grown in beds on a mini farm, lodging can be entirely eliminated by using deck screws to screw some four foot uprights to the corners of the bed and running some stout string that is resistant to UV degradation around the bed and through holes drilled near the top of the uprights.

Harvest

Field corns such as dent and flint corn are harvested at their dry stage. Harvest as soon as the green husk fades to tan by holding the corn stalk in one hand, and pulling the ear down with the other while twisting slightly. The ears should be shucked immediately, meaning that the husks and as much silk removed as possible. Then the husked ears should be hung in bunches out of the weather where there is good air circulation for a month or more. Once the kernels are well dried, the kernels can be removed from the cobs by shelling. On a small scale, you can remove the dry kernels from the ears by wearing gloves (so you don't get blisters) and rubbing two ears together and twisting the cob in your hands. Collect the kernels and allow to dry further. On a larger scale, you can use a simple hand sheller, or a manually operated mechanical sheller. Mechanical shellers are operated with a hand crank and are pretty fun to use. My cousins and I used to shell corn for my grandfather using a mechanical sheller, and we thought it was a lot of fun. As he had never told us to do it, we never realized it was supposed to be work.

The timing of sweet corn harvest is a bit more tricky. If you harvest too early, the kernels are imperfectly formed and there is insufficient sugar. If you harvest too late, it becomes starchy and hard. To complicate matters, especially with open-pollinated varieties, not all the ears mature at once. This is one reason why hybrids are used in large-scale farming—they allow all of the corn to be harvested in one session. Nevertheless, all of the ears of open-pollinated sweet corn can be harvested within a week of each other.

Corn will mature at a different rate each year, depending on temperature, amount of sunlight, and the amount of water it receives, so the "days to harvest" given in the seed catalog is an approximation. Start checking the ears twenty-one days after silk has appeared. When the silk has turned brown and started to dry, feel the ears to see if

When the silk has turned brown and started to dry, check your sweet corn for ripeness.

they are firm. If so, gently separate some of the husk midway down the ear, and puncture one of the kernels with your thumb. If the juice is clear, the corn isn't ready yet. If the juice is milky, it is time to harvest. If it is creamy, then the corn is over-ripe. All is not lost with slightly overripe sweet corn because at that stage it is perfect for canning.

To harvest, remove the ears using the same technique as for field corn, but leave the husks

⊗ Sweet corn should be shucked and used as soon as possible after harvest.

on. Store at a cool temperature, preferably in a refrigerator until used to help slow down the conversion of sugar to starch. With Su varieties, use or preserve within a few hours. With Se varieties, you have 2-3 days. With Sh2 varieties, you have a week.

Seed Saving

Corn is a strongly out-breeding plant, meaning that it is subject to inbreeding depression if a large number of plants aren't used as the breeding pool. In the case of corn, so many plants are needed that it may not even be feasible to save seed at a small scale. You need at least 200 plants, from which you cull any that are clearly inferior or off-type. Because corn is wind pollinated and readily crosses with all other varieties of corn, if you are trying to maintain pure seed it should be separated from other corn by at least a mile, but preferably more.

The seeds of field corn are harvested as described above in the section on harvesting. In order to save seed from sweet corn, treat it like field corn and allow the ear to reach maturity rather than harvesting at its milk stage. I recommend shelling all of the corn into a large container, mixing it thoroughly so that seeds are saved from as many unique plants as possible, and taking a random sample of at least a quart from the container as seed. The dried corn that isn't used for seed can also be ground into corn meal.

Preparation and Preservation

Dried corn should be stored in an airtight container in a cool, dry place. Ideally, that container will be free of oxygen in order to prevent pests. There are a lot of ways to do this. One way is to put a metal plate on top of the corn and place an amount of dry ice (solidified carbon dioxide) on the plate. Because carbon dioxide is heavier than air, as it vaporizes, it will supplant all of the oxygen in the container. When the dry ice is almost gone, put the lid on the container. Another way is to use an airtight metal container, put a very stable heat-proof plate on top of the corn, put an unscented candle on it, light the candle and close the lid. Though this won't remove all the oxygen, it will alter the oxygen/carbon dioxide proportions sufficiently to be inimical to animal life. You'll need to re-light the candle each time the lid is opened. Flint and dent corn can be ground into truly excellent corn meal using a hand grinder with proper burrs such as the Corona grain mill.

Sweet corn is ideally prepared within a few hours of harvest to prevent the conversion of sugars to starches. The most popular way to eat sweet corn is on the cob. The corn is shucked, and the ears are boiled for twenty minutes or so. I prefer to slather mine with enough butter and salt to make a cardiologist wince, but there are plenty of other toppings. Corn on the cob can also be grilled. Peel back the husk but leave it attached, remove the silk, coat the kernels with plentiful olive oil, put the husk back and tie closed with cotton string. Then grill, turning frequently, on a medium-hot grill for fifteen to twenty minutes. If you don't want to bother with the husk, wrap the shucked ears in aluminum foil and use butter instead of oil.

Sweet corn can be frozen either on or off the cob. Blanch for four minutes, cool for four minutes, dry off the water, and put in freezer bags from which the air has been evacuated. Off the cob, it can also be dehydrated following blanching. corn" holds up to pressure canning pretty well, especially if harvested a couple of days late.

Canned Corn

Ingredients:

2 pounds of husked corn on the cob per pint
salt
water

Procedure:

Husk the corn and remove the silk. Use a sharp knife to cut the kernels from the cob. Place the kernels in jars, add (optionally) ½ tsp salt per pint or 1 tsp per quart, ladle boiling water over the corn in the jars leaving one inch of head space, and then process in a pressure canner at ten pounds of pressure for 55 minutes for pints, or 80 minutes for quarts.

Fresh Corn Salsa

Ingredients:

5 ears of fresh corn
1 jalapeño pepper
½ pound of tomatillos (preferred) or tomatoes
1 red pepper, chopped small with membranes removed
1 small onion, sliced thinly
1 lemon
½ tsp ground coriander
1 Tbsp chopped fresh cilantro
water

Procedure:

Husk the corn and cut the kernels from the cobs. Remove membranes and chop the jalapeño pepper finely. Chop up the tomatillos after removing the husks. Add all of the ingredients to a frying pan, squeeze the juice of the lemon into the mixture, add enough water to prevent scorching, and bring to a light boil over medium heat. Stir frequently for 5 minutes, and then remove from heat. Put it in the refrigerator to cool, and then stir in the cilantro before serving. Note: this is a fresh salsa and is not intended for canning as it isn't acidic enough to be canned safely.

8

Cucumbers

Cucumbers are in close competition with tomatoes as the quintessential vegetable announcing the joy of summer. Eaten alone, as part of a salad or as a pickle, cucumbers lend a distinctively fresh and wholesome flavor to any meal. A member of the gourd family along with gourds, melons and squash, cucumbers were originally cultivated in India, and spread from there to ancient Greece, Rome and eventually to France where they graced Charlemagne's table.

Cucumbers contain caffeic acid and vitamin C, as well as being a good source of molybdenum, vitamin A, fiber and folate in the diet. Their silica content is good for the skin, and they have been used as a cosmetic for hundreds of years to reduce puffiness in and around the eyes either sliced or as a paste.

Variety Selection

In general, cucumbers are classified as *slicers*, *picklers* or *burpless*, though at the right stage of development their uses are interchangeable to some degree. Slicers are usually long and straight, and are intended for fresh eating. Picklers usually grow no longer than four inches, and have been bred specifically for their quality as pickles. Burpless cucumbers are supposed to be more easily digested without burping when eaten fresh, but as I've never had a problem with either slicers or picklers causing burping, I can't say with certainty that burpless cucumbers solve the problem.

When growing in raised beds, space is an issue. Cucumbers are usually a vining crop, though some bush varieties have been introduced. In general, bush varieties aren't very productive. Using raised beds, the best space efficiency is gained by growing vining varieties on a trellis on the Northern one foot of a bed, and using the rest of the bed for growing a shorter crop such as lettuce or carrots. Trellised cucumbers also tend to grow straighter.

One additional complication in choosing cucumber varieties is bacterial wilt disease, spread by cucumber beetles. There are very few resistant cultivars, but if you run into trouble with this pest and the accompanying disease, your best bet may be to switch to a variety of cucumber that is resistant.

⊗ Pickling and slicing cucumbers ready for a salad.

Among slicers, good vining varieties include Muncher, Marketmore 76, Tendergreen Burpless and Straight 8. My favorite vining picklers are Homemade Pickles and Boston Pickling Improved. If you have difficulty with cucumber beetles carrying bacterial wilt disease, you might want to consider the hybrid pickler County Fair which has demonstrated resistance to bacterial wilt disease in controlled studies.

Soil Preparation

Cucumbers like fertile, well-drained soils with lots of organic matter. Add at least 5 cubic feet of compost per 4'x8' bed, adjust the pH to between 6 and 7, and amend for NPK as indicated by a soil test. Cucumbers like trace minerals, so make sure these are added as well. Organic fertilizers are well-matched to cucumbers as continuous harvest creates long-term needs for fertility. Organic fertilizers buffered with plenty of compost are a recipe for impressive success with cucumbers, and also reduce the uneven growth spurts that make cucumbers more vulnerable to disease.

Starting and Planting

Cucumbers can be grown either from seed or from transplants. I prefer to start the seeds indoors a week before last frost, and then plant them out a week after last frost to give them a head start. If you prefer direct seeding, wait until a week after last frost, put the seeds in soil ½" to 1" deep and water thoroughly daily until the seedlings emerge.

As mentioned earlier, cucumbers are most productive and most space-efficient when trellised. A six foot trellis is sufficient. Plant cucum-

⊗ Growing cucumbers on a trellis makes them straighter and saves space.

bers spaced 8"–12" apart in a single row along the Northern one foot of a bed. As the seedlings grow, train the vines onto the trellis. Once they have a foothold on the trellis, you'll only have to train the occasional errant vine.

Weeds, Pests and Diseases

Plant cucumbers in a weed-free bed and weed by hand weekly. Once established, cucumbers will outgrow most weed problems, but you want to get the weeds out anyway so they don't set seed and create a problem for future crops.

Cucumbers are vulnerable to three major pests: leaf miners, aphids and cucumber beetles.

They also are vulnerable to squash bugs and squash vine borers, though they aren't a preferred food for those creatures. (For more information on these latter two pests, please see the section on squash.) Leaf miners are the larvae of a small yellow and black fly. The eggs are laid on the upper surface of the leaf, and the hatched larvae burrow through the leaf, leaving tracks. When ready, they cut a semi-circular hole on the underside of the leaf, and drop to the ground to pupate. Usually, leaf miners pose little or no economic risk to cucumbers. Crop rotation and cleaning up debris are sufficient to keep them at bay.

Various species of aphids affect nearly every soft plant in existence. They suck out the plant juices and excrete a sticky honeydew that serves as food for ants and fungi. At low levels of infestation, aphids aren't usually an economic threat, but at higher levels they can weaken and stunt plants. Aphids are tiny oval creatures about $\frac{1}{16}$th of an inch long when full grown. Some have wings and some don't. They can be controlled with insecticidal soap or a light horticultural oil applied to tops and bottoms of leaf surfaces and along the stem.

Cucumber beetles are a serious threat because they carry bacterial wilt disease. They can do serious feeding damage as well, with adults feeding on fruit, flowers, stems and foliage and larvae feeding on the roots. But overall, bacterial wilt disease is their greatest threat because the disease kills the plants outright. Organic control focuses mainly on prevention because botanical insecticides are only moderately effective at best, especially given that all it takes to kill a plant is a single bite. Because cucumber beetles overwinter away from the garden, feed on a variety of wild

plants and trees until cucurbits are available and can be carried hundreds of miles on high altitude wind currents; crop rotation and composting debris are not as effective in controlling them as controlling other pests.

Some people grow cucumbers for decades and never encounter a cucumber beetle, while another farmer less than a mile away can suffer serious infestation year after year. You never really know unless you encounter them. If you encounter them, here are some strategies for their management:

Grow resistant varieties. Only two resistant varieties exist as far as I know: County Fair (a pickler) and Saladin (a European greenhouse slicer). Use transplants instead of seeds to get a head start. Use **floating row cover** (well-anchored) to exclude the beetles until the first flowers appear. If you use this strategy, you should thoroughly weed the bed and then flame the soil before transplanting, as opening up the row cover

to weed will defeat its purpose. Use aluminum foil or mylar (you can get this cheap as a so-called "emergency blanket") as a **mulch** because studies show this sort of **mulch** can reduce pest levels below the threshold of economic damage.[6]

Once you see cucumber beetles on your vines (they often hide in the flowers), it's too late for any organic sprays to have much of an effect. Plus, those sprays (particularly those containing pyrethrin) would likely be far more toxic to bees, and bees are critical pollinators for cucumbers.

Other than bacterial wilt, the most likely disease you will see in cucumbers is powdery mildew. Powdery mildew is caused by a fungal spoor taking root on (usually) the underside of the leaves. It appears like baby powder, and is often accompanied by a yellowing of the upper side of the leaf opposite the fungus colony. As the

---

6   Diver, S. & Hinman, T. (2008), *Cucumber Beetles: Organic and Biorational Integrated Pest Management.*

disease progresses, it can spread to the upper sides of leaves and even (although rarely) to the fruit. Powdery mildew infections, if uncontrolled, will cause the death of the associated leaves and poor quality fruit.

Conditions favoring powdery mildew development are high humidity, shade, and poor air circulation. It overwinters in crop debris, so even though the spoors are widespread, risk of reinfection can be diminished through sanitation. Likewise, the variation and species of powdery mildew fungus is usually specific to a given family of plants, so crop rotation will help. So growing cucumbers on trellises for better air circulation and locating them in full sun, along with crop rotation and sanitation will go a long way toward prevention.

Another thing to consider, because a lot of resistant varieties of cucumber are available, is planting a variety of cucumber that is resistant to powdery mildew. Examples include Marketmore 76 and Tendergreen Burpless among others.

Once an infection is noted, immediate treatment can eliminate the problem. Because development of fungicide resistance has been observed in many variations of powdery mildew, I recommend a fungicide cocktail approach. The fungicides used in organic production, particularly bicarbonate and horticultural oils, have the potential to harm or kill garden plants. So during this treatment regimen, please make sure the plants are well-hydrated, and test bicarbonate and horticultural oils on a single leaf first and wait a day to assure no harm is done before making a wider application.

Use a pressure sprayer to spray the plants and leaves, making sure to get the undersides of the leaves, with a solution *Bacillus subtilis* (such as Serenade™) according to label directions. Wait two days, then spray with light horticultural oil mixed according to label directions and to which you have added one tablespoon baking soda (sodium bicarbonate) per one gallon of water. Spray to the point of run-off. Wait three days, and then repeat the cycle. Continue repeating the cycle until no powdery mildew remains, and then spray every other week with the bacillus subtilis preparation.

Harvest

Cucumbers should be harvested when they have reached the size for the particular variety grown and well before they have started to turn from green to yellow. Keep a watchful eye for cucumbers that manage to hide among the leaves while they ripen, because once a cucumber on a particular vine starts ripening, that vine will stop producing new fruit. To pick a cucumber with minimal damage to the vine, gently hold the

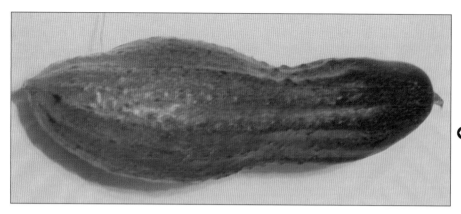

◀ Cucumbers will bulge due to uneven watering. Assuring the equivalent of 1″ of rain weekly will prevent this.

cucumber with one hand, while using a pair of scissors in the other hand to cut the stem.

Saving Seed

Cucumber seeds are saved via the wet method. Allow a couple of cucumbers on each vine to grow to maturity—meaning they grow large, yellow and soft. Leave these on the vines until they are dead from frost, and then bring them in to ripen out of direct sunlight for another couple of weeks. Slice the cucumbers open lengthwise, and scoop out the seed mass into a plastic cup. Add some warm water, stir, and allow to sit for five days. At the end of five days there will be mold growing on top. Give it a swirl, and the bad seeds will float while the good ones will sink. Empty out the water, discard the mold and bad seeds, and rinse the good seeds thoroughly. Dry the good seeds with a paper towel, and then allow them to dry on a screen until they are brittle. You can dehydrate them further using a silica gel desiccant. Store in a sealed container in a cool, dry place away from sunlight.

Preparation and Preservation

Cucumbers keep best at a humidity of 95 percent and temperature of 45 degrees. In practical terms, this environment doesn't exist in most homes. For short term storage—five days or less—putting cucumbers in sealed bags in the refrigerator works well. For longer storage, up to two weeks, wrap each cucumber individually in plastic wrap in plastic wrap and store in the refrigerator. That is the effective limit of how long cucumbers can be stored fresh, but they will keep for several years as pickles using any of a number of available recipes. They neither freeze nor dehydrate well, though you can freeze them with moderate success if you bake them first at 350 degrees for thirty minutes.

⊗ Sesame cucumber salad is a quick and delicious summer dish.

Sesame Cucumber Salad

3 slicing cucumbers
1 tsp sesame seeds
1 Tbsp sesame oil
1 tsp soy sauce
½ tsp salt
¼ of a lemon
½ tsp dill

Peel the cucumbers and cut into chunks. Add salt and stir thoroughly. Squeeze the lemon over the cucumber and mix. Mix the remaining ingredients together, then pour over the cucumber and mix thoroughly. Serve chilled.

9

Greens

The term "greens" includes any plant whose leaves are eaten as food, including cabbage, kale, collard greens, beet greens, chard, spinach and lettuce. But it also includes a wide array of under-appreciated leaf vegetables rich in nutrients that you can seldom—if ever—find in the store. Examples include orach, lettuce, mustard, garden purslane, water cress, garden cress and corn salad just to name a few. Greens are eaten both raw and cooked, depending upon culinary tastes.

Some of the plants in this category are covered in other chapters, such as chard. In the case of plants where I've given more detailed information in another chapter, that more specific information should be preferred. Nevertheless, greens have enough in common in spite of their diversity that a chapter dedicated to their general growth and properties is useful, especially given that having separate chapters on orach and lettuce would be wasteful.

Leafy greens are a nutritional powerhouse that combine high nutrient density with compounds that lower the risks for serious diseases such as cancer and atherosclerosis. Some work better raw, and some work better cooked. But in either state, leafy greens in many cases literally contain more vitamins than a vitamin tablet from the store. As a mini farmer, you have the ability to eat these greens as fresh as humanly possible, along with growing a diversity of greens unavailable in stores. You'll discover amazing taste sensations.

Growing Greens

By definition, greens are grown for their leafy vegetation. As such, they require a substantial amount of nitrogen. As key dietary sources of everything from minerals to Omega 3 fatty acids, they should be provided with soil rich in compost and properly managed for trace nutrients. Most greens grow best in cooler weather and are grown from seed. Raised beds are ideal as they allow the soil to be worked earlier in the spring, thereby extending the season while preventing over-saturation with moisture.

With the exception of collards and kale which should be started from seed in the same manner as cabbage and transplanted at a spacing of at least twelve inches, greens are usually harvested in two stages: early in their growth as salad greens that are eaten raw, and later in the season as pot greens that are steamed, boiled or fried. In order to accommodate this, greens are usually sowed as closely together as an inch. They are harvested as they grow, leaving an increasing amount of spacing between plants until all that is left are the plants being grown for pot greens.

Often, so-called "mesclun" mixes are sowed. Mesclun mixes contain seeds for a variety of greens that have different tastes and textures. Common mixes contain lettuces, arugula, endive and chervil; but quite a few also include mustard, chard, spinach and sorrel. You can buy these pre-mixed, or mix your own.

To grow mesclun mixes or use the dual-harvest method described; put narrow furrows in the soil of the bed spaced four inches apart. Sprinkle the seed in the furrows at about a one-inch spacing, and then cover the seeds with soil and water thoroughly daily until they sprout. Start harvesting when plants are four inches tall, and do so in a fashion that will leave increasing spaces between what remains. This way you can harvest baby lettuce and mature lettuce from the same planting, or both small mustard greens for salad and large mustard greens for steaming.

Pests and Diseases

The most troublesome pest of greens, especially milder greens, is the slug. Slugs gobble holes in the vegetation, leaving a slimy trail in their wake. They can be large or small, and seem to be able to work their way through the smallest crevasse. Luckily, there are a lot of ways to deter slugs.

Caffeine is deadly to slugs. Spread coffee grounds around plants that the slugs like, and as they crawl across the grounds they will absorb the caffeine through their bellies and die. As a bonus, coffee grounds are a good nitrogen-containing organic fertilizer.

Corn meal is also deadly to slugs, as well as being an attractant. Put a few tablespoons of corn meal in a jar, and lay that jar on its side near plants requiring protection. The slugs will crawl into the jar, eat the corn meal, and die.

Beer is an extremely effective lure. You can fill a container 75 percent full of beer, bury it so the lip is at ground level, and provide it with a canopy of some sort to keep out rain and debris. Slugs will crawl in and drown (my wife uses cleaned cat food cans for this trap).

Slugs are physically delicate creatures. Sand, egg shells and similar substances will cut them severely, causing them to dehydrate and die.

Outside of this, all you need to be concerned about are grasshoppers, leaf hoppers and similar insects migrating from nearby vegetation. These can be avoided by keeping the lawn trimmed near the beds. Diseases are not a problem so long as you practice crop rotation and sanitation.

Purslane

Though purslane is often considered a weed, I grow it every year in my garden. It contains more Omega 3 fatty acids than any other land plant[7], and is also a rich source of vitamins A and C, as well as pigment-based anti-oxidants. The leaves, stems and flowers can be eaten raw, steamed or fried. When harvested in the morning, it has a tangy apple-like taste; when harvested in the afternoon it has a sweeter and more grass-like taste. If you are eating a diet free of starches that are used as thickeners keep in mind that purslane has mucilaginous properties similar to okra that make it a good thickener for soups, stews and gravies. Blanch it, dehydrate it, and then turn it into a powder in your blender. Use the powder as a thickener in place of corn starch or flour.

Sow purslane seeds directly after danger of frost has passed. If you let it go to seed, it will regrow every year in that spot in your garden. The bed where I originally planted purslane has been used to grow greens, corn, carrots and more, yet

⊗ Purslane is delicious fresh and makes a good thickener for soups.

purslane now grows there every year with no effort.

Corn Salad

Like purslane, corn salad is often considered a weed; it can be an invasive weed in corn and wheat fields. It is delicately flavored, and rich in vitamins E, C, A, B6, B9 and Omega 3s. It is best when harvested before the flowers appear, and is best raw in salads, though it can be good when steamed lightly for about four minutes. It can be sown in late fall for an early spring harvest, or in early fall for a late spring harvest. It is an ideal crop to grow late in an unheated hoop house. Germination is slow at 10–14 days. Plant thinly—one seed per inch—and use the thinned plants in salads. Leave at a final spacing of 4" and harvest the entire rosette.

Orach

I grow Red Orach every year mainly for the colorful zest it adds to salads. It is best when sowed

---

7   A. P. Simopoulos, H. A. Norman, J. E. Gillaspy and J. A. Duke. (1992) "Common purslane: a source of omega-3 fatty acids and antioxidants." *Journal of the American College of Nutrition*, Vol 11, Issue 4 374-382.

early in the spring and the young leaves harvested and eaten like young spinach. Sow seeds every two inches. As they grow, thin out to eight inches between plants and eat the thinnings.

Lettuce

Lettuce" (also known as Claytonia) is native to North America and was called Miner's lettuce because it was used extensively by Gold Rush miners as a source of vitamin C to prevent scurvy. It tastes more like spinach than lettuce, and some consider its taste superior to both. It can be eaten either raw or gently steamed. If you have difficulty growing spinach, consider lettuce instead as it grows more easily. Lettuce will grow year round in a greenhouse, hoop house or cold frame. Plant directly in the spring at ½" spacing, thinning out to six-inch spacing as the plants grow.

Mustard

Mustard is a culinary delight, and this fact is demonstrated in the dozens of varieties available reflecting every size, shape and flavor imaginable. Sow in the early spring, harvest the small leaves for salads and then use the larger leaves for steaming and stir-fries. The pungent character in the fresh leaves is diminished by cooking. The seeds can be harvested as a spice for pickling. A single cup of raw mustard greens has almost double the U.S. RDA of vitamin A, and 500 percent of the RDA of vitamin K. It is high in folate and a number of other important vitamins and minerals too. As a member of the same family as broccoli, it also contains a number of cancer-fighting compounds. And, it happens to be delicious, so I grow a lot of it.

Plant the seeds directly in the ground every six inches as early as the ground can be worked in the spring, and then every week thereafter for the next month so you have a continuous harvest until it bolts. Once the mustard bolts, let it go to seed if you plan to use mustard seed in pickle or other recipes. Collect the seed pods by stripping them from the plant when brown, break up the delicate pods and separate the seeds by winnowing.

Cress

Cress grows both wild and cultivated, both in the form of watercress along stream banks and in the form of dry land cress in fields and gardens. Cress, watercress particularly, has shown a number of anti-cancer properties, including the ability to inhibit the formation of blood supply to tumors. It is tangy and peppery, and usually eaten raw—though it can also be steamed or boiled. It is best harvested before it goes to seed. Starting in the spring and every two weeks thereafter until fall, plant the seeds for cress directly, spaced every two inches.

Sorrel

Sorrel is a member of the dock family, and contains sufficiently high levels of oxalic acid that it could cause poisoning if eaten in large quantities. Thus, its tangy leaves are best eaten young as small additions to salads for variety rather than as a main-course pot herb when fully grown. Sorrel

⚙ Rich in folate and vitamin K, spinach is a super-food.

grows best in light shade but will tolerate full sun. It is a hardy perennial, so if not dug up or killed it will come back every year from the roots. Directly seed at twelve inch spacing. These plants spread, so growing them in a raised bed is a good idea.

Arugula

Arugula (also known as rocket) has an assertive, peppery taste. It's young leaves are often used in mesclun mix for salads, and its older leaves as pot herbs. Starting in mid spring and every three weeks thereafter until summer, sow the seeds two inches apart. Harvest by pulling up the plants and cutting off the roots.

Endive

Endive is a member of the chicory family that has bitter leaves that promote salivation and appetite. It is an excellent source of fiber, vitamins A, C and K and folate and other vitamins and

❷ Leaf lettuces pack a more powerful nutritional punch than iceberg lettuce.

minerals. Endive can be started indoors for a head start, or it can be directly seeded. Space the plants at eight inch intervals.

Chervil

Chervil is a member of the same family as parsley and has a distinctive yet mild flavor. It is used in mesclun, but also as an herb in French cooking. Chervil is best started indoors four weeks before last frost, and transplanted at eight inch spacing once the danger of frost has passed.

Spinach

Spinach is, for all practical purposes, a super-food. A single cup of cooked spinach contains ⅔ of the RDA of folate, 25 percent of the RDA of calcium, 300+ percent of vitamin A and over 1,000 percent of the RDA of vitamin K. It is indeed powerful stuff. And for such good medicine, it is also quite tasty harvested young in salads or steamed when older.

Sow spinach six to eight weeks before last frost. I recommend "broadcast" seeding in a bed, so there is approximately one seed per inch. As the plants start growing, thin to a three-inch spacing while using the thinnings in salad. You can also grow a fall crop by using the same method, starting six weeks before the first expected frost in fall. Spinach will grow up until hard frosts.

Lettuce

Lettuce has a reputation for being nutritionally vapid, but this only applies to the common iceberg lettuce found in stores. When growing your own, you can grow any of dozens of varieties of cos (also known as romaine) lettuce, leaf lettuce and butter lettuce; all of these pack a greater nutritional punch than standard iceberg lettuce. Two cups of romaine lettuce deliver 58 percent of the RDA of vitamin A, 45 percent of the RDA of vitamin C, and a substantial dose of vitamins" as well. The array of textures, tastes and colors available in lettuce is unequaled in any other leaf vegetable. My favorite varieties are Parris Island Cos, Buttercrunch and Lollo Rossa.

Lettuce can be directly seeded, or planted out from transplants grown indoors. I do both. I grow the headed varieties such as romaine indoors, and plant them out about six weeks before last frost so they have time to grow a large head. I sow the leaf varieties directly starting eight weeks before

last frost and every two weeks thereafter until last frost. I make little furrows six inches apart across the beds, sprinkle seed in the furrows at the rate of one seed per inch, and lightly cover. I harvest the plants for salads until they reach a final spacing of six inches and allow those to grow into full heads.

Greenery Broth (a base for soups)

Ingredients:

1 head romaine lettuce, chopped
1 small onion, chopped
3 sticks of celery, chopped
2 cups of purslane, chopped
½ tsp salt (optional)
8 cups of water

Procedure:

Chop up the ingredients while the salted water is coming to a simmer in a medium pot. Add the ingredients, return to a simmer, cover, and allow to simmer for another hour. Strain out the greens and reserve the liquid as a soup base. This is surprisingly good!

Herbs

A few years ago I ran out of oregano, so I headed down to the supermarket to buy some. Talk about sticker shock! The good stuff in the glass containers was selling for $10/ounce! That's when I decided that I needed a bed full of herbs.

Herbs are, of course, used in naturopathic medicine. But for my purposes, I use them a lot in cooking to add taste and variety. Being oriented toward self-sufficiency, what I don't want to do is make the guys who own the grocery store rich in the process. I'd rather keep that money in the family budget while simultaneously making sure my herbs are fresh.

It isn't likely that you'll be growing your own nutmeg, cloves or cinnamon. For those, you'll remain beholden to the supermarket for the foreseeable future because the conditions required to grow them aren't favorable. But other common herbs such as basil, thyme, rosemary, sage, parsley, dill, mint, lovage and more can be grown easily at home. Some, in fact, are perennials or self-seeding annuals that will become established and return every year with little to no effort required.

Another benefit of growing your own herbs is variety. Down at the store, basil is just basil and thyme is just thyme. It is a standardized commodity product. But when you start looking through seed catalogs, you'll discover dozens of varieties of common herbs, each with subtle (or not so subtle) differences in color, flavor, aroma and texture. In one catalog I receive, there are two pages dedicated just to different varieties of basil. With this variety available, you can literally grow herbs that cannot be purchased at any price.

In addition, fresh herbs are simply amazingly tasteful and fragrant. Some of the finest dishes I prepare include herbs such as rosemary, thyme or dill that I have literally taken directly from a bed to the kitchen. The dimensions these add to taste are impossible to describe and have to be experienced to be understood. Dried herbs are good, but not as good as something harvested fresh. Some of the compounds responsible for the tastes and smells of fresh herbs are volatile at low temperatures, and they are lost in the drying process. So even though drying your own herbs is a great thing that will save a lot of money over time, it is the culinary experience of access to fresh herbs that will get you hooked on growing your own.

I grow most of my herbs in one 4'x8' bed. Most herbs aren't bothered by bugs so rotation isn't an issue, and those that aren't perennial often self-seed. Some herbs, mints in particular, seem to harbor ambitions for world domination, so pulling up the excess every year as part of bed maintenance is a good idea.

Basil

Basil is an essential herb in Italian cooking, salad dressings and pesto; it also goes well in broiled or roasted meats and stews. There are many varieties of basil available. For pesto, try Genovese or Napoletano. For a real treat, try one of the red varieties like Red Rubin. As a spice for dressings, try Lemon Basil or Fine Verde. Basil can be directly sown after last frost at 4" spacing and then thinned to 8" spacing or it can be started indoors three weeks before last frost and then transplanted at 8" spacing.

Borage

Borage has cucumber-flavored leaves that go well in salads, and its blue flowers are a nice edible garnish. Sow the seeds directly at 4" spacing after last frost. Once they have sprouted, thin to 8" spacing. Borage's greatest value may lie in its non-culinary benefits. It's flowers are a bee-magnet, and they will draw beneficial pollinators to

⊗ Chopped borage leaves go well in salads.

your garden and thereby improve crops as diverse as cucumbers and okra. Inter-planted with tomatoes it will repel tomato horn worms; some gardeners claim that they improve the flavor of tomatoes. Dried and powdered borage leaves make a very worthwhile addition to meat stews, making them more savory.

Chives

Chives have a mild onion flavor that goes well in everything from omelets to mashed potatoes. Chives are perennial and can either be directly seeded starting three weeks before last frost or started inside six weeks before last frost and transplanted at a final spacing of eight inches. The grass-like leaves are snipped as needed, or they can be dried for convenient use. The purple flowers are edible and make a wonderful garnish for salads.

Cilantro/Coriander

The leaves of this fresh herb are known as "cilantro" and the seeds are known as "coriander." Cilantro is used in salsas and other spicy dishes, giving them an air of cool freshness to offset the

❷ Fresh cilantro contributes a sense of freshness to salads and salsas.

spice; coriander seeds are used in curries and roast poultry. Cilantro is directly seeded starting four weeks before last frost at a spacing of three inches. It becomes bitter when temperatures start averaging over 75 degrees. For culinary use, the seeds should be heated in a dry hot pan until the scent is notable, then cooled and ground with a mortar and pestle.

Dill

Dill is obviously used in pickles, but it is also used to spice fish, salad dressings, cooked vegetables and more. I enjoy chewing on a sprig of dill as I work in the garden. Both the foliage and the seeds can be used. It will re-seed itself every year, making for a bountiful supply. I grow "Mammoth" dill, but other common varieties include Dukat and Bouquet. It can be directly seeded starting a month before last frost, or started indoors two months before last frost and transplanted. Thereafter, it will re-seed itself impressively.

Fennel

Fennel has a flavor like anise or black licorice and is popular in Italian cooking; it is also used for flavoring fish, lamb and pork. The seeds are used as a spice, the leaves and flowers are used in salads, and the bulbs can be cooked as a root vegetable. Fennel re-seeds itself so aggressively it could become invasive; be merciless when culling unwanted volunteers. Directly seed at four-inch spacing.

Garlic

An entire book can be written about garlic. It is one of the most popular herbs in all forms of cooking, and dozens of varieties are available. **Garlic** falls into two broad categories: hardneck (also known as "stiffneck") and softneck. This differentiation is based upon whether or not the particular variety of garlic creates a flower stalk. The flower stalk, if allowed to grow, becomes hard, thus giving the garlic a hard neck. The flower stalks, also known as *scapes*, if cut young, make an excellent stir-fry vegetable. Cutting the scapes also makes the garlic more productive. Softneck garlic has a more flexible neck, and once harvested, those necks can be braided together to hang the garlic.

Best soil conditions are the same as for onions. Though garlic can be planted in spring, it is less productive. Likewise, even though all cloves of garlic will grow, the larger the clove you plant, the larger the bulb it will produce. So garlic is best planted in the fall around the first frost date for harvest the next year. Plant the cloves with the root side down, two inches deep at six inch intervals in all directions, and then mulch heavily with straw to assist survival through the winter. If you live in a very cold place like Maine or Minnesota, you may need to plant the more winter-hardy hardneck varieties.

When you see the foliage starting to die back, stop watering your garlic. Once the bottom leaves are brown, it is ready to harvest. Don't just try to pull it up by the dead foliage. Instead, loosen the soil by inserting a digging fork six inches away from the garlic and levering up the soil. Then dig out the bulbs. Brush off any dirt, leave the tops attached, and let it cure by drying in a shady well-ventilated place away from rain. After curing, you can remove the tops and store in the dark in mesh bags. Softneck varieties can keep for as long as eight months, but hardneck varieties will only keep for four months.

All garlic varieties can be successfully pickled in vinegar for long-term storage, and can likewise be blanched for four minutes and then frozen or dehydrated. (Once dehydrated, you can make your own garlic powder by putting the dehydrated garlic in a blender.) Though it is a popular practice, I would discourage putting fresh garlic cloves in olive oil for storage, as this provides good conditions for growth of undetectable botulism. In fact, people have died as a result. In 1989 the FDA issued the following statement about fresh garlic in olive oil:

"To be safe . . . garlic-in-oil products should contain additional ingredients—specific levels of microbial inhibitors or acidifying agents such as phosphoric or citric acid. . . . Unrefrigerated garlic-in-oil mixes lacking antimicrobial agents can permit the growth of Clostridium botulinum bacteria with subsequent toxin production without affecting the taste and smell of the products. Toxin production can occur even when a small number of Clostridium botulinum spores are present in the garlic. When the spore-containing garlic is bottled and covered with oil, an oxygen-free environment is created that promotes the germination of spores and the growth of microorganisms at temperatures as low as 50 degrees Fahrenheit."[8]

Lemon Balm

Lemon balm makes a pleasant tea, but is also a welcome addition to mushroom and aspara-

---

8   The FDA Memo on Garlic-in-Oil Preparations, 4/17/1989.

⊗ Like lemon balm, lemon verbena contributes a citrus and savory essence to marinades.

gus dishes, as well as sauces and marinades for fish and meats. It is a perennial herb that will overwinter throughout most of the continental United States. The seeds won't germinate below 70 degrees, and can be started indoors and then transplanted, or sprinkled outdoors but not covered, and then watered frequently until they sprout.

Lovage

Lovage's unique celery-like flavor goes well in all sorts of stews and stuffings while adding new possibilities for salad dressings, herb butters and fruit dishes. Lovage will grow to be about six feet tall and comes back every year, so you only need one plant. Start a few seeds indoors about six weeks before last frost, and then transplant the best one outside on the North side of your herb bed. Lovage is best used fresh; the dried herb is marginally useful although blanching and freezing works pretty well. In place of the dried herb, you can use the seeds year-round. They are a bit

sweeter than the leaves, but otherwise carry the same excellent flavor.

Marjoram

Marjoram is a close relative of oregano, it is more mild and sweet, complementing practically any meat dish. Although it is a perennial herb in its native regions, it is somewhat cold-sensitive and won't survive the winters in the Northern parts of the country. All is not lost, however, because it can be successfully grown as an annual by starting the seeds inside six weeks before last frost and putting out the transplants just after the last frost. Transplant at a spacing of twelve inches. The herb is harvested by cutting a section of growth and hanging it upside down in the shade until dry.

Mint

There are many mint varieties available, ranging from the common spearmint, catnip and peppermint to more exotic mints with flavors such as lemon and chocolate. Mint is best started indoors six weeks before last frost, and then planted outside at twelve inch spacing after last frost. It is a hardy perennial that will come back year after year throughout the continental United States. It's flowers attract bees in abundance, and it can self-seed to the point of becoming invasive if you don't keep an eye on it and ruthlessly cull invaders. In most mint varieties, the greatest concentration of flavor is in the top five to seven inches of growth. Snip that completely—stem and all—near midsummer, hang upside down in a shady but well-ventilated place to dry, and then

⊗ This chocolate mint makes excellent teas but will take over the beds if you allow it!

use the leaves as seasoning, in tea, etc. Mints, in general, can attract cats.

Mustard

Growing mustard and harvesting the seed is covered in the chapter on greens. The seeds are used as a spice, both in whole form when making pickles, and ground as an addition to practically anything that can be cooked. It is especially good when used as a flavoring for boiled cabbage, but likely the biggest attraction for purposes of self-sufficiency is the ability to make your own prepared mustard, so I'll include a recipe at the end of this chapter.

Oregano

Oregano is a perennial that is more cold-hardy than its cousin marjoram, and will overwinter well throughout the continental United States.

It should be started indoors six weeks before last frost and then transplanted outdoors at a spacing of 12" sometime after last frost. Don't cover the seeds because they need light to germinate. Oregano is known as the essential Italian herb, but it goes well with almost everything. I like to add a small amount to portabella mushrooms fried in butter. Oregano is best harvested before the plant flowers. Cut a stalk all the way down to the ground to encourage a bushy habit. You can then hang it upside-down to dry in the shade away from weather and then strip the leaves, or strip the leaves from the stem directly for fresh use.

Parsley

Everyone has seen parsley used as a garnish, and many swear by parsley as a remedy for halitosis, but by far my favorite use is an ingredient in vegetable juices that I make with my juice machine. I use a half pound of carrots, two stalks of celery and a handful of parsley to make the juice. The parsley makes the juice taste fresh and vibrant. There are two primary types of parsley: flat-leaved and curly-leaved varieties. Though some claim one variety to taste better than the other; I think they are both quite good.

Parsley is hard to start from seed. To start it, put the seeds in the freezer for a week, then put them in a wet paper towel sealed in a zippered plastic bag overnight before planting inside. They will take nearly a month to germinate. Once they have been established for a couple of weeks, transplant them outside at a spacing of twelve inches. Harvest by cutting entire stems back to the ground to encourage more growth. It is best eaten fresh, but it can be quickly blanched (one minute) and dehydrated as well.

Rosemary

Rosemary is a perennial herb best known for its use in poultry seasoning, but it is also useful in marinades and vegetables. Though it is supposedly only winter-hardy through zone six, my rosemary comes back every year in the more chilly zone five. Rosemary is most easily started as a purchased plant from a nursery or from a cutting taken from an established plant; it is nevertheless possible to start from seed using the same method as described with parsley. The germination rate is very low, so plant five times as much seed as you think you'll need. Put out the transplants at eight inch spacing two weeks before last frost. Harvest rosemary by cutting healthy branches, tying them together and hanging them upside down out of the weather until dry.

Sage

The uses of sage overlap those of rosemary; I have found that in marinades for various meats, one spice will be better than the other. Like rosemary, sage is most easily started from a nursery plant or a cutting, but it can be started from seed using the same method as with parsley with difficulty. Space plants at twelve-inch intervals, and don't harvest the first year. In subsequent years, harvest healthy branches that are hung upside-down inside to dry. Sage is also excellent in stews when used fresh from the plant.

Tarragon

There are two varieties of tarragon: Russian and French. The French variety (*Artemisia dracunculus*) is more flavorful but seldom produces

⊗ Sage will reward you abundantly year after year.

seeds, and therefore must be started from a cutting or purchased from a nursery. The Russian variety (*Artemisia dracunculoides*) can be started from seed, is more prolific and has a milder flavor. Both are superb as flavorings for various species of white fish, as well as for making herbal vinegars for salads. Sow Russian Tarragon seeds indoors six weeks before last frost, and plant out shortly after last frost. You'll probably only want or need one plant, as it grows to be two feet tall and two feet wide.

The leaves don't smell like much when growing, but once harvested the flavor starts to concentrate. The heat of cooking releases even more flavor, so it is easy to over-use tarragon. Tarragon can be used fresh, it can be dried on a dehydrator, or the sprigs can be sealed in air-tight bags and frozen.

Thyme

A classic and essential herb, thyme lends its flavors to dressings, vegetables and meats alike. Thyme is a perennial, though different varieties have different cold tolerance, so make sure the variety you choose will overwinter in your area. Sow the seeds indoors six weeks before last frost, and then transplant shortly after last frost at eighteen inch spacing. Early in its life, thyme grows slowly, so weed control is important. Also, for its first year, don't harvest from the plants. From the second year and thereafter, harvest around midsummer, just before it blooms, or just as it is blooming. Cut off the top four or five inches, and dry it inside in the shade.

How to Make Mustard

The prepared mustard available in the store is made from vinegar, water, mustard seed, salt, turmeric and other spices such as garlic. Each of these ingredients serves a particular purpose due to the nature of the active ingredients in mustard seed.

Just as the irritant substances in onions and garlic are released by mechanical damage to the cells of the bulbs, the distinctive tastes and smells

⊗ This creeping thyme is featured in homemade salad dressings.

of mustard seed are released by mechanical damage to the seed. Likewise, applying heat to the damaged mustard seed inactivates the compounds, so the degree of spiciness of mustard can be controlled by the amount of heat applied.

There are three types of mustard seed: the milder white/yellow mustard used in American mustards, the tangier brown prevalent in European mustards and the fiery black that predominates Asian cuisine. For your first experiments with making mustard, I recommend using mostly yellow and a bit of brown.

For processing, whole mustard seed should be soaked overnight in water. Once it has soaked, process it with the soaking water in a blender. Just as-is, the properties of the mustard would dissipate in a few days. Wait ten minutes or so, and then add the vinegar and process further in the blender. Salt is also needed to fix the qualities of the mustard, and anywhere from one teaspoon to two teaspoons is used per cup of product. The turmeric is used for imparting a yellow color. The reason why the famous "Grey Poupon" mustard lacks the distinctive fluorescent yellow color of American mustard is because it lacks turmeric. Turmeric lends a taste all its own, so if you are used to American-style mustards you'll want to add this ingredient as well. Freshly made mustard is unbearably bitter, but this bitterness will disappear once it has been refrigerated for twenty-four hours. I have only provided one recipe, but by explaining the process, you can branch out to create your own.

Down-Home Mustard

Ingredients:

⅓ cup water
½ cup wine vinegar
½ cup mustard seed, yellow and brown
2 tsp salt
½ tsp turmeric
½ tsp garlic powder

Procedure.

Soak the seeds in the water overnight at room temperature. Dump in the blender, and blend until it is smooth enough for your purposes. Add the remaining ingredients, blend thoroughly, and then dump into a sealed container. Store in the refrigerator, and allow to sit at least a day before sampling.

11

Melons

The quintessential taste of summer is the melon. Whether it be watermelon, honeydew or cantaloupe, melons just seem to concentrate summer's essential sweetness. And even though they are nature's candy, they are very healthful as well. Watermelon contains citrulline, an arginine precursor that relaxes blood vessels and indirectly supports nitric oxide synthesis.[9] It likewise contains a great deal of lycopene, known to help prevent prostate, breast and lung cancer. Cantaloupe is so tasty that it is hard to believe that a single cup contains more than the RDA of both vitamins A and C.

Melons are members of the same family as cucumbers and squash, and there are likely a hundred varieties around the world. Many are eaten fresh, but just as many are pickled as condiments or used to make preserves.

In the United States, we typically think in terms of three melon variations: watermelons, cantaloupes and honeydew. In reality the melon with netted skin that we in the United States call a "cantaloupe"

---

9   Nitric oxide synthesis is necessary for achieving and maintaining erections. Studies show that watermelon can assist in that regard. *Science Daily,* July 1, 2008, "Watermelon May Have Viagra-Effect."

is a muskmelon, Cucumis melo *var. reticulatus.* True cantaloupes, cucumis melo *var. cantalupensis,* have scaled rinds and are much more common in Europe than in the United States. Honeydew, crenshaw and casaba melons are Cucumis melo *var. inodorus.* But all variations of Cucumis melo can interbreed with each other, so if you are growing them for seed, you will need to practice isolation techniques to keep seedlines pure.

Watermelons are Citrullus lanatus and will cross with other watermelons and citron, but not with any other melons grown in the United States.

Variety Selection

Plants that make fruits require sun to make them, so melons in particular tend to be long-season crops with some requiring more than 100 frost-free days—preferably warm days. Particularly if you live in the Northern parts of the country, you should choose a variety that will produce ripe fruit within your growing season with some room to spare.

Another consideration is disease resistance. Watermelons are pretty much resistant to bacterial wilt, but all varieties of muskmelon are susceptible. Powdery mildew and mosaic virus can pose a problem with melons, but resistant cultivars are available.

In New Hampshire, I have successfully grown Moon and Stars and Sugarbaby watermelons, and Hale's Best and Green Machine melon varieties.

Soil Preparation

Like other members of the cucumber family, melons prefer fertile, well-drained soils with lots of organic matter. The use of raised beds assists with drainage. Add at least three cubic feet of compost per 4'x8' bed, adjust the pH to between 6 and 7, and amend for NPK as indicated by a soil test. Melons use a lot of nitrogen, so make sure to combine nitrogen sources that release both quickly (such as blood meal) and slowly (such as alfalfa meal) when amending the soil.

Starting and Planting

Melons can be grown either from seed or from transplants. I prefer to start the seeds indoors a week before last frost, and then plant them out a week after last frost to give them a head start. If you prefer direct seeding, wait until a week after last frost or until soil temperature is 65 degrees, put the seeds in soil 1" deep and water thoroughly daily until the seedlings emerge. Space melon plants at one per foot. If planting from seed, plant two seeds every foot and then use scissors to snip off the least strong of the two that sprout.

Melons, theoretically, can be grown in the Northern one foot of a bed on a trellis for highest space efficiency—just as cucumbers—and I have successfully done this with muskmelons by supporting the growing melons with a sling made from old washed nylons (aka panty hose). It turned out to be labor intensive, and would work better with true cantaloupes because those don't slip off the vine. What I recommend instead is planting the melons six to twelve inches back from the South side of the bed, allowing the vines to trail along the yard or the area between beds. I mulch the area covered by vines with grass clippings (or hay can be used) and set boards under the growing melons to keep them off the ground. The Northern portion of the bed can be planted with other crops.

One thing to consider is planting trellised cucumbers on the North side of a bed, free-running melons on the South side of the bed, and closely spaced bush beans treated with inoculant down the center for a continuous supply of nitrogen.

Melons tend to have shallow root systems. Considering their need for water, it is important to establish the deepest root systems possible. To this end, then, watering should be only weekly unless the weather is abominably hot; the watering should be extremely thorough each time it is done. Use a rain gage, and in any week where less than an inch of water was received, give them an inch of water on top of what they already have. If an inch or more of water was received that week, you can let it pass as long as the vines look okay.

Weeds, Pests and Diseases

Melons are fast-growing once they get started and tend to shade out weed competition, so weeds aren't usually a direct problem, but they can be an indirect problem as a reservoir of disease organisms and a hiding place for pests. It is practically impossible to weed efficiently around melon vines without risk of harming the vines, so mulching is the best option. In my own mini-farm, I usually use grass clippings because they are abundant and free and return their elements to the soil. But if you have trouble getting melons to ripen within your season, I recommend killing two birds with one stone by using black weed barrier that suppresses weeds while allowing water and air to penetrate.

Once watermelon plants have grown to have ten leaves or more, they are immune to the bac-terial wilt disease transmitted by cucumber beetles. Even so, if present in large numbers they can decrease the vigor of the plant through the mechanical damage of feeding, and their larvae can hurt the roots, causing the vines to wilt and die. Planting nasturtiums around the stems of watermelons can help prevent the adults from laying eggs around the stem and thus prevent root damage, but once adult numbers are noticeable, chemical controls may become necessary. Natural alternatives include using a fine clay product called Surround™, or the use of a mixture of pyrethrin, rotenone and neem.

Muskmelons are not immune to bacterial wilt and, in fact, are almost as susceptible as cucumbers. The most effective natural way of dealing with cucumber beetles spreading bacterial wilt to muskmelons is to seal them up tightly under floating row covers until the flowers appear.

Aphids can sometimes spread from surrounding vegetation to melons in sufficient quantities to pose a risk to the plant. If this happens, two applications of insecticidal soap spaced five days apart will usually get rid of them.

Other than bacterial wilt, the next most likely disease to be encountered is powdery mildew. Powdery mildew starts on the underside of the leaf and then spreads. It can become a serious problem if conditions are shady. If you have a problem with bacterial wilt, resistant varieties of melon are available, and you should grow resistant varieties in future seasons.

Once an infection is discovered, fast treatment can eliminate the problem. Because development of fungicide resistance has been observed in many variations of powdery mildew, I recommend a fungicide cocktail approach. The fungicides used in organic production, particularly bicarbonate and horticultural oils, have the potential to harm or kill garden plants. So during this treatment regimen, make sure the plants are well-hydrated, and test bicarbonate and horticultural oils on a single leaf first and wait a day to assure no harm is done before making a wider application.

Use a pressure sprayer to spray the plants and leaves, making sure to get the undersides of the leaves, with a solution *Bacillus subtilis* (such as Serenade™) according to label directions. Wait two days, then spray with light horticultural oil mixed according to label directions and to which you have added one tablespoon baking soda (sodium bicarbonate) per one gallon of water. Spray to the point of run-off. Wait three days, and then repeat the cycle. Continue repeating the cycle until no powdery mildew remains, and then spray every other week with the bacillus subtilis preparation.

Harvest

Timing the harvest of watermelons is sometimes seen as a black art, where only those initiated to the secrets of the unique sounds melons make when rapped can make such determinations. Most certainly, with watermelons, a very experienced person can do so. But you can also tell by looking for three signs: the curly tendril opposite the stem of the melon has turned brown and/or died, the spot here the watermelon was touching the ground has changed from white to

⊗ This watermelon shows yellow instead of white where it was touching the ground, and so it is ready for harvest.

⊗ The netting is well defined and it slipped from the vine easily, indicating ripeness.

yellow, and the rind of the melon has become a bit less shiny. The stem to the watermelon should be cut with a sharp knife to harvest. It should never just be pulled.

Muskmelons should be harvested when the netting is well defined, they are fragrant, and there is a bit of "give" when the blossom end is pushed. A ripe muskmelon will also slip easily from the vine when pulled. If it is stubborn, it isn't ripe yet—give it another couple of days. Muskmelons are harvested by pulling them from the vines.

Over-ripe watermelons, incidentally, will explode. When I first started growing watermelons, I had no idea how to tell when they were ripe, so I just let them grow until the vines they were on were dead, then I brought them in the house. For some reason, I also suffered under the notion that they would keep for a long time sitting out, just like squash. So I brought in some 30+-pound melons, put them on the kitchen table, and let them sit for a couple of weeks. One day when I was in the living room, I heard a "thud" reminiscent of a sledgehammer hitting something. I ran into the kitchen to find a most impressive mess all over the table, chairs, floor, walls and more. You have been warned!

Seed Saving

Melons are insect-pollinated, and if pollinated naturally, only one variety should be grown, or it should be isolated from other varieties by at least ¼ mile. The seeds are ready when the melon is ripe to eat, and they are best collected using the wet method. Put the seeds and a bit of the pulp into a large plastic cup, add a cup of water, stir and allow to sit for three days. At the end of three days, clean off any scum and discard any floating seeds. Then, wash and dry the seeds that remain, and dry them over a dessicant for a week before storing in a dark, cool place in a sealed container (see *Mini Farming* for more information on dessicants).

Preparation and Preservation

Melons don't keep long—maybe a week at room temperature or two weeks in the refrigerator tops. Preparation consists of just slicing it up and eating it!

You could dehydrate melons, but as they are mostly water you wouldn't get much after the dehydrating process. Muskmelons can be cubed and frozen with some success, but watermelon won't come out well at all.

The only effective way to make sure excess melons don't go to waste is to turn them into preserves, pickles, sorbets or even wines. The good news is that even in such states, many of the preserves still retain important nutritional components such as vitamins and antioxidants. That makes me happy because watermelon rind pickles have been my favorite since childhood!

Muskmelon Ice

Ingredients:

4 cups cubed muskmelon
2 cups water
½ cup sugar
2 Tbsp fresh-squeezed lime juice (don't use the bottled kind)
¼ tsp vanilla extract
⅛ tsp cinnamon

Procedure:

Place all the ingredients in a blender and process until smooth. Pour into clean ice cube trays and allow to freeze. Once frozen, store the cubes in sealed freezer bags. To serve, put the cubes into the blender and break them up, or just put them in a bowl and use the edge of a spoon to eat them a little at a time.

Watermelon Rind Pickles

Ingredients:

4 quarts of cubed watermelon rind
4 quarts of cold water
1 cup coarse sea salt
9 cups of sugar
4 cups of distilled (white) vinegar
4 cups of water

2 lemons, thinly sliced

4 tsp whole cloves

8 cinnamon sticks broken into one-inch pieces

Procedure:

Remove the pink flesh and the outermost green rind from the watermelon, and cut the remaining rind into 1-inch cubes. Add the 1 cup of sea salt to the 4 quarts of water to make a brine, and pour this over the cubed watermelon rind in a large bowl. Allow to sit for 3 hours, then drain and rinse. Put the drained cubes into a large pot, add just enough water to cover, and bring to a simmer. Simmer for 10 minutes, then drain and set the cubes aside.

Make the pickling brine by putting the spices in a spice bag, and adding the bag to the mixture of vinegar, water, sugar and sliced lemon in a medium pot. Bring to a boil, then reduce to a simmer and stir occasionally for half.

Pack the rinds into pint jars, add one of the pieces of cinnamon from the spice bag, cover with hot pickling brine leaving ½" of head space, and process for 15 minutes in a boiling water canner. Allow to sit a month before consuming.

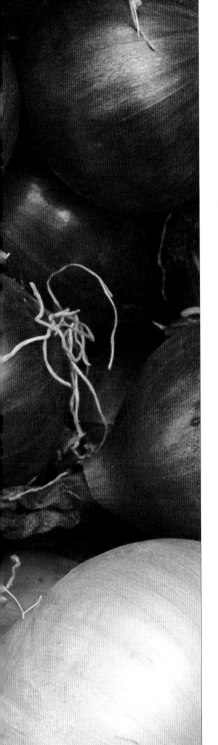

12

Onions

I have it on good authority that, without onions, food would still exist in some form or fashion, but it would hardly be an exaggeration to state that *good* food would be rare. Onions lend their unique flavor and pungency to everything from spaghetti sauce to chicken soup. And along with flavor, they have so many health benefits that even the World Health Organization recognizes them as a medicinal treatment and preventative for chronic diseases.

Onions are well known as a preventative for atherosclerosis, and when used regularly the fibrinolytic substances they contain suppress the platelet aggregation that can give rise to heart attacks. Several studies have shown that eating as little as half an onion a day reduces the risk of stomach cancer by 40 percent.

Given proper care and conditions, and using intensive spacing methods, you will easily reap over 180 onions from a single 4'x6' bed. The trick lies in the proper care and conditions, along with selecting the right variety for your purposes—so that's what this chapter is all about.

Selecting the Right Variety

Onions can be categorized in a number of different ways. There are bulb-forming and non-bulb-forming onions, sweet and pungent varieties, multiplier onions and seed-bearing onions, and that's just for starters. For now we're just going to discuss the common bulb-forming and seed-bearing onion that people usually grow in their gardens or buy in stores.

This onion, typified by the red, white and yellow varieties in the grocery store produce department, can be divided into short-day, long-day and intermediate-day onions based upon how much sunlight they need to receive in order to properly form a bulb. Long-day onions require 15+ hours of sunlight, intermediate-day onions require 12-13 hours of sunlight and short-day onions require only 9-10 hours of sunlight.

The number of hours of sunlight your garden receives at mid-summer is determined by your latitude. Though it may be counter-intuitive, the closer you are to either the North or South Pole, the greater the hours of sunlight you'll see at midsummer. In practice, this means you can grow a long-day onion in latitudes greater than 40 degrees. In latitudes less than 40 degrees, you'll grow an intermediate-day onion. Short-day onions are used in areas with mild winters and are planted in the fall for a spring harvest.

Not everyone walks around with a globe in their back pocket, but there's an easy rule of thumb for the United States. If you are on the East Coast, 40 degrees runs through Newark, NJ, and Pittsburgh, PA. If you are in the Midwest, it runs through Columbus, OH. If you are in the Great Plains it runs through Lincoln, NE, and Denver, CO. If you are on the West Coast, it runs about 100 miles north of Sacramento, CA.

The choice of intermediate-day or long-day onion is made for you based upon where you live, but there are still other considerations including taste and keeping qualities. When it comes to storage ability, Northern growers have a definite advantage. As a general rule, the more pungent a variety, the better it keeps, and long-day onions usually (but don't always) store better than short-day onions. The following table is far from exhaustive, but lists some common and heirloom onion varieties that are successful in home gardens.

Keeping Qualities	Short Day	Intermediate Day	Long Day
Good for storage	Red Creole	Long Yellow Sweet Spanish, California Early Red	White Sweet Spanish, Yellow Sweet Spanish, Walla Walla, Brunswick, Stuttgarter
Best for fresh eating	Bermuda, Grano, Granex, Torpedo, Excel	Yellow Globe, Long Yellow Globe, Candy	Ailsa Craig

Common onion varieties for your location and intended use.

Starting Onions

Onions usually require a long season, so it is a good thing that they are not terribly sensitive to frost! You can start or plant onions in three ways: from seed, from transplants, and from bulbs.

In areas such as Southern California, Georgia, Florida or Alabama, you can plant seeds in the fall for harvest in the spring. And, in fact, this is exactly what growers of the famous Vidalia onion do. The Vidalia onion is not its own unique variety, but is rather a Grano or Granex onion that is sweet due to the unique conditions of the soil in that region combined with being grown from seed over the winter months. So if you live in a warmer climate, it could be worthwhile to experiment with growing onions from seed. However, if you live in a cooler climate, you will find that planting onions from seed, even as early as possible in the spring, will give very small bulbs. In this case, you can plant the seeds closely together and use the resultant sprouts, once they are the size of a pencil, as "bunching onions." These are a delightful addition to salads and soups.

In order to form a bulb, onions need to gather a lot of energy from the sun; outside of very warm areas, will need a head start in order to form a bulb. Thus, onions are typically planted as either bulbs (knows as "sets") or transplants. Onions grown from transplants usually have the best keeping qualities, so if you are growing onions for storage, this is definitely the way to go. Onions should be started indoors approximately twelve weeks before last frost, and the sets planted outside about six weeks before last frost. This gives them the head start they need to form a good bulb. The seeds can be started within a wide temperature range—anywhere from 65 to 80 degrees; once they have sprouted, try to keep them cooler at around 60 degrees for best growth.

« Onions can be started indoors from seed. This technique usually grows the best onions.

Many find growing onions from bulbs to be more convenient, and this can easily be done. Simply sow seeds close together in a small patch of ground about six weeks before last frost. Then, about three or four weeks after midsummer, pull the plants when the bulbs are no more than ¾" in diameter. Discard the largest ones or use them for pickling or salads because they will go to seed early if planted. Lay your sets out in the sun (but protect them from rain) for 7 to 10 days to cure, then remove the dry tops and store just as you would an onion for eating. Come spring, six weeks prior to last frost, plant them out at their optimal distance for the expected size of that particular variety of onion.

Planting Onions

Soil for onions should already be corrected for the major macronutrients (nitrogen, phosphorus and potassium) before planting. Raw manures and the like should be strictly avoided, and only very well matured compost employed. This is the case, incidentally, for all root crops that come into direct contact with the soil, because fresh manures draw pests, leach nutrients and worst of all lend their flavor to what is grown in them.

The compound in onions that makes them pungent is a sulfur compound. Therefore, onions can be made sweeter by depriving them of sulfur. This, however, can make them keep poorly and be more susceptible to pest damage because sulfur is a crucial element in certain amino acids that are a part of DNA structure. This is why you can only get the famously sweet Vidalia onion during a short time of the year—the low sulfur soil in which it is grown makes it a very poor keeper. Thus, you can make sweeter onions by depriving the soil of sulfur, but you do so at the expense of keeping quality.

Potassium and phosphorus are particularly crucial for onions, and should be present in sufficient quantities prior to planting. If needed, they can be added later in the season as a side dressing in the form of ashes, greensand, bone meal, etc. Nitrogen, as a key constituent of amino acids, is likewise needful and should be present at adequate levels at the beginning of the season. However, it should not be added later in the season, as doing so will delay or otherwise inhibit the formation of bulbs in favor of excessive top-growth. This is where slow-release organic forms of nitrogen such as alfalfa meal have a definite advantage over chemicals easily washed from the soil.

Onions taste better when grown in sweeter (i.e. less acidic) soils with pH between 6 and 6.8. Lime in either pelleted or powdered form should be applied well in advance of the season because it takes months to affect the pH of the soil. So it is best applied in the fall. If, come spring, the soil pH is still too low, you can use a mixture of lime" (which acts slowly) and wood ashes (which act quickly) to raise the pH. These should be mixed into the top 6" of soil very thoroughly as ashes contain potassium hydroxide (wood lye) which can be highly corrosive and therefore toxic to plants in heavy concentrations.

Weeds are the Nemesis of Onions

Early in the season, onions' greatest vulnerability due to their slow growth is being choked out by weeds—particularly grasses. This is especially problematic as distinguishing between an onion and blades of grass can make weeding difficult. As a result, onions are definitely a case where applying the proverbial "ounce of prevention" is wise.

For beds that will be growing onions, soil solarization as covered in the chapter on weeds is a very effective strategy. This requires some advanced planning because solarization is most effective in July and August when the sun is at its hottest. So you'll need to know in advance which bed you'll be using for onions.

The following step-by-step strategy will allow you to effectively prevent weed problems without need for chemicals. As an added bonus, as part of a bed rotation combined with solarization, nutrients will be more available and diseases will be suppressed.

- Previous Spring: Grow a spring crop such as broccoli that is harvested in midsummer.
- Previous Summer: Harvest the spring crop.
- Mix in amendments, then smooth out the bed so it is nice and flat.
- Water the bed very thoroughly with the equivalent of 2" of rain.
- Cover with 6 mil thickness plastic attached to the bed with staples. Leave plastic in place until late August.
- Late August: Remove the plastic and sow with a cover crop.
- Early Spring: Harvest cover crop and add to compost pile.
- Cover with dark breathable landscape fabric.
- When the transplants are ready, cut Xs in the landscape fabric and plant them in the Xs.
- Cover the landscape fabric between plants with straw and water thoroughly.

Diseases: Rare but Preventable

Though not typically a problem for home gardeners, onions are vulnerable to a number of fungal and bacterial diseases that can be spread via soil; most notable among these diseases are

⊗ Well-controlled weeds make for happy onions.

sclerotinia, botrytis and pink root. Primary prevention for these is crop rotation, with pre-solarizing also being a great help.

Sclerotinia of onions shows up as small dark brown spots on the blades that can expsand to kill the entire blade while infecting others. The organism responsible is *Sclerotinia homoeocarpa*, which is the same organism that causes dollar spot on turf grasses, which are its primary host.[10] Using bark mulch or similar mulching to prevent grasses between and around growing beds will help prevent inoculation.

Botrytis infection looks like small white or yellow spots on the blades of the onion where cells have died. These spots appear sunken. Successful infection will usually bring about the death of the tops of the onions in as little as a week. Though botrytis spoors are ubiquitous, the most common source of infection is debris from the prior year's crop where the spoors have over-wintered.

In industrial agriculture where onions are grown on a large scale and often re-planted in the same fields year after year, crop losses from

---

10 Saharan, G. & Mehta, N. (2008) *Sclerotinia Diseases of Crop Plants: Biology, Ecology and Disease Management.* ISBN: 978-1-4020-8407-2.

botrytis can approach 50 percent annually. However, on the scale of a mini farm, simple preventative measures can keep you from ever seeing it. The conditions that favor development of the mold are cool and wet weather, particularly later in the season. However, this factor alone is insufficient to cause infection. Botritis spoors require a wound in the onion in order to enter. All you need to do in order to prevent botrytis is the following:

- Rotate so that onions aren't grown in the same bed more often than once every four years,
- clear and compost all crop debris at the end of the season so spoors have nowhere to overwinter,
- avoid disturbing the onions during damp or wet weather, and
- respond to the rare pests of onions that can cause breaks in the leaves leaving them vulnerable to infection.

Pink root is common in industrial agriculture, but something you will hopefully never see. It manifests in dead onions that die back as though affected by drought, and the bulbs are shriveled and pink. Pink root infestation is ubiquitous in poorly drained soils with low levels of organic matter and nutrient deficiencies that have been used to grow onions or other susceptible crops for year after year. The fungus responsible, Pyrenochaeta Terrestris, is only weakly pathogenic, and if it is infecting your onions, you are doing something wrong.

Using the mini farming method, by growing in raised beds your soil should be well drained, and by using plenty of mature compost for organic matter, rotating crops and amending soil

as needed for proper nutrient levels, your onions should be practically invulnerable.

Onion Pests

Most insects don't like to eat onions, and for good reason: when onion tissues are injured, they release a compound that, when mixed with water, produces sulfuric acid. This is why cut onions make your eyes water. But just as there are some intrepid souls who can eat even the most pungent onions as though they were apples; there are a couple of insects who seem not to notice the onion's natural defense mechanism.

Thrips are a common garden pest. They are tiny, with the winged adult being no more than $\frac{1}{10}$ of an inch long. Damage from thrips can be twofold. First, in the direct damage they can do to the crop, but most importantly the cuts they make provide an entry for botrytis. A thrip infestation combined with a week of cold, wet weather can spell doom for the whole crop. They plant their eggs—anywhere from 10 to 100 of them—in the leaves, and when the eggs hatch, the larvae can do considerable damage to the host plant. Thrips are not unique to onions and eat practically anything grown in the garden, so crop rotation won't help.

Prevention requires a combination of cover crop selection, vegetation control, proper soil fertility and garden hygiene. Clearing crop debris at the end of the season to reduce overwintering populations of thrips is crucial. Their eggs won't survive the composting process. Using a mulch between and around beds to keep extraneous vegetation away will also reduce thrip populations. Thrips have a preference for wheat and rye, so if a cereal grain is anticipated as a cover-crop choose oats instead. Finally, many studies have shown that inadequate levels of calcium as well as trace minerals predispose thrip infestation, so adequate lime plus the addition of sea minerals would be wise. Likewise, excess nitrogen is a risk factor, so maintaining optimal fertility of the soil will ward off this pest.

If all efforts at prevention fail, and severe crop damage is likely or occurring, a number of natural insecticides are effective against thrips including pyrethrin with rotenone, Hot Pepper Wax™ and others. Be certain to follow label directions including safety precautions.

The other likely pest problem is onion maggots which are the larvae of a fly that lays its eggs near the roots of the plant. The first symptom you'd likely see, as the flies stay hidden, is wilting plants. When you dig them up, you'll find onions that are a rotten and putrid mess. Once an area is infested, it will likely remain so. Meticulous hygiene in debris removal, solarization and application of parasitic nematodes will help, as will avoiding white onion varieties because these are most susceptible. But of these, removal of onion debris, including making sure no onions are left in the ground, is the most important. Overwintering onion maggots need onions for their survival, and removal of onion debris and burying it deep in the compost pile will substantially reduce their population.

Harvesting Onions

An onion can be pulled and eaten at any stage, but for purposes of storage and marketing, they should be harvested when mature. Onions are mature when the tops of 80 percent of them have weakened, turned brown, and flopped over. When this happens, go ahead and bend over the remaining tops, and then allow the onions to remain in the ground until the next sunny day five to ten days away. When harvest day comes, pull up the onions in the morning, and leave them outside in the sun until evening. This will kill the little rootlets at the bottom of the bulb. Then bring the onions out of the weather into a place that is shaded, protected from rain, and with good air circulation. Leave them for a couple of weeks, turning every couple of days. This yields a fully cured onion of the best keeping quality for its variety.

Preparation and Preservation

Whole onions should be stored either braided or in mesh bags with good air circulation in a cool, dark, dry place. Don't let them freeze. Onions can be frozen raw (without blanching) by peeling, quartering, and placing in freezer bags from which as much air as possible has been removed. Onions can also be successfully dehydrated with or without blanching, but are likely to discolor unless first dipped in a bowl containing one cup of water to which either a tablespoon of lemon juice or a 250mg vitamin C tablet has been added. The discoloration is harmless and doesn't adversely affect the quality of the onions. Onions can also be pickled in vinegar for preservation using water bath canning; they will turn into a shapeless blob if pressure-canned.

Onions play a key role in food preparation generally, and are prepared in every imaginable way ranging from breaded onion rings to creamed pearl onions.

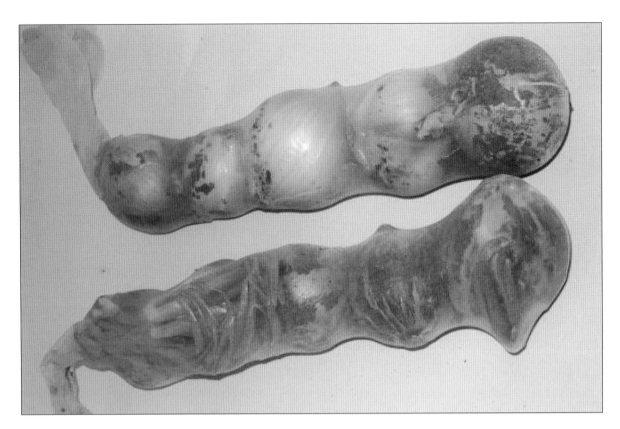

⊗ The onions on the bottom have sprouted because they were allowed to freeze.

Dilled Salad Onions

Ingredients:

3 lbs onions, sliced thinly
1½ cup vinegar
1½ cup sugar
¾ cup water
1 Tbsp salt
1½ tsp dill weed

Procedure:

Peel the onions and slice thinly. Pack into sterilized pint jars. Bring the remaining ingredients to a boil, and use the resulting pickling mixture to pour into the pint jars leaving ½" of head space. Process in a boiling water bath canner for 15 minutes.

13

Peas

Sometimes kids aren't impressed by peas, but they will likely enjoy classic dishes such as peas with carrots, peas with pearl onions, split pea soup and more. Naturally, peas fresh out of the garden are far superior to the canned peas from the supermarket, with a bursting sweetness that makes them almost like candy. In addition, peas are high in fiber, protein, vitamin C, vitamin K and a variety of phytonutrients that make our mothers' advice to eat them quite wise.

Another great thing about peas is that, being legumes, they improve the soil by fixing nitrogen from the air. So using peas (as well as other legumes such as beans) as part of your bed rotation will reduce the need for nitrogen fertilizers.

There are a great many types of peas, representing not just varieties of a given species, but two different species. Garden peas (also known as English peas) that are removed from the pod for eating, and snap peas and snow peas whose pods are eaten, are members of the species *Pisum sativum*. These peas are a cool-weather crop started in the spring once soil temperatures reach 50 degrees. Split peas are dried peas that have been mechanically split after the shell has been removed.

Cowpeas, also known as peas, are members of the species *vigna unguiculata*; they are adapted to warm seasons and near-drought conditions. Peas are usually prepared from a dried state in a fashion identical to dried beans.

Variety Selection

In order to select a variety, you need to determine the type of pea you want to eat. Do you want snow peas for Asian cooking? Sugar snap peas? Shelled garden peas? Split peas for soup? Black-eyed peas?

Among garden peas, my favorites are Laxton's Progress #9 and Little Marvel. These are short vines—no more than 18"—that can be very easily trellised around the edges of a bed.

There are now a large variety of sugar snap peas available. My pick of the bunch is a variety known simply as Sugar Snap. These grow a massive six-foot vine requiring a trellis like pole beans.

Flat-podded snow peas are popular in Asian cuisine, and my selection in this category is Oregon Giant. The vines are three feet long, and the pods are harvested while still flat.

I grow the same variety of peas that my grandfather grew, because I haven't found any varieties I like better. The Black Crowder Cowpea makes an extra-long pod that is easily shelled. At first, the peas are purple but they become black when dried.

Soil Preparation and Planting

Peas prefer deeply worked and well-drained soils with a pH of between 5.8 and 7. You should check macronutrient levels with a soil testing kit and amend as needed with appropriate organic additives. Organic matter is not as important for peas as with other crops, but adding one or two cubic feet of compost per 4'x8' bed would still be a good idea as it would supply micronutrients; as well as biological content that will help assure the success of the inoculant.

Like beans and other legumes, peas perform best when the seeds are treated at planting time with an inoculant containing nitrogen fixing bacteria. The bacteria turn nitrogen from the air into a form usable by peas and other plants, as well as assisting with the symbiotic bacterial interface that provides other nutrients to the roots. I put my pea seeds in a pint canning jar, moisten slightly, and then add a heaping tablespoon of inoculant to the jar. The pea seeds are planted after they are swirled around in the jar so they will be evenly coated with inoculant.

Garden, sugar and snow peas should be planted in the spring as soon as the soil can be worked. This is because the heat of summer shuts them down. If you happen to have apple trees, I have found that the optimal time for planting peas corresponds to the proper time for spring pruning. Otherwise, a soil temperature of 50 degrees is a good guide.

Unlike garden peas, cowpeas are very vulnerable to frost, so they can be planted at the same time as other crops that are susceptible to frost.

Seeds for peas and cowpeas should be planted more deeply than is immediately evident. Usually, seeds are planted at a depth of double the size of the seed, but peas are best planted two inches deep. This is necessary to establish a sufficient root system. If they are planted more shallowly, the plants will be more vulnerable to drought and weaker generally.

Every variety grows a bit differently. Some only grow a vine that is 18 inches long, so they are easily

⊗ Three rows of peas trellised in a single bed.

vines are more delicate, you have to be more careful when weeding. For this reason, I like to get off to a good start by pre-sprouting weeds where peas will be grown, followed by flaming. This way, hand weeding won't be required until the vines are strong and well established.

Pre-sprouting is a straight-forward process. You cover a bed with clear plastic in early spring so that it heats more rapidly than it would otherwise, thereby inducing weed seeds to sprout. Two weeks is enough. Once that is done, you can dispose of the weeds by hand pulling, using a stirrup hoe, tilling or flame weeding. Flame weeding offers the advantage of bringing up no new seeds. But if the bed needs tilled anyway, the best approach is to till the bed (adding any needed amendments) before the plastic is employed.

Crop rotation between beds and composting all crop debris at the end of the season goes a long way toward keeping disease and pest problems in check. Fusarium wilt and powdery mildew are the most likely diseases to be encountered. Fusarium wilt can be diagnosed by the symptoms: the leaves start browning at the bottom of the plant, and then the disease progresses along the vine's length until the plant is dead. Powdery mildew is aptly named, because it appears as a white, powdery mold on the leaves and other plant parts. Thankfully, a large number of pea varieties are

trellised on a few branches stuck in the ground. (Traditionally these are the branches pruned from fruit trees, though anything other than poison sumac will do fine.) Other varieties might grow as tall as six feet, requiring a more extensive trellis similar to that used for beans. The shorter varieties of peas can be grown around the perimeter of the garden without shading other crops; however, the taller varieties can be grown on the North side of a bed to avoid shading other crops. Peas should be planted at a two-inch interval.

Weeds, Pests and Diseases

Peas are more vulnerable to weeds than many of their other legume cousins, and because the resistant to these diseases. Just check the seed catalog when ordering your seeds, and if you have experienced these problems in the past, select resistant varieties.

Though other pests such as Japanese beetles will feed on peas, the primary pests likely to cause difficulties are cutworms, aphids and slugs.

If you walk out to inspect your garden one morning and find a young seedling snipped off at ground level just as neatly as if it had been done with scissors, you'll know you have a cutworm. The next night, that particular cutworm will get a different plant. Cutworms are little caterpillars about an inch and a half long, usually colored in a motley fashion so that they blend in with the soil. After making a meal of your seedling, the cutworm will usually burrow down into the soil no more than a four inches from the seedling and make its bed during the day in preparation for the next night. So if you dig around the cut seedling, you'll dig up the cutworm. My chickens like them, so I save them in a jar along with other grubs, wireworms and so forth, and feed them to the grateful poultry.

Cutworms can be largely—though not entirely—prevented by timing your planting so that at least two weeks have passed after tilling other organic materials into the ground. For example, if you are cutting a cover crop and tilling it into the ground, wait at least two weeks after incorporating the cover crop before planting the next one, as the fresh organic matter attracts the cutworms.

One thing I have often seen recommended is the use of cardboard collars. This does work, but it can be time-consuming if you are trying to protect 50 plants. There is also a matter of timing in that a cutworm can feed on anything from a new sprout to a transplant as big around as a pencil.

The stems expand as the plant grows. So rather than attaching collars directly to plants, it is more efficient to surround them with a wall at the time the seed is planted or the transplant is put in the ground. For this purpose, I use scissors to snip paper towel or toilet paper tubes into 1½" sections. You push them into the ground about ¼" around the seed, seedling or transplant and you're all set. Eventually they'll become soggy and start to decompose, but by then danger from cutworms will have passed.

I've mentioned aphids in connection with many plants, and that's because they affect practically every plant to some degree. In most cases their numbers are insufficient to create a problem, so they can be ignored. But if their numbers become too great, they will weaken the plants they infest and predispose those plants to mold or other diseases. If aphids are a problem, they can be dispatched with insecticidal soap sprayed twice, four days apart. Make sure to get under the leaves and along the stems.

Harvest

Garden peas are somewhat like corn in that their sugars will turn to starch if left too long, so the timing of harvest is important. The key is to catch them when they are fully expanded yet immature. Once the pods have started to become round, pick a pod and sample the peas raw every day. The pods on the bottom become ripe first, followed by those on the middle of the vine three days later and those toward the top another three days later. So you'll get three harvests. At the third harvest, just pull up the plant and add it to the compost pile. Once garden peas are harvested, they should be shelled

⊗ Garden peas should be shelled and used within a couple hours of harvest.

and either eaten or preserved within a couple of hours because from the moment they are picked, their sugars start converting to starch.

Unlike garden peas, the vines of sugar snap peas and snow peas will continue to grow and produce new blooms and pods so long as they are kept harvested. The pods closest to the root are ready first, and once those are ready count on harvesting every other day until the vines stop producing. Snap peas are harvested when they first start to fatten, but they still snap like a green bean. If you let them stay on the vine longer, the pods will become fibrous and inedible. If this happens, don't despair—just treat it like a garden pea. Snow peas are harvested at an even earlier stage—when the pods are still flat and the peas inside make little

lumps no larger than a BB. (The diameter of a BB, incidentally, is 0.177 inches.) Once harvest is started, they need to be harvested daily to keep any pods from becoming overly mature.

Snow peas and sugar snap peas can be stored in a plastic bag in the refrigerator for as long as two weeks without deterioration.

Any of the peas discussed so far can be used as a dried split pea for soup-making. All you need to do is leave the pods on the plant until they turn brown and you can hear the peas rattling when you shake the pod. Pick the pods, and set them aside either in the sun or in a well-ventilated place for a couple of days. Then, split open the pod by pressing on the seam and remove the peas. You can split the peas as you go along by using a thumbnail and the work progresses pretty quickly. It's the sort of thing you can do if forced to watch a bad movie on television with a family member. Put the peas in a large bowl and allow to sit out for a couple of weeks to dry, mixing with your hand every once in a while. Then, store them in an airtight container in a cool place away from sunlight.

Cowpeas or black-eyed peas are treated the same as split peas. Harvest when the pods are brown and you can hear the peas rattling when you shake the pod.

Preparation and Preservation

As I explained above, garden peas should be shelled and then eaten or preserved as soon as possible after harvest to preserve their sweetness. Split peas and cowpeas should be harvested when the pods are brown. Shell, and then allow them to dry before being stored in an airtight container. Sugar snap and snow peas can be sealed in a plastic bag and kept in the refrigerator for up to two weeks without loss of quality.

Garden peas, sugar snap and snow peas are all at their best fresh, but freeze very well. Steam blanch garden peas for two and half minutes or edible-podded peas for four minutes. Dump them into ice water for an equal amount of time to cool, dry them, and then seal in freezer bags with as much air removed as possible.

Sesame Snow Peas

Ingredients:

1 lb snow peas
1 Tbsp sesame seeds
2 Tbsp canola oil
1 Tbsp toasted sesame seed oil
2 tsp soy sauce
½ tsp ground ginger
4 green onions, chopped small
2 carrots, julienned

Procedure:

Prepare the snow peas by pinching off the stem end and pulling the strings down the pod. (Strings may not be present depending upon pea variety and timing of harvest.) Toast the sesame seeds in a dry pain, stirring constantly over low heat for 5 minutes. Set the toasted sesame seeds aside. Bring a large skillet to high heat, add the oils, then add the remaining ingredients. Keep in constant motion so nothing burns (peas burn easily due to high sugar content) until the peas are a bright green and slightly tender. Then add the soy sauce, put in the sesame seeds, give everything another good stir and then transfer to a heated dish for serving.

❖ Garden peas

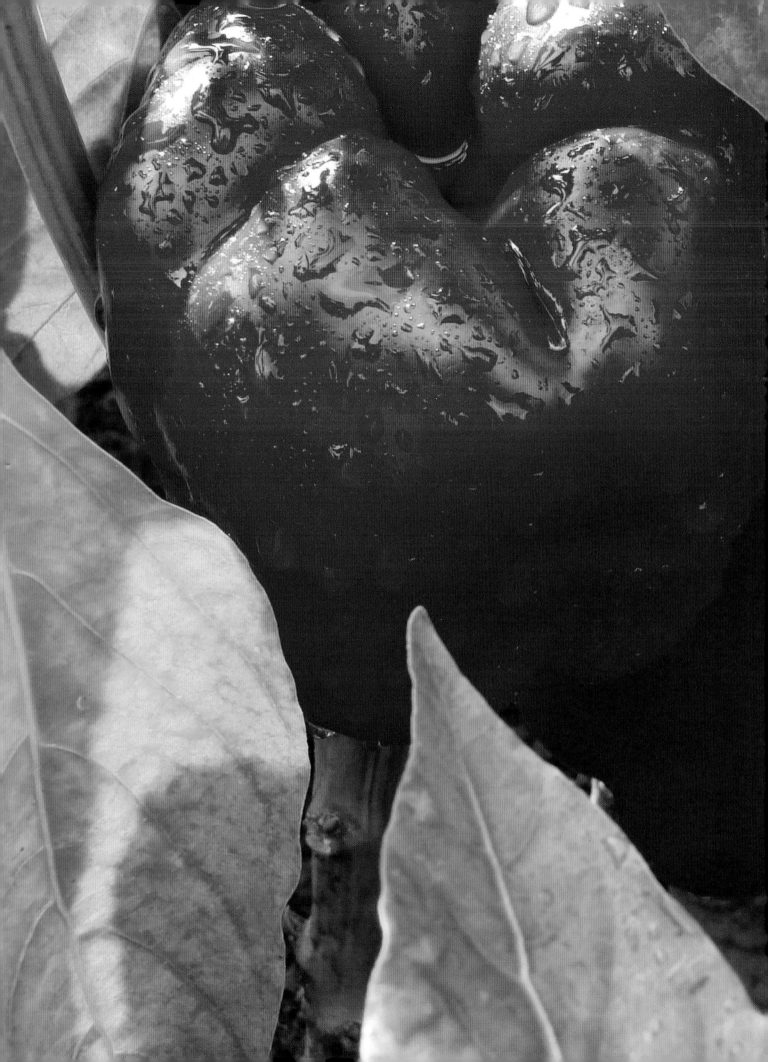

14

Peppers

Native to Mexico, South America and Central America, peppers have become an important ingredient in cuisines worldwide, both in the form of sweet peppers and hot peppers. The peppers available in the store represent only a tiny fraction of the range of this versatile fruit, and growing your own peppers is an ideal way to experience the array of flavors available. A cup of ripe sweet peppers contains two days' supply of vitamin C and more than a days' supply of vitamin A, along with a goodly dose of vitamin B6, fiber and important antioxidants.

Peppers can be divided into two broad categories: sweet and hot. Sweet peppers carry two copies of a recessive gene that inhibits the production of the capsaicin and closely related compounds that give hot peppers their bite. Many sweet peppers have been bred, and the standard blocky bell pepper is the one with which most people are familiar, though there are many other sweet pepper cultivars that have a wide array of shapes, flavors and colors.

Hot peppers either lack the gene that inhibits capsaicin, or have only one copy of the gene. Because the gene is recessive, with only one copy (rather than two), capsaicin production is not inhibited. Open-pollinated hot peppers always lack the gene altogether, but in some hybrids there is only one copy. Once capsaicin production is enabled, however, there are other genes that modulate the amount that is produced in a given variety of hot pepper as well as genes that have the effect of creating different flavors and colors.

The degree of hotness of a pepper is measured in either Scoville Heat Units or ASTA pungency units. The Scoville Heat Units are a measure of how much an alcoholic extract of the dried pepper must be diluted before it is just barely detectable by a panel of five tasters; the larger the number, the hotter the pepper. ASTA pungency units are derived through use of High Performance Liquid Chromatography (HPLC) to measure the absolute amount of capsaicinoid content. Most people are familiar with the Scoville Heat Units, and in my personal opinion, because there are

⊗ This little yellow pepper is mildly hot.

elements to taste outside of just a specific set of related chemicals, SHUs are a better measure of a person's likely subjective reaction.

The peperoncini peppers on a Greek salad and the pimentos stuffed into olives usually have fewer than 200 Scoville Heat Units, so they are pretty mild. Banana peppers will have up to 500 SHUs. Jalapeño peppers will have more than 2,500 SHUs. The world's hottest pepper is the Naga Viper, with more than 1,300,000 SHUs.

Variety Selection

Peppers are indigenous to warm zones with long growing seasons, though over time varieties have been selected that will do fine in cooler zones with shorter seasons. So the most important aspect of a cultivar to consider is its growing season. Keep in mind that there are two maturity dates for peppers: one for green peppers, and another for ripe peppers. Usually a catalog listing will give the number of days for green peppers and then specify an additional number of days for those peppers to ripen. Especially if you plan to save seeds, you want to choose a variety whose time to a mature and fully ripened fruit is at least ten days less than the length of your growing season. My area only has ninety-six frost-free days on average, so I have to pick varieties that are ripe in eighty-six days or less.

Another consideration is whether you prefer peppers that are sweet or hot and whether the peppers are for use in salads, salsa, frying or other specific uses.

Because my mini farm is in the Northeast, my particular choices might not be the best for other parts of the country, so you can use these as a starting point only for your own experimen-

⊗ A frying pepper awaiting my frying pan.

tation: I grow Jimmy Nardello's both for frying and drying, Ozark Giant or California Wonder for salads, and Black Hungarian as a hot pepper for salsas and spice. This latter is about half as hot as a jalapeño and has a nice smoky flavor.

Starting and Planting

Peppers should be started indoors seven weeks before last frost, and planted out a week after last frost after they have two sets of true leaves. They germinate slowly at lower temperatures, so use a heat mat when growing seedlings indoors to achieve the best temperature of 70 to 80 degrees. In addition, make sure to keep the fluorescent lights to within an inch of the leaves so the stems are stocky and strong. In order to avoid bacterial leaf spot (unless you are planting a variety of pepper that is resistant to that disease) the seed should be pre-treated via the method described in the section on weeds, pests and diseases.

Prepare the bed for the peppers by correcting the pH to between 6.0 and 6.5, thoroughly incorporating three cubic feet of finished compost or well-rotted manure per 4'x8' bed. Correct the soil for the major macronutrients, and then add an additional two pounds of bone meal per 4'x8' bed.

When transplanting, sprinkle a tablespoon of Epsom salt (magnesium sulfate) into the hole that will receive the transplant and mix it into the soil. Space transplants at 12"-18". Water transplants daily for the first week, and then make sure they get the equivalent of an inch of rain every week in the form of a deep soaking rather than multiple shallow waterings.

Weeds, Pests and Diseases

Because peppers are spaced a good distance apart, if you make sure the bed is weed-free before planting, weeds can be either handpicked or controlled by carefully using a stirrup hoe.

Bacterial leaf spot (BLS) is an economically important disease of peppers that has caused failure of entire crops. It starts with water-soaked spots on leaves that turn brown. Subsequently, the affected leaf may turn yellow, wither and die. The reduced foliage reduces yield and delays fruit maturity, and the spots can affect the peppers as well. It is spread primarily via infected seeds, though once the infection is present it will inhabit the soil and can be spread from plant to plant, especially in wet conditions, via hand contact. Once an infection is noticed, it can be controlled and kept from spreading by applying copper sulfate as indicated on the package. If you run into trouble with bacterial leaf spot, keep in mind that crop rotation and thoroughly cleaning up crop debris at the end of season are the best preventatives. If that is insufficient, seed pre-treatment and growing resistant cultivars will help.

Seeds can be pre-treated with scalding water to kill the bacteria. Unfortunately, this is a delicate process because the bacteria are inside the seed, so anything that would kill the bacteria would adversely affect the vigor of the seed as well. Ideally, this would be accomplished using laboratory equipment such as stirring hotplates and so forth, but the gear to do that would easily cost $400. Thankfully, there is another way that is a lot less expensive. The only gear you'll need that you may not already have is a high quality laboratory-grade thermometer such as the Fischer Scientific 14-983-15B.

Procedure: Seed Pre-Treatment

Equipment:

3 large Styrofoam coffee cups
1 fitted lid for one of the coffee cups
1 saucepan holding 8 cups of water
1 quart jar of cool water, uncovered
2 ice cubes
1 laboratory grade thermometer with a Fahrenheit scale
1 clean handkerchief, cut in four squares—use one of the squares
2 rubber bands
1 large nut

Procedure:

1. Nest two of the coffee cups together and set the lid next to them. These are for the hot water.

2. Fill the other coffee cup ⅔ with cold water and add the two ice cubes.

3. Twist the nut into a pocket in the square of handkerchief, and secure with a rubber band. Put the seeds in an adjacent pocket formed similarly, and secure with the other rubber band.

4. Bring the water in the pot to a temperature of exactly 122 degrees F. Test by swirling the water with the thermometer and then observing the reading. If the temperature goes higher than that, turn off the burner and add cool water a little at a time, stirring each time until the temperature is exactly 122 degrees.

5. Pour the water from the pot into the two nested cups until ⅔ full.

6. Add the handkerchief and assure it sinks.

7. Attach the lid.

8. Wait 25 minutes.

9. Remove the handkerchief from the hot water, and put it in the cup containing ice water, and leave it there for another 25 minutes.

10. Removed the handkerchief, unwrap the seeds, dry them on paper towels and plant as usual.

Phytophthera root rot, also known as "chile wilt" occurs throughout the United States but is most economically important in irrigated fields. The conditions that give rise to it—"wet feet" or waterlogged soil—simply do not exist in raised beds. Furthermore, as it is caused by a microorganism, standard sanitation and rotation practices will keep it even further suppressed, so you are unlikely to ever encounter this problem on your mini farm.

There are about twenty other bacterial and viral diseases that could theoretically infect your peppers, but just as with phytophthera, standard mini-farming practices will make most of them a theory rather than a fact. The one exception is Tobacco Mosaic Virus" (TMV). TMV can be present in the tobacco in cigarettes, and it is easily transmitted by hand to peppers, tomatoes, potatoes and other plants in that family. If anyone who touches your plants smokes, uses snuff, etc. make sure they wash their hands thoroughly before touching the plants. Other viruses, such as Tobacco Etch Virus, and Pepper Mosaic, are transmitted by aphids. If you keep aphids controlled, the lawn mowed and border weeds well away from your garden, these are an unlikely problem.

Aphids are a pest of all pepper species. Because of their role in transmitting diseases in peppers, you want to keep them under control. Aphids are a small, soft-bodied insect, green for camouflage, and they are usually kept controlled by natural predators. You can often prevent them by growing a bed of something they really like, such as marigolds, at some distance from the crop you are trying to protect. (This is called a *trap crop*.) But if they become prolific, you can keep them controlled by spraying weekly with a dilute solution (one tablespoon/gallon of water) of pure soap such as Dr. Bronner's or a specific insecticidal soap.

Slugs can also be an issue. You'd think, especially with hot peppers, that slugs would avoid them, but evidently they have no taste and will eat foliage and the peppers alike. Ground up egg shells combined with coffee grounds (renewed every couple of weeks) will create a deadly barrier around your pepper plants. The coffee grounds are poisonous to them and the egg shells cut their skin so they dehydrate. Other ways to deal with slugs are explained in Chapter 9: Greens.

Root knot nematodes are microscopic roundworms that can affect many garden plants including peppers. Symptoms include wilting and loss of productivity. When the plants are pulled, the roots have little nodules that can be as big as a pea, though they are usually smaller. Root knot nematodes prefer sandy soils low in organic matter, so if you use plenty of cured compost to start with, they won't likely become a problem. Use plenty of compost, practice crop rotation, pull up and compost old pepper plants and you won't have troubles.

Pepper maggots are the larvae of a fly with green eyes and a yellow head that is the same size as an ordinary housefly. The females use an ovipositor to punch a hole in the surface of the pepper, laying a tiny egg that grows into a white-yellow larva a bit under half an inch long. The larva eats inside the pepper, burrows back out, falls to the ground and then pupates in the soil. The injury to the fruit opens it up to diseases, and the insides become discolored. Pepper maggots aren't a problem for thin-skinned hot peppers, but tend to adversely affect sweet bell peppers. Keep in mind that you can grow peppers for years without seeing a pepper maggot and then suddenly have an entire crop wiped out. Remedies are the usual: sanitation and rotation. Sanitation in the form of burying old/dead/rotting peppers deep in the compost pile is particularly important because it is the scent of rotting peppers that draws the adult flies.

Harvest

Peppers can be harvested at any stage, though hot and sweet peppers alike have more sweetness and flavor when harvested fully ripe.

Each pepper plant has what is called a "fruit load." This is the maximum number of peppers that the plant can sustain given its foliage and root system. Once a plant has reached its fruit load, it will cease to flower or produce new fruits. In general, then, it is best to harvest some early fruits while green to make room for more peppers, and to allow some of these latter peppers to stay through full maturity and ripening.

Peppers vary in color as they ripen. Some ripen to orange, and others to red or even purple. A good rule of thumb is the less green you see on the pepper, the more ripe it is. Once they start to lose their green color, they ripen quickly—sometimes in just a day or two. Peppers start to lose quality quickly once fully ripe, so keep an eye on them and harvest when ready. Letting a pepper stay on the plant overlong will not improve its flavor. If you are planning to can or pickle your peppers, they maintain their crispness better when harvested a day or two prematurely.

The stems of pepper plants are brittle and delicate. You can harvest peppers, especially when ripe, just by lifting up the fruit and the fruit stem will separate from the plant easily enough. But when the peppers are green, this happens with difficulty and there is possibility of breaking the plant stems. So I use a pair of garden sheers to cut the fruit stem with minimal disturbance to the plant.

As noted previously, hot peppers contain an oily substance called capsaicin. Capsaicin can wreak havoc with mucus membranes at even low concentrations, and burn or blister skin at higher concentrations. In fact, law enforcement officers use the substance to disable people resisting arrest, so it is pretty powerful stuff. When harvesting hot peppers, resist any urge to scratch your nose or rub your eyes. If your skin starts to burn, you can

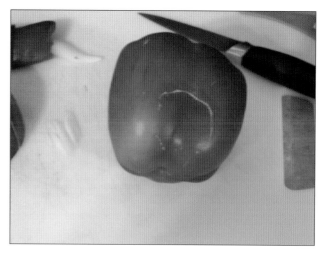

These striations occur most often on hot peppers, but if you see them harvest immediately so the pepper isn't over-ripe.

remove the capsaicin from your skin (but *not* eyes, nose, etc.!) with rubbing alcohol. Internally, milk can be helpful.

Seed Saving

Peppers are both self-fertile (meaning they will self-pollinate from the male and female parts inside the same flower and that they are receptive to their own pollen), and can be insect pollinated. All peppers are the same species, so they will interbreed freely. If you are planning to save seed, you either have to practice isolation techniques or grow only one variety of pepper. Isolation is as simple as covering the flower with a bag made from spun polyester. (Floating row cover is made from spun polyester; this is plentiful and cheap.) Cover the flower before it opens and gently shake the plant a couple of times a day to encourage self-pollination. Once a fruit starts to form, remove the bag, but mark that pepper as one that will be used for seeds.

Pepper seeds have greater vigor and higher germination rates if the peppers from which they are taken are allowed to become over-ripe. So allow the marked peppers to mature for an extra week or two after becoming fully ripe.

Seeds are collected by cutting open the pepper and removing them. Put the seeds, separated from any internal membranes, on a paper plate and allow to dry for a month. Then dehydrate further over a silica gel desiccant and store in a sealed container in a cool place away from sunlight.

Preparation and Preservation

Peppers can be eaten raw or cooked. They will keep in the refrigerator for one or two weeks in sealed plastic bags, and can be pickled, canned, dehydrated and frozen.

For freezing and dehydrating, first blanch the peppers in water (two minutes for rings, three minutes for halves) or steam (three minutes for rings, five minutes for halves) and then cool in ice water for several minutes. Then the peppers can be blotted dry and either frozen in evacuated freezer bags or dehydrated and stored in airtight jars.

Un-pickled peppers must be pressure-canned. But pickled peppers can be canned in a water bath canner. In either case, the process of canning makes the skin tough, so the skin is best removed. The skin is removed via a process known as "blistering." This consists of heating the skin, thereby causing it to become easily removed. You can do this in the microwave, oven or frying pan. To use the frying pan method, cut off the top and bottom of the peppers, split them lengthwise and remove the seeds. Heat the pan to medium. Put the split peppers in the pan skin-side down until the skins start to blister. Allow the peppers to cool, and then peel off the skin.

Though it varies with the variety of pepper, sometimes you can skip blistering by steam blanching the peppers for four minutes first, which sufficiently softens the skin. You can try it both ways and note the difference. In general, if I am cutting up the peppers small for a relish, I blanch them, but if I am leaving them long, I blister them.

Pickled Peppers

Ingredients:

8 lbs peppers, cleaned, seeds removed, sliced lengthwise and blistered or blanched

7 cups vinegar (5 percent acetic acid. Either cider vinegar or distilled vinegar is fine.)

1⅓ cups water

2 Tbsp pickling salt

3 Tbsp sugar

2 cloves of garlic

1 tsp peppercorns

1 tsp whole coriander seeds

Procedure:

Prepare the peppers. (They can be hot, sweet or a mix.) Combine the remaining ingredients in a large saucepan to make the brine, bring to a boil, and allow to simmer for 10 minutes. Pack the peppers into sterilized jars leaving one inch of head space, then fill the jars with brine leaving ½ inch of head space. Adjust the two-piece caps and process in a boiling water canner for 10 minutes. Makes 8–9 pints.

15

Potatoes

Originating in the Andes mountains and spread throughout the world by European explorers, potatoes have become a staple crop throughout the world. In fact, though you are unlikely to find potatoes at a Chinese or Indian restaurant, China and India are the world's first and third ranked producers of potatoes respectively. Potatoes are calorically dense, easy to grow, delicious and packed with vitamin C, potassium, vitamin B6 and fiber.

Potatoes also contain what is called resistant starch. This is starch that can't be broken down into sugars by enzymes in the small intestine, and is instead fermented in the large intestine. Research indicates that this resistant starch helps in the synthesis of important short-chain fatty acids and acts as a probiotic encouraging the growth of beneficial bacteria in the colon. Potatoes, especially purple and red ones, contain a substantial amount of antioxidants as well.

Because of the glycemic index[11] of potatoes and the growing problem with weight management in the United States, there are many who would counsel not to eat potatoes (or any other concentrated

---

11 Glycemic index is a measure of how much a person's blood sugar levels are raised by eating the food. The higher the glycemic index, the more (or more quickly) the blood glucose level is raised.

carbohydrate such as grains or breads) for reasons of health. This subject is fiercely debated by experts, and I'm not about to definitively address the issue in a book on gardening. Instead, I will point out that the glycemic index of a potato is influenced by the variety grown, where it is grown and even how it is prepared.

Potatoes are a member of the nightshade family, and the foliage and fruits of potato plants are poisonous, containing a number of toxic compounds. Solanine is the toxic compound most likely to be a concern for humans.

In general, the actual tubers of potato plants contain a safely low concentration of solanine. However, there are two circumstances where this may not be true. If potatoes are exposed to light their skin starts to turn green and solanine concentrations within the tuber increase rapidly. Do not eat any potatoes with green skin! If you live in South America, there are some wild closely-related species that have toxic tubers. If you grow potatoes from true seed in such an area, be sure to use isolation practices. Otherwise, the plants grown from the true seed could yield a toxic potato. This is not an issue in the United States or Europe as toxic wild potatoes don't grow in those areas.

There is also some concern about acrylamide—a suspected carcinogen in tobacco smoke. The problem is that acrylamide is formed in carbohydrate-rich foods when they are cooked[12] and can provide a level of acrylamide exposure similar to smoking. If this is a matter of concern for you, two things can be done to lessen the amount of acrylamide derived from eating potatoes. First, do not eat stored potatoes once they have become soft. This softness comes from the starch turning to sugar, and the higher sugar content leads to higher acrylamide formation on cooking. The second is to cook potatoes by boiling and then cool them for consumption. This decreases the amount of acrylamide formed and simultaneously increases the amount of beneficial resistant starch.

Variety Selection

Though there are literally thousands of varieties of potatoes, only a few dozen are commercially available. The primary consideration in choosing a potato cultivar is the purpose for which the potatoes will be used. Different varieties of potatoes have different amounts of starch as well as different ratios of amylose and amylopectin. High levels of starch create qualities desirable in a baking potato, high levels of amylose are best in mashed potatoes and higher levels of amylopectin allow for better boiled potatoes for potato salads. All of these characteristics are different for each variety of potato, so it is best to select a variety suitable for the end use.

Potatoes are also susceptible to a number of diseases including late blight, scab, verticillum wilt, potato viruses, blackspot and more. For most of these diseases, resistant varieties have been bred. If you have difficulty with a given disease, look in the seed catalogs to see what resistant varieties are available.

Starting and Planting

Potatoes can be started either from tubers or true botanical seeds. By far the most popular

12 Tarake, E. et. al. (2002) *J Agric Food Chem.* 2002 Aug 14;50(17):4998-5006.

	Baking	Mashed	Salad
Early/New Potatoes	All Blue, Purple Viking, Red Gold	German Butterball, Mountain Rose, Red Gold	Red Pontiac, Nicola, Sangre
Main Crop	Burbank Russet, Gold Rush, Katahdin	Burbank Russet, Kennebec	Yukon Gold, Yellow Finn, La Ratte

method is using the tubers. The eyes that form on potatoes are a small plant that, if planted in soil and allowed to grow, will turn into a full potato plant that will grow more potatoes.

Potatoes can accumulate many blights and viral diseases that can be passed in the tubers. For this reason, using potatoes from the supermarket is a very bad idea. Will it work? Usually it will. I've done it. But just because I've done something foolish and gotten away with it doesn't mean it should be emulated. The fact is that potatoes in the supermarket are not screened for diseases and

⊗ These potatoes are ready for planting.

using them as seed stock can be a recipe for crop failure.

There are a great many sources for certified seed potatoes. These are grown in isolation and tested for diseases. You can use them on your farm with a high degree of confidence that you aren't importing something nasty.

In terms of productivity, certified seed potatoes are usually superior to true botanical seed. Seed potatoes are cloned from the most productive plants available to the seed producer, whereas the results of heterosexual reproduction in true seed never reproduce either parent's characteristics exactly. So using seed potatoes that have been certified disease-free from a reputable supplier is generally most productive in the short term.

Nevertheless, I recommend growing potatoes from true botanical seed because most of the potatoes commercially available are from just a handful of cloned varieties representing a tiny segment of genetic diversity that leaves our food supply far more vulnerable than it should be to unknown pest and disease threats. True botanical seed gives and preserves the greatest genetic diversity, giving greater odds of maintaining a crop in the face of unknown future hazards. Furthermore, it gives you the ability to save your own seeds to cut costs and increase self-sufficiency.

Potatoes grow best in loose soil that is rich in organic matter, so mix in two to four cubic feet of well-finished compost per 4'x8' bed. Don't use immature compost or fresh animal feces as these can suck certain nutrients out of the soil as well as imparting off-flavors and potential human pathogens to the crop. Furthermore, fresh manures can cause unsightly scab on potatoes. Potatoes will grow fine in soils with pH as low as 4.8, and in fact these lower pH levels inhibit the fungus that causes scab, so skip the lime. Beyond that, if you add micronutrients (including boron) and correct the soil levels of macronutrients using appropriate organic amendments, you'll be fine. Potatoes also need soil to be well drained, but using raised beds solves that problem in advance.

Potatoes are a cool weather crop and should be planted around a month before the last frost. This is important, as the productivity of potatoes falls in 90 degree weather, and 95 degree weather may even kill the plants. So get started early!

If you use true botanical seed rather than seed potatoes, start those seeds indoors ten weeks before last frost so they can be planted outside at four weeks before last frost. Plant twice as many seeds as you think you'll need because germination rates on true seed aren't very good. If using certified seed potatoes, set them in a warm window for a week in advance of planting to help them break dormancy. Small- and medium-sized seed potatoes can be planted whole, but large ones should be cut into sections such that there are at least two buds in each section. Allow the cut potatoes to scab over in the open air for a day before planting. Plant either the seed potatoes or the transplants grown from true seed at 18" intervals in all directions. If your beds are so narrow you can only fit in two rows at that distance, you can space the seed potatoes or trans-

plants at one foot lengthwise and allow two feet between those rows. Plant the transplants as you would any other, and put seed potatoes two to three inches underground.

When the plants have grown to six inches, mound the dirt over them and let them grow some more. This will maximize the total number of potatoes grown from each plant. There are limits to this: the plants need foliage to make tubers, and the more stem you put underground, the less foliage there is to make tubers. I have tried mounding potatoes as much as two feet high, and have found their productivity to be no greater than in instances where I have planted the seed potatoes two inches deep in a six inch trench, and then filled in the trench with more dirt once the potato plants had grow up above the edge of the trench. You can continue mounding up until the plants start to flower, at which point new tubers stop being produced.

Potatoes need sufficient water to prevent hollow tubers and to grow them to optimal sizes. The equivalent of one inch of water weekly is sufficient.

Weeds, Pests and Diseases

Potato vines grow quickly. Planted as closely as I've recommended, all you need to do is make sure all the weeds in the bed are pulled prior to planting, and the vines will shade out competition in short order. All that will remain is keeping weeds at the edge of the bed pulled before they set seed. Potatoes have a few pests. Colorado potato beetles are pretty much a given anytime you plant potatoes. Wireworms can be a serious problem, especially in areas that abut or were previously grass. These two are the most likely to be of eco-

⊗ Colorado potato beetles are an important pest of potatoes.

nomic importance, but you can also experience damage from flea beetles, aphids and cutworms.

Colorado potato beetles and their larvae eat the foliage of potato plants. A single female can lay hundreds of eggs, so if left unchecked just a couple of beetles can devastate a crop in a couple of weeks. When the beetles are done with the potatoes, they may also jump to any tomato or eggplant plants they can find. The adult beetles are up to ⅜ of an inch long, bright yellow or orange, and each wing has five distinct brown stripes. They lay yellow eggs underneath the leaves in clusters of thirty, which hatch in a few days. The larva are reddish-orange with a row of black spots on each side.

In practice, because of their high fecundity, natural predators are almost always insufficient to keep potato beetles in check even using the best practices. The only alternatives available are to grow a resistant variety of potato (such as King Harry, Dakota Diamond or Elba) or spray them with something that will kill them.

Adult potato beetles overwinter just under the ground so in large-scale operations the practices of flaming, plastic trenches and similar physical controls have an aggregate effect that can mitigate the need for spraying when combined with crop rotation involving fields separated by long distances. Unfortunately, in a small scale operation like a mini farm, crop rotation doesn't give enough separation. And, if you flame the beds in which potatoes were previously grown, the beetles arrive anyway from alternate natural hosts such as horse nettle or woody nightshade (two common weeds). Thus, if resistant varieties aren't grown, we are left with spraying.

When spraying for Colorado potato beetles, I use a three-part mix that includes natural pyrethrin, rotenone and spinosad, each added in concentrations specified by the manufacturers. Pyrethrin is a contact poison highly toxic to bees, so spray it at dusk once all bees have left your plants to avoid hurting them. It's effects last a couple of days before it is rendered harmless through fresh air and sunshine.

Rotenone is an organic poison from the roots of certain tropical plants. It needs to be ingested to work, and will last on plants for up to six days. Pyrethrin and rotenone are both neurotoxins, but they work in different ways so that when combined, resistance is less likely to develop. Both of these target the adult beetles to keep them from laying more eggs and stop them from doing damage, though they will also kill any larvae. Spinosad is a bacterial toxin derived from a unique bacteria found in a rum distillery in the 1980s. It has to be ingested and is especially toxic to larvae. It takes a couple of days to kill the larvae, but they stop feeding immediately. I have found full control with only two sprayings a week apart.

Wireworms are a serious problem for potatoes as well as carrots, parsnips, beets, Jerusalem

⊗ This stackable frame with a landscape fabric bottom allows potatoes to be progressively hilled and excludes wireworms.

artichokes and practically any other edible root save those in the onion family. They will also damage directly planted corn seeds. They will be in soil that was previously lawn or is near lawn. Grassy cover-crops such as rye will likewise attract them. Rotations with crops they don't like, such as mustard or onions, have no practical effect in reducing their presence.

Up until soil temperatures reach 60 degrees, as many as a quarter of wireworms are two or three feet underground—far deeper than you will dig. But once the soil temperatures are that high, the preponderance of the wireworm population will be in the top one foot of soil. Though poisoning them is the modus operandi in industrial agriculture, the poisons used are among the most toxic imaginable and often require special permits for use as some of them, such as chlor-

picrin and methyl bromide are chemical warfare gases usable as weapons of mass destruction. Others, such as carbofuran and imidacloprid, are systemic insecticides that are absorbed into the plant tissues of the treated crop, which is a valid cause for concern.

Obviously, I'm not going to encourage this approach on a mini farm. What I do, as part of preparing a bed for potatoes or any other root crop, is dig through the soil looking for wireworms with a fine-toothed comb. As I find them, I put them in a jar, and when I'm done, I feed them to the chickens. Also, prior to planting I turn the chickens loose in the yard. They inevitably forage through the beds pulling weeds and eating various bugs, including wireworms. This is not 100 percent effective, but over time it has reduced crop damage to tolerable levels.

With potatoes, another very viable approach is to grow them in containers. As long as there are holes in the bottom (blocked with a water-permeable barrier that will exclude wireworms) to allow for drainage, growing them in containers such as five gallon buckets is entirely feasible and works well.

Potatoes are susceptible to several economically important diseases, including early blight, late blight, scab, and black leg. Black leg is not a problem in raised beds because they provide adequate drainage to prevent the disease. The most important weapon against the other diseases is crop rotation such that the same bed is not used to grow anything from the nightshade family (potato, tomato, pepper, eggplant, etc.) any more often than once every four years. Spoors also overwinter in crop debris and culled potatoes; crop debris and culled potatoes should be routinely buried deeply in the hottest section of the compost pile.

Early blight affects potatoes and tomatoes. It is caused by *Alternia solani*, and shows up first on the lowest leaves of the plant; it can ultimately kill the entire plant and adversely affect the tubers. It starts as a small, sunken brown spot on the leaf that expands. Usually, there is more than one such spot. As the spot progresses, the leaf turns yellow, then brown, and dies. In my experience, this disease will also affect cabbage-family crops once it is in the soil, so make sure to rotate crops such that nothing in either the nightshade or cabbage family is grown in that bed for four years to help deny it a host.

One thing that can help with this, as the fungus usually affects leaves rather than stems, is to grow your potato vines on a trellis and remove any leaves within one foot of the ground. This minimizes opportunities for the fungal spoors to be splashed up onto the lower foliage by rain or watering. I have also completely avoided this problem by planting my potatoes in an established living clover cover crop.

If all else fails and early blight visits your potatoes anyway, you can spray with a bacillus subtilis based preparation used according to label directions starting as soon as the infection is noticed, and this will usually control the disease.

Like early blight, late blight also affects tomatoes. Late blight is also known as potato blight, and was the disease responsible for the Irish potato famine. The water-soaked areas on the leaves that serve as the first symptom usually escape notice, but those areas then turn brown and as the leaf dies, it turns black. The spoors are washed from the leaves into the soil where they infect the tubers. Warm, wet weather favors its growth and you may see gray hairy mold growing under affected leaves in humid weather. Crop rotation is very important to prevent this disease, and because the spoors overwinter on potatoes left in the soil, plants growing in cull piles and so forth, meticulous sanitation is equally valuable.

Yet, in spite of the best rotation and sanitation, some of the spoors may blow in to your beds; if they take hold, it can be a serious problem. Sprays are more effective as preventatives than curatives, and those with greatest utility in that regard are copper sulfate and *Bacillus subtilis*. A program of regular spraying at least once every fourteen days, with particular attention to getting the undersides of the leaves, is generally effective. Copper can accumulate in the soil and reach toxic levels, so I would generally recommend using the bacillus subtilis instead; it is also more effective. If you see signs of infection in the plants, you can mix both together as the mixture is synergistic. If you grow a large crop of potatoes and you see some of them are affected, you can cut off the affected plants immediately and burn or thermophilically compost them. This will often stop the spread of infection.

Potato scab is another fungus. It leaves unsightly scab-like blemishes on the surface of potatoes, but doesn't pose a risk to the plant overall and the potatoes, once peeled, are perfectly edible. Even so, it makes the potatoes unsaleable. The best preventative is to grow the potatoes in beds where the pH is lower than 5.2; the fungus that causes scab doesn't survive well below that pH but the potatoes will do just fine. This, however, may not be practical as crops are rotated between beds and most crops prefer a pH of 6 or higher. If lowering the pH that much is not practical, a rotation of at least three years substantially diminishes scab. Using plenty of compost to enrich the soil provides competitive organisms that diminish the incidence of scab even further.

⊗ The symptoms of early blight when it starts on the lower leaves are distinctive.

Harvest

As long as they are not green, which indicates the presence of poisonous solanine, potatoes can be harvested at any stage. Early or so-called "new" potatoes can be harvested a week after the potato plants start to flower. New potatoes do not keep well, so they must be used soon after harvest. If you are careful, you can gently dig around under the plants with your bare hands and take a few new potatoes and leave the plants otherwise undisturbed. The potatoes that remain will continue to mature.

Or, you can pull up entire plants and dig around. Because the soil in my beds is uncompressed and practically ideal, I can harvest with my hands and nothing more than a garden trowel. If your beds aren't yet at the point, you can use a digging fork. Stick it in the dirt twelve to sixteen inches from the base of the plant, making sure to insert it as deeply as possible, and then lean back using the digging fork as a lever until the tines emerge from the soil. Do this along one side of the plants, and then along the other side, and then dig out the potatoes with your hands.

This same technique is applicable when harvesting fully mature potatoes. Fully mature potatoes have a toughened skin and are more suitable for long-term storage. Potatoes are mature when the foliage starts to die back later in the season. In my area, that is usually late August.

Mature potatoes harvested this way should be harvested in the morning, laid out in the sun to dry, and then turned at mid-day for even sun exposure. After that, the dirt can be brushed off with a large clean paint brush, and the potatoes can be stored.

Seed Saving

If you use tubers to start your potatoes, you are best off not trying to use your own tubers as seed potatoes except in an emergency, because as I mentioned earlier, a number of diseases will tend to accumulate and within just a couple of years you are likely to have seemingly intractable disease issues. So if you use tubers, you should order or otherwise obtain certified seed potatoes every year.

I have previously discussed using true botanical potato seed as the only practical way for a mini farmer to save potato seeds at all without concentrating diseases. So if total self-sufficiency is your goal, using true seed—even if productivity may be a bit less—is the way to go.

If you are going to grow your potatoes from true seed, it would be best to start by ordering true seeds rather than tubers. You shouldn't use just any old potato variety as a starting point for collecting true seed. Many commercial strains of potatoes (though the breeders will not say which ones for trade secret reasons) have beneficial characteristics such as disease resistance that have been imparted through crosses with wild potato varieties that have toxic properties that are reliably suppressed in the first generation hybrids which are cloned for certified seed potatoes, but would **not** be reliably suppressed in the next generation grown from true seed. Growing random poisonous potatoes probably wouldn't be a big hit with the family.

In theory, if you have the facilities to measure solanine content, you could select the plants from that second generation whose tubers were non-poisonous, pull the other plants, and ultimately create a variety that bred true without potential for poisonous potatoes. But in practice, it is a lot easier to stick with heirloom varieties provided as true seed.

There are very few sources for true potato seed that you can use to start. One unlikely but very productive place to get a small quantity of seed for research purposes is the USDA Germplasm Repository at www.ars-grin.gov/npgs/orders.html. Another source is New World Crops (www.newworldcrops.com). Some other sources can be found by using an Internet search engine, but these are mostly private individuals and seed savers.

Potatoes are an outbreeding plant, and as such you want to grow at least twenty potato plants to avoid inbreeding depression. Then, collect the berries from those plants that were the most resistant to diseases and pests, excluding berries from the runts or those that seemed particularly susceptible to problems. (Warning: when ripe, the berries smell appetizing but are poisonous to eat. Keep out of reach of children!) Put the berries in a blender with a cup of water, and process just enough at low speed to break up the berries and free the seed. Dump that into an open container to ferment for a couple of days, then pour off the water, rinse the seed, and let it dry for a few days on paper towels before dehydrating over a dessicant and storing in a cool, dark place in a sealed container.

Within just a few years you will end up with your own strain of potatoes that grows optimally in your location and soil and that has also accumulated robust multiple-gene resistances to a variety of diseases and maybe even a pest or two.

Preparation and Preservation

Mature potatoes last longest in locations that are cool (42 to 50 degrees), dark, and humid with good ventilation. They should be checked weekly and any rotting potatoes removed before the rot spreads to other potatoes. In these conditions, the potatoes will remain sound and free of sprouts for up to 140 days; the specific time will vary with the particular potato. Commercial storage facilities with computer-controlled storage conditions can keep some potatoes as long as 210 days, but you are unlikely to create such perfect conditions at home.

New potatoes—those that have been harvested before the plant starts to die back and have not been sun cured—can't be stored this way as they go bad quickly. The alternative for both new and mature potatoes is freezing. To freeze potatoes, wash, dry, chop into slices or fries no more than ¼" thick, water blanch for four minutes, cool in ice water for five minutes, pat dry, and then seal in freezer bags excluding as much air as possible.

Potatoes can also be dehydrated. Wash the potatoes, cut into ⅛-inch-thick rounds, water blanch for eight minutes, cool in ice water for fifteen minutes, pat dry, and dehydrate according to the recommendations of the manufacturer of your dehydrator. The results can be stored in airtight jars for a year or more, and if you are ambitious can be ground into a powder for making your own instant mashed potatoes.

Oven French Fries

Ingredients:

Non-stick cooking spray
Several large baking potatoes

Procedure:

Wash and dry the potatoes and pre-heat the oven to 450 degrees. Cut the potatoes into ¼" strips. Spray liberally with the non-stick cooking spray, season as desired, and place flat in a single layer on a non-stick baking sheet in the oven. Cook for 25 minutes, turning over after the first 10 minutes for even browning.

⮉ Oven french fries

Squash

16

Squash have been cultivated starting more than 8,000 years ago in the Americas, and are now grown in almost endless variety in every region on the planet that supports agriculture. Their culinary uses extend from soups and salads to even pies, so their popularity is understandable.

In a culinary sense, squash are divided into two categories: summer squash (including zucchini, patty pan and yellow) and winter squash (including acorn, hubbard, butternut, spaghetti, pumpkins and others). But in a botanical sense, squash are divided into four distinct species. Hubbard and buttercup squash are *Cucurbita maxima*; Cushaw squash are *Cucurbita mixta*; butternut squash is *Cucurbita moschata*; and acorn squash, pumpkins, zucchini and other squash are *Cucurbita pepo*.

All varieties of squash are rich in fiber, vitamin C and carotenes that exert a protective influence against cancers. Squash also provide useful amounts of folic acid, omega-3 fatty acids, pantothenic acid, vitamin B1, vitamin B6 and niacin. With the exception of hubbard squash (because the woody seed capsule is generally too tough) all squash seeds are edible. The seeds are high in minerals such as zinc, manganese, phosphorus and iron, and studies have shown pumpkin seeds to reduce the symptoms of BPH (benign prostatic hypoplasia).

Variety Selection

The three most important things to consider in selecting varieties of squash to grow are the types of squash your family prefers to eat, the length of your growing season and disease resistance. Most supermarkets carry a variety of squash year-round and summer squash seasonally. You can try various types to find out what you and your family prefer. Growing season is not generally a consideration for squash as they are harvested early, but some squash require a growing season well in excess of 100 days. The time to maturity for squash is measured from the time the seed is planted, so if you start your squash inside three weeks before planting out as a transplant, you can often squeeze a variety of squash into your season that otherwise wouldn't have enough time.

Powdery mildew is quite common in all varieties of squash, and is the only disease for which a wide variety of resistant cultivars is available. If you have serious economic impact from powdery

⊗ Zucchini and squash are prolific and grow in a short season.

mildew, then consider growing squash varieties that are resistant.

Starting and Planting

In typical gardens, squash seeds are planted directly in hills or rows. However, both to maximize productivity in terms of season extension and to get a head start against pests or diseases, I recommend starting them indoors two weeks before last frost and putting out the transplants a week after last frost.

Optimum soil pH is between 6.5 and 6.8, though squash will grow satisfactorily at pH levels as low as 5.5 if the soil's fertility is otherwise optimal. Squash grow best with even soil moisture. Uneven moisture can cause blossom end rot and malformed fruit. As rain is unpredictable, the best way to assure the most even moisture uptake possible is to establish deep root systems and provide a great deal of organic matter in the soil. This can be accomplished by adding at least five cubic feet of compost per 4'x8' bed so that the organic matter will buffer and hold moisture, and through deep watering equivalent to one inch of rain at least once a week, but twice weekly in hot weather. Using raised beds will help to compensate for over-watering due to heavy rains by allowing excessive moisture to drain.

Squash require full sun so the bed location should be optimally located for minimum shade. Some squash varieties, notably yellow, patty pan and zucchini, grow on bushes. These should be spaced at two foot intervals throughout the bed. Others, such as acorn squash and pumpkins, grow a long vining system.

For smaller squash varieties such as acorn squash, it is fine to put your transplants at 1'

Small squash can be trellised on the north side of a bed.

Larger winter squash grow fine on a trellis.

intervals along the northern one foot of the bed and train the vines onto a trellis. But for larger squash varieties such as hubbard squash or large pumpkins, this isn't practical. The larger squash plants should be planted at 1' intervals along the southern one foot of the bed, and their vines allowed to grow across the yard. This way, the rest of the bed real estate can be used for another crop. You could grow small squash trellised along the northern foot of the bed, large squash along the southern foot of the bed, and a crop such as lettuce or chard in the two feet in between to make maximum use of space.

If the vines for larger squash are allowed to grow across the yard, you won't be able to control grass and weeds in that area that could serve as a reservoir for pests and disease. To cut down on weeds and the pests/diseases they carry, that area can be heavily mulched with grass clippings, hay, or something similar.

Squash will also grow well planted in between corn stalks as long as you space the corn a bit wider than usual. It is also one of the very few plants that will do fine in companion plantings with onions.

Weeds, Pests and Diseases

Weeds can sap nutrients, block sunlight and give a safe-haven to pests and diseases. Bush-type squash are planted far enough apart that a stirrup hoe, used shallowly once a week, can deal with the weeds. Weeding is likewise easy on smaller squash that are trellised, but the squash vines that are allowed to grow across the yard outside of the beds really need to be mulched under the vines to control weeds as using a hoe or weeding by hand just isn't practical. Lots of materials can be used for mulch. I use grass clippings because they are free. Some studies indicate that using very shiny mulch such as aluminum foil or mylar may help deter cucumber beetles; these should be placed on top of a regular mulch because all by themselves they won't hold back weeds.

The most common disease of squash is powdery mildew. This appears as a white or gray powdery-looking mold that results in deformed and dead leaves. It spreads rapidly and can wipe out a plant or even several plants within a few days of emerging. Prevention is better than attempting a cure, and the best preventatives are growing resistant varieties, planting in full sun, and avoiding nighttime watering. If the disease still takes hold, remove affected leaves and discard in the trash. (Make sure that the tools you use to cut off the leaves are disinfected after each cut by dipping in a 1:10 bleach solution before being used on other leaves or plants.) If that fails to halt the progress of the disease, try a milk and baking soda spray composed of one pint of milk and three teaspoons of baking soda for every gallon of spray. Spray twice weekly, being sure to get both the tops and bottoms of the leaves.

Other important diseases of squash include bacterial wilt, anthracnose, angular leafspot and mosaic viruses. All of these are either spread by pests that can be controlled, overwinter in the previous year's crop refuse, or both. So the most important preventative measures are crop rotation, cleaning up debris at the end of each season, and controlling pests.

Bacterial wilt is spread by cucumber beetles and organic control is quite difficult which is one reason organic squash varieties (pumpkins especially) from the U.S. are hard to find. Preventative measures include giving seedlings a head start through transplanting instead of sowing seed directly, covering the plants with floating row cover until the blossoms appear so they can produce at least some mature fruit before succumbing, planting trap crops that are more attractive than those being grown and that have been treated with a non-organic insecticide, and using organic insecticides such as pyrethrin mixed with canola oil or diatomaceous earth prophylactically. In non-organic gardens carbaryl applied regularly according to package directions from the moment of seed emergence is effective.

Anthracnose fungus overwinters in crop debris and in seed collected from infected fruit. It usually starts as yellow spots on older leaves, but especially in warm damp weather it can quickly spread to affect younger leaves, stems and fruit. As the disease progresses, the spots get larger and turn brown, followed by the vine dying. Crop rotation and cleaning up the prior year's debris are the most important steps to prevent anthracnose. If your seed is of dubious origin, you can treat it with hot water as described in the chapter on peppers, but this will substantially reduce germination rates so start three times as many seedlings if you do this. Once anthracnose has made itself known, if you catch it early you can cut off and throw away infected leaves—this may prevent further spreading. Thereafter, spray neem oil according to package directions every seven to ten days as a preventative, making sure to get the undersides of leaves. Once the disease is clearly actively spreading, Soap Shield[13] **copper** fungicidal soap will control it if used quickly, as will Bordeaux mixtures of **copper sulfate** and **lime**.

Angular leafspot overwinters in crop debris, so crop rotation and sanitation will effectively prevent it. Angular leafspot gets its name from the spots it produces on leaves; they are confined to the leaf area between veins. The spots start as water-soaked spots that later turn brown and develop tears. It spreads like wildfire in wet weather, and is spread by people working with the fruits, leaves and vines when they are damp. Prevention is better than cure, but if prevention fails a copper fungicide will usually work if used soon after detection. Copper fungicides, used excessively, can harm soil biology and the runoff can harm fish. So, again, a concentration on prevention is wise.

Squash are affected by both squash mosaic and cucumber mosiac, transmitted by cucumber beetles and aphids respectively. Cucumber beetle control has already been discussed in relation to bacterial wilt disease, and aphids can be controlled in a variety of ways. Insecticidal soap applied according to label directions is effective, as are the encapsulated natural pyrethrins. Garlic oil sprays will kill aphids, and most varieties of aphids can be deterred or killed with a tea made from potato or tomato leaves.

Squash (as well as cucumbers and melons to a lesser degree) are also affected by squash bugs. They suck the plant juices and inject a toxin that can weaken and kill the vines. Even worse, in four states (Oklahoma, Kentucky, Texas and Ohio) they have been found to transmit Cucurbit Yellow Vine Disease virus. Squash bugs are about ⅝" long, dark brown or mottled with brown and gray, and hard-shelled. They are shield-shaped and make a disagreeable odor when crushed. They lay their orange-yellow eggs in clusters of twelve or more on the underside of leaves. Adult squash bugs overwinter in crop debris, under mulches and under boards. Avoiding mulches (other than hay, which seems to repel them) in beds that will be used for cucurbit family crops is a good idea, as is removal and composting of crop debris.

The best organic control of squash bugs is to cover the vines with floating row cover that is well-anchored so bugs can't sneak in from the moment the crop is planted until the first flowers emerge. This will at least reduce the timeframe available for them to do damage. You can try interplanting buckwheat to attract parasitic wasps that will prey on the squash bugs, but the results of this are marginal. Likewise, interplanting with marigolds or nasturtiums may have some marginal effect. On the scale of a minifarm you can pick off the bugs and put them in some soapy water and smash the egg clusters by hand. If infestation can't be controlled that way, a pyrethrin/rotenone spray used according to label directions can control them.

The larvae of squash vine borers burrow into vines and destroy the tissue, thereby killing any part of the vine beyond where they entered. The adult is a moth whose coloration often leads to it being mistaken for a bee or wasp. It lays small blackish pin-head eggs, usually along the six inches of a vine just above where it emerges from the soil. When the eggs hatch, the larvae burrow into the vine, growing as they eat until they are

---

13 Soap Shield is a registered trademark of Gardens Alive, Inc.

⊗ Squash bugs inject a poison into the vine.

through it with a pin and leaving the pin in place. You can sometimes cut the stem along its length, extract the borer, push the vine back together where it was cut and bury the cut section in soil.

Industrial agriculture depends on insecticides sprayed on a regular schedule to kill the larvae as they emerge from the eggs, but they are seldom a large enough problem on a mini farm to justify default use of insecticides "just in case."

Particularly in summer squash, blossom end rot is a possibility. As the name of the condition implies, the blossom end of the squash simply rots. This is caused by uneven uptake of calcium due to variations in water availability such as two weeks without water followed by a sudden soaking rain. Often the first fruits of summer squash will have this problem and it is nothing to worry about. But overall the problem can be prevented by making sure the beds have plenty of compost to buffer the water supply and watering regularly (once a week in normal weather but twice a week if it is hot and dry) and deeply to the equivalent of an inch of rain each time.

Harvest

Summer and winter squash are harvested differently. Summer squash are harvested while still immature like cucumbers so the plants will continue to make new flowers and squash. For best flavor, yellow squash and zucchini should be harvested when no more than six to eight inches long, and patty pan squash should be harvested when no more than four inches in diameter. Once you allow a summer squash to mature, the plant stops making new ones, so make sure none escape your notice, which can easily happen under the heavy cover provided by squash leaves.

ultimately large enough that their burrowing physically disrupts the plant.

Squash vines will put roots into the soil anywhere the vine is covered with soil, so one thing that will help diminish the damage from borers is burying parts of the vine as it grows so that the vine has a diversified source of nutrients and water. Another thing you can try is wrapping some aluminum foil around the bottom six inches of the vine so the moth has no place to lay its eggs or has to settle for a less damaging place.

Observing your plants daily, and particularly looking for "frass"—the sawdust-like leavings that borers leave behind them as they eat into the stems—can allow you to react before too much damage is done. If you catch it before the vine wilts, you can kill the borer in the vine by poking

A couple of times I've missed squash that easily grew to several pounds. Not only did the plant stop making more squash, but the large squash was not very tasty.

Winter squash, on the other hand, are harvested when mature and they are cured for longer keeping. In fact, in most cases the flavor of winter squash varieties improves over the first several weeks after harvest. Winter squash are harvested when they have developed full color and their rinds are hard enough that they can't be dented with a thumb nail and the rind has become dull-looking as opposed to glossy. Don't pull them off the vine or their keeping quality will be adversely affected. Instead, cut the vine using pruners or a sharp knife, leaving two or three inches of vine still attached to the squash. With the exception of acorn types, other winter squash should then be cured by leaving them in the shade at temperatures exceeding 80 degrees for five to ten days before storing.

Seed Saving

The biggest challenge with seed saving is that squash require bees or other pollinators to pollinate, and interbreeding between varieties within the same species is quite easy. If you want to save seed, I would recommend growing only one type of squash of a given species each year.

Cucurbita pepo: Yellow, zucchini, patty pan, acorn, spaghetti, common pumpkin

Cucurbita moschata: butternut, naples, kentucky field pumpkin, neck pumpkin

Cucurbita mixta: cushaw squash (looks like a pumpkin)

Cucurbita maxima: buttercup, hubbard, banana, Lakota

There is room for confusion, particularly with squash known as pumpkins, because there are many varieties of pumpkins, and the term encompasses squash from more than one species. Just to be on the safe side, when ordering seeds for squash, check the catalog to make sure what species it is.

Winter squash used for seeds should be taken three or even four weeks later than the squash would normally be harvested. Also, those squash that grow closest to the root of the plant are likely to produce seeds with the highest rate of germination. Scoop out the seeds, swirl around in a bowl of lukewarm water, dry off with some paper towels and allow to sit for a couple of weeks before drying further over a dessicant. Store in an airtight container in a cool, dark place.

Summer squash are treated identically. If you leave them long enough, they will get large and grow a tough rind. Once this rind is tough enough you can't dent it with your thumbnail, let the squash mature for another three weeks before harvesting.

⊗ Squash flowers are very attractive to bees and rely on them for pollination.

Preparation and Preservation

Summer squash can be kept in a plastic bag in the crisper drawer of your refrigerator, but it will only keep for three to five days. Like corn, it is one of those vegetables best eaten or preserved soon after harvest. The best way to preserve summer squash is freezing. Cut off the ends, slice uniformly, water blanch for three minutes or steam blanch for five minutes, cool in ice water for five minutes, pat dry and then store in freezer bags with as much air excluded as possible.

Winter squash should be stored at a temperature of 50-55 degrees. Acorn type squash will keep for one or two months, butternut, turban and butternut squash will keep for two or three months, and hubbard squash for as long as six months. Storage life can be enhanced even longer if, after the fruits have been cured and before you store them, you wash the surface using a cloth dipped in soapy water (dish liquid is fine) that contains one part of bleach for every ten parts of soapy water. This kills many of the pathogens that would normally affect the squash, thus prolonging storage life. Check your stored squash frequently and discard those showing signs of rotting promptly so spoors don't spread to adjacent fruit. The optimal humidity for storage is 50 percent to 70 percent. Higher than that will decrease storage life due to increased rotting and lower than that will decrease storage life due to dehydration of the fruit. Don't store winter squash near apples as the ethylene gas that apples generate will cause the squash to rot.

The seeds of this acorn squash will make a nutritious high-energy snack.

The seeds of any edible squash (including pumpkins) can be eaten (though those of the largest varieties may be too tough), and they make a tasty high-energy snack. There are several ways to prepare them depending upon one's preferences and health-consciousness. To preserve the healthful character of the oils in squash seeds, they shouldn't be cooked at a temperature higher than 170 degrees. On the other hand, cooking at higher temperatures is preferred by many because it results in a different taste. Seeds prepared either way will keep for a week if stored in an airtight container in the refrigerator.

To prepare in this fashion, clean the seeds by swishing them around in a big bowl of warm water, then strain them out of the water and dry them on paper towels overnight. Preheat your oven to 160-170 degrees, and spread the seeds in a single layer on a baking sheet. Bake for twenty minutes, use a spatula to flip the seeds, and then bake for another ten minutes.

To go all-out on snack food, clean the seeds as above, preheat the oven to 450 degrees, mix the seeds in a large bowl with canola oil and a bit of Adobo,[14] and then put in a single layer on the baking sheet. Cook for ten minutes, flip with a spatula, and then cook for another ten minutes.

Baked Acorn Squash

Ingredients:

2 acorn squash (will also work with butternut, buttercup, delicata, etc.)

4 Tbsp butter

¼ cup packed brown sugar

salt and pepper to taste

Procedure:

Preheat oven to 400 degrees. Cut the squash in half lengthwise and remove the seeds. Cook the halves in a shallow pan with the cut side down for 30 minutes. Turn them with the cut side up, then add the butter, sugar, salt and pepper. Return to the oven and cook for another 30–40 minutes until a fork can be easily inserted.

Squash Casserole

Ingredients:

2 lbs squash (yellow, zucchini, patty pan or any combination)

1 beaten egg

2 cups of chopped tomatoes

1 onion, chopped

1 cup bread crumbs

2 Tbsp melted butter

½ tsp salt

Procedure:

Preheat the oven to 350 degrees. Slice the squash and cook in a bowl in the microwave for 5 minutes, stopping to stir at the halfway point. Thoroughly combine the bread crumbs, salt, beaten egg and tomatoes and salt thoroughly, then stir in the squash. Use the butter to grease a casserole dish. Dump all the ingredients into the casserole dish and bake for 45 minutes.

---

14 "Adobo" in this case is a seasoning available in the Latin section of the supermarket. I use the Adobo con Cumin for this recipe.

Tomatoes

17

If there is any one thing that motivates more people to take up gardening, it is the desire to eat a tomato right off the vine. The tomatoes in the supermarket usually look perfect, but they taste unripe and have little flavor. Many people remember the taste of tomatoes right out of their mother's or grandfather's garden, and they know they don't have to settle for the unappetizing fare at the store.

Not only are tomatoes are a nutritional powerhouse rich in vitamins A and C along with various minerals and B vitamins, but study after study has shown that a diet rich in tomatoes is protective against a variety of cancers, including prostate and pancreatic. Other studies have shown that important antioxidants in tomatoes, such as lycopene, are present in greater quantities when the tomatoes are raised organically, so growing your own would be a tremendous benefit in more than just taste.

One thing you may find helpful in your quest for higher levels of self-sufficiency is how easy it is to make your own spaghetti sauce, salsa and even ketchup from your own tomatoes.

Variety Selection

There are literally hundreds of different varieties of tomatoes encompassing colors from yellow to purple, as well as variations in growing habits, disease resistance, early or late maturities and a range of taste that makes tomatoes the subject of tastings similar to wine. There is no way to even make a dent in all the varieties available, but there are a number of ways to make sense of them.

Tomatoes are either determinate, meaning bush-like, or indeterminate, meaning vine-like. Determinate varieties can be grown using just a short tomato cage, but indeterminate varieties will need a trellis to maximize their potential. Determinate tomatoes also tend to ripen more closely together, whereas the tomatoes on indeterminate vines will ripen at different times. For purposes of processing large numbers of tomatoes for spaghetti sauce or ketchup, determinate varieties are usually best, but for adding to salads throughout the summer or for drying in batches, you might find indeterminate varieties more convenient.

The maturity date for tomatoes listed in seed catalogs is based on the number of days since they were put in the garden as transplants. Usually, you will want tomatoes for both early in the season and later in the season, so you might grow a couple of varieties to have your harvest spread out.

Though in most respects tomatoes can be readily substituted for each other, there are differences in moisture content that make some tomatoes more suitable for sauces and other more suitable for fresh eating. For example, the Italian plum varieties tend to have a lower moisture content, so they don't have to be simmered as long to make a thick sauce.

Tomatoes come in a variety of colors ranging from white to purple. There are even varieties that remain green when ripe! In general, the tomatoes rated most highly in taste tests are pink, purple or black varieties. (These latter aren't really black. They have a complex darker color.) Examples include Pruden's Purple and Brandywine. However, your taste and opinion is the only one that matters.

In my garden, I usually grow an indeterminate cherry tomato for salad tomatoes all season, an early slicer for sandwiches and a late slicer for even more sandwiches, and a group of determinate paste tomatoes for sauce and salsa. I like Peacevine cherry for salads, Moskvich and Stupice for early season slicing, Brandywine and Pruden's Purple for late season slicing and Amish Paste, Black Plum and Plum for sauces among others. But those are just my own preferences!

Starting and Planting

Tomatoes are a warm weather crop and as long as they are supplied with sufficient water, the more sun and heat the better. This makes tomatoes a bit of a challenge for Northern growers, but breeders have put a great deal of effort into producing early tomatoes, especially in Eastern Europe. So with proper variety selection, tomatoes certainly belong in gardens across the continental United States.

If you've ever had tomatoes rot in the garden and been faced with dozens if not hundreds of volunteer plants the following year, you know that tomatoes can be directly seeded in the garden. Volunteers need to be ruthlessly culled because they can serve as a reservoir of disease (for both tomatoes and potatoes) that negates the value of crop rotation. Even so, putting seeds in the ground directly is not very reliable and in most of the country tomatoes could definitely benefit from a head start. Maturity dates given for tomatoes in catalogs assume the use of transplants started six weeks earlier, so a bit of math shows that sowing them directly from seed won't allow for enough time before frost sets in in the fall in most of the country. Start them indoors six weeks before last frost, and plant them out right after the last expected frost.

If you are growing indeterminate tomatoes, plant them spaced 18" apart in the northern one foot of the bed, and train them onto a trellis six feet tall. Prune the tops back once they reach that high. If you are growing determinate tomatoes, use the cheap wire tomato cages, and space them 18" to 24" apart. Ideally, these will be in a bed that has the long sides on the East and West so the tomatoes will benefit from sun on both sides of the bed.

The soil for tomatoes should be deeply worked, incorporating a lot of organic matter. I would recommend at least five cubic feet of compost per 4'x8' bed. The pH should ideally be in the 6.5 to 7 range, though closer to 6.5 is better for prevention of a condition known as yellow shoulder. Uneven uptake of calcium due to uneven uptake of water causes blossom end rot and splitting in tomatoes. The organic matter will help hold and buffer the water while using a raised bed will help prevent an overabundance.

Too much nitrogen can cause tomato plants to create lots of foliage but bland tomatoes. So when you add amendments in accordance with a soil test, use slow release nitrogen sources such as alfalfa meal, cotton seed meal and compost as opposed to sodium nitrate, urea or blood meal, and don't add any more than the soil testing indicates. If you mix a tablespoon of garden gypsum

» Lay the stem horizontally when transplanting for maximum strength roots.

into the soil of the hole where you plant tomatoes, it will also help prevent blossom end rot.

Tomatoes will send down roots anywhere the stem is covered with soil. For the most robust root system and plants, put the tomatoes deep in the soil with the stem horizontal and only four inches of the plant above ground. As the plant grows, strip off the leaves that are within a foot of the ground, as this will help prevent a variety of blights and other diseases that start with infecting the lower leaves.

Weeds, Pests and Diseases

Because tomatoes are planted with such wide spacing, controlling weeds via careful periodic hoeing is straightforward, and the foliage is often so plentiful at close spacing that much weed competition is shaded out once the plants are growing well.

Because tomato foliage is poisonous to most things, tomatoes only have a few notable pests; among these are hornworms, cutworms, flea beetles, aphids, whiteflies and root knot nematodes.

Aphids will always exist to some degree on tomato plants and they don't usually pose a problem, but if their numbers become too large they can weaken the plants. They can be controlled with a couple sprays of insecticidal soap. Cutworms will exist in any bed that has had fresh organic matter (such as cover crops or heavy weeds) cut and turned into the bed within a couple of weeks of planting. Protect the seedlings with cardboard collars four inches long and buried an inch deep in the soil when they are first planted, and you'll have no trouble.

Hornworms are such a unique creature that once you've seen one you'll never forget it. They have a prominent horn at one end, are as much as three inches long, and green with stripes and eye-like markings over their body. They gobble foliage extensively, even chopping off entire branches of the plant at times. You can pick these off and feed them to the chickens. I've never found more than a few of these in a single season, but if your plants are suffering from an extensive infestation, they can be controlled overnight with a single complete spraying with a bacillus thuringiensis preparation used according to label directions.

Whiteflies are not usually a problem when using home-grown transplants; they often hitchhike on plants purchased from nurseries or garden stores. In small quantities, these don't adversely affect the plant. In large populations they can leave a lot of honeydew on the plant that gives room for sooty mold to take hold. Sooty mold looks like a sooty coating on leaves and fruits. It doesn't actually infect the plant, but rather lives in the honeydew on the surface. It isn't economi-

😞 Tomato hornworms have a unique beauty, but they are voracious.

cally important unless it becomes so extensive as to block sunlight and photosynthesis. Whiteflies are ubiquitous in garden stores, greenhouses and the like because over the decades they have become immune to practically all insecticides. If you develop a substantial infestation of whiteflies, about the only thing that will control them is a light horticultural oil. Don't use such oils during a drought or they can kill the plant.

Flea beetles resemble fleas. A few of them won't hurt anything, but if the populations are high they can defoliate and weaken the plants. If their damage crosses an economic threshold, they can be easily controlled with a pyrethrin/rotenone spray used according to package directions.

Perhaps the most dreaded pest of tomatoes is root knot nematodes. These microscopic worms burrow into the roots causing knots that interfere with nutrient absorption and the full cycle of photosynthesis. The preparations used to control them on a commercial scale are breathtakingly toxic and expensive and thus impractical on a mini farm; they are better off prevented. Luckily, they can be prevented easily through crop rotation and sanitation. At the end of the season, pull out all plants including as much of the roots as you can and compost them. If you develop an infestation in a bed, I would recommend growing mustard in that bed for a couple of years, followed by onions the next year. Then try a crop such as beets that is susceptible to root knot nematodes and where the damage is easily seen to see if you've successfully abolished them. If not, go back to the mustard and onions for another couple of years.

A common but seldom recognized pest of tomatoes is the tomato russet mite. The symptoms start with the lower leaves turning brown and then moving up the plant with the stem taking on a bronze-like appearance. If they appear, you can control tomato russet mites with a commercial wettable sulfur preparation.

Diseases of tomatoes include fusarium wilt, verticillium wilt and mosaic viruses among others, though tomatoes can also be affected by potato early and late blight, manifesting identical symptoms to potatoes. The key to controlling diseases is crop rotation and sanitation. Only once have I ever had a problem with disease in tomatoes, and those seedlings were brought home from a nursery (purchased after an unexpected late and hard frost killed our seedlings). Otherwise, following the simple precautions of rotation, sanitation and keeping tobacco products away from the plants I've never had a problem.

Fusarium wilt affects all nightshade-family plants including tomatoes, eggplant, peppers and potatoes. Fusarium usually times its arrival for damp weather when there is already lots of full-sized green fruit on the plant, turning the leaves yellow. There seems to be no rhyme or reason to which leaves will be affected, and sometime it will infect one half of the leaves but not the other. Those leaves lose the power of photosynthesis, and the fruit doesn't get enough energy to ripen. Fusarium is a soil-born fungus that can be controlled by crop rotation. If problems persist, there are many varieties of tomatoes that are resistant, so if you choose a resistant variety it won't be an issue.

Verticillium wilt usually starts on the older leaves with the edges turning first yellow than brown. Unlike fusarium it doesn't kill the plant, but it definitely hurts productivity. Crop rotation and sanitation are your biggest preventatives; as the pathogen is soil-born I have found another solution. What I do is sow my tomato bed in clover, and grow indeterminate varieties trellised on the North side of the bed. The clover creates a dense ground cover that keeps rain from splattering fungus spoors from the soil up onto the leaves. I plant the transplants in the clover patch, take off the bottom leaves once they get big enough, and train them onto a trellis. For determinate plants where trellising isn't feasible, they tend to shade out the clover so the protection isn't as full, but a number of verticillium resistant varieties of tomato are also available.

There are many mosaic viruses, but they all have the same symptoms on tomatoes. The leaves develop a mottled appearance, wilt, and grow small—almost like a fern. The result is a plant that fails to thrive. Plants infected with such viruses should be discarded in the rubbish.

Now for the good news: your tomatoes will never suffer from this virus. The reason is because 99.9 percent of the time mosaic virus comes from tobacco in cigarettes where the gardener fails to wash his or her hands after smoking and then transmits the virus to the tomatoes. If you smoke, all you need to do is avoid smoking in or around your garden and wash your hands after smoking before touching tomato (or potato or pepper) plants and you will never see this.

Pinching and Pruning Tomatoes

As mentioned earlier, tomatoes can be divided into determinate and indeterminate types. Determinate plants only reach a certain size and do not require extensive pruning or a trellis; indeterminate plants, given proper conditions, will literally grow with no limits. Determinate plants only need a cage or a stake—though I much prefer cages. Indeterminate plants will grow adjunct stems at leaf axils in an infinite variety, and if left unchecked will outgrow practically any trellis and start creeping along the ground.

Because of soil-borne diseases, it is important to keep tomatoes off the ground. Thus cages for determinate tomatoes and trellising for indeterminate tomatoes are absolutely necessary. Pruning indeterminate tomatoes is an exercise in discretion; understanding why it is needed will help put it in context.

The more vegetative growth a tomato plant produces, the more of that growth will be shaded and thus consuming more sugar than it produces. Furthermore, the more vegetation, the more fruit clusters, the smaller the fruit, and the later it will ripen. Too much vegetation will also favor disease conditions due to the prolonged time required for moisture to evaporate from the leaves. There is an optimal trade-off between the number of stems and the size, and the number and speed of maturation of fruits. In most cases, this is just three or at most four adjunct stems.

How high up on the plant these stems grow is important. You don't want them growing from below the first fruit cluster because they will put too much strain on the root. You don't want them growing too high on the plant, because then they will be too weak to support fruits of their own. What I recommend is allowing a new stem to grow from the leaf axils immediately above the first, second and third fruit clusters, and ruthlessly pinching off any others.

In between the leaves and the stems (an area known as the axil) is where the new stems emerge. Once you see it growing small leaves, you'll know it is a new stem. These new stems are most easily removed by "pinching." Just grasp between

⊗ Excess stems can be easily pinched off when they are small.

your thumb and forefinger, and literally pinch it off. This method exposes the least amount of remaining tissue to disease. Sometimes, though, the plants get away from you and you'll have a stem three feet long before you realize it; such stems that can't be removed by pinching should be removed with the least tissue damage possible by using a razor knife in preference to tools such as scissors or pruners.

Indeterminate tomatoes should also be "topped." About a month before your first expected frost, you want to cut the top off of any growing stems. This will force all energy production to go into ripening the fruit.

Because damp conditions favor the spread of disease, never prune tomatoes when the plants are damp. And because diseases spread easily between plants, I recommend dipping any tools used in a 10 percent bleach/water solution after each cut.

Harvest

Tomatoes can be eaten at any time and size. Though green tomatoes contain small amounts of the poisonous alkaloid tomatine, no cases of poisoning have been reported from their consumption and studies indicate that the tomatine binds to cholesterol in the digestive tract, preventing absorption of both the tomatine and the cholesterol. In the concentrations present in green tomatoes, consumption has been shown to lower bad LDL cholesterol, inhibit certain cancers and enhance immune response.[15] So green tomatoes are safe to harvest and eat.

Even so, I much prefer my tomatoes ripe—especially for fresh eating—and I suspect most folks share my preference. Vine-ripened fruits are by far the most tasty, with those ripening indoors rating a very close second.

Timing the harvest is straightforward: pick the tomato when it has developed maximum color for its variety but has not become soft. There are two exceptions to this rule. The first is cherry tomatoes because of their tendency to split. Harvest these when the color has changed but before maximum ripeness to avoid splitting. The second is any variety of tomato that is prone to cracking. These should also be harvested before maximum color.

Problems with cracking can occur in any tomato that has been water-deprived for an extended period of time and then given an overabundance of water. Incorporating plenty of organic matter into the soil as a buffer to absorb and release water as needed will be helpful, as will growing in raised beds and making sure tomatoes are watered properly. But even with the best care, some varieties are prone to splitting as ripeness approaches, and these should be harvested before they crack.

Tomatoes harvested a little early will continue to ripen indoors. Ideally, put them in a closed paper bag at room temperature. A paper bag will retain and concentrate ripening factors such as the ethylene gas released by the ripening fruit that also triggers further ripening, but also keep the fruit from becoming water-laden and rotten as would happen with a plastic bag. You can hasten the ripening process by putting a ripe (but not overripe) banana in the bag with the tomatoes.

If you know a frost is coming and you have a lot of green fruits on your plants, you can either harvest the green fruits and use them in appropriate recipes or cut the vines and hang them upside down indoors in the dark. Surprisingly, a lot of the fruit will ripen.

Saving Seeds

Tomatoes usually self-pollinate. That is, the pollen fertilizes the ovum within the flower; sometimes before the flower even opens. To help this process, you can give your tomato plants a little shake now and then. Even though tomatoes are self-pollinating, they can also be cross-pollinated by insects, so maintain several feet of separation between plants of different varieties from which you want to save seeds. Also, use only open-pollinated or heirloom varieties for seed saving as hybrids will not make seed that re-creates the characteristics of the immediate parent.

When you save tomato seeds, you want to save them from the very best tomatoes on the very best plants. Pick the tomato slightly before it is fully ripe. If you wait until it is fully ripe it will hurt the germination rates of the seeds you save. Tomato seeds are processed using a fermentation method.

Cut the tomato across the equator, and use your clean fingers or a spoon to scoop the gelatin and seeds (but not the meat of the tomato) into a clean container. I use small plastic cups, but can-

---

15 McGee, H. (2009), "Accused but Probably not a Killer," *New York Times*, July 18, 2009, ISSN 0362-4331.

ning jars will also work fine. Add water equivalent to about half the volume of tomato gelatin in the cups, and swirl it around with a spoon. Cover the top with cheesecloth to keep out bugs, and set aside for two to four days until a mold starts growing on top. If four days have elapsed and there is still no mold, don't worry. Add water to the cups, swish it around, and pour off any mold or floating seeds. Rinse off with water a few times, and then spread the seeds on multiple layers of paper towels to dry. After about a week, put the seeds on a paper plate to dry further. After another week, you can dry further over a dessicant before storing for up to four years in a sealed container in a cool, dry, dark place.

Preparation and Preservation

If you wash and dry your tomatoes when you bring them in, they'll keep for a week without loss of flavor just sitting on the kitchen counter; longer if they are not yet ripe. They will keep for yet another week in the refrigerator, but at the cost of some loss of flavor and a sort of graininess being imparted to the flesh. Between the two methods you can save up your tomatoes for a couple of weeks (if you are saving for a batch of sauce).

Tomatoes can also be dehydrated, canned and even frozen. Though vegetables are usually blanched before dehydrating and freezing, this is not needed with tomatoes, though many prefer to remove the skin, and the procedure for doing so tends to blanch them a bit anyway.

Many recipes call for removing the skin from the tomatoes because especially when canned, the skin can become tough and a detracting annoyance in some dishes. Once you get the hang of removing the skin, it is easy. Bring some water in a pot to a gentle boil. Make sure it is deep enough to fully cover the tomato. Lower the tomato into the water on a slotted metal spoon. Leave it in the water until the skin starts cracking—about a minute—and then put the tomato in ice water for three minutes. The skin is then easily removed. Once the skin is removed, you can also remove the hard core from the tomato by using a simple apple corer. Once the tomato has been skinned and cored, you can cut it, remove the gelatinous portion containing the seeds, and either freeze directly in a freezer bag from which air has been excluded or dehydrate according to the directions that came with your dehydrator.

For making sauces, I don't bother with removing seeds, skins or cores. Instead, I boil up the tomatoes in a big pot until they are mushy and process them through a hand-cranked strainer that separates these portions out.

Canning tomatoes is a borderline proposition; that is, the pH of tomatoes is right on the borderline between foods that can be safely canned in a water bath and foods that require pressure canning. Most recipes in canning books specify the addition of an acidifying substance—usually commercial bottled lemon juice—as a means of lowering the pH sufficiently to allow for safe water bath canning. The reason they specify commercially bottled lemon juice is because it contains a predictable and standardized amount of citric acid. The problem is that the stuff usually contains potassium sorbate as a preservative. Even though as far as I know potassium sorbate is not harmful, it has been my experience that when used in products that are cooked it imparts off-flavors. So instead I recommend that you go on the Internet to any wine-making hobby store and order pure citric acid. Substitute ¼ teaspoon of citric acid for one tablespoon of lemon juice, and you will achieve the same effect without imparting unintended off flavors. Also, keep in mind that if you add any other vegetable or meat to a tomato recipe (excepting salsa because salsa is actually a pickle), you will need to pressure can that product for the longest length of time for any of the ingredients. Failure to do so can result in botulism.

There are a host of recipes for relishes, salsas, chutneys and pies (for the adventurous) made from green tomatoes. Some like to slice them, dip them in egg and then seasoned flour, and fry them. All of these are wonderful.

Homemade Ketchup

20–25 lbs of tomatoes

3 cups vinegar

1 cup of chopped onions

1 cup of chopped sweet red pepper

1 cup sugar

1 clove garlic

2 tsp celery seed

1 tsp salt

1 tsp whole black pepper

2 tsp whole allspice

2 tsp mustard seed

1 stick of cinnamon

½ tsp cayenne pepper

Clean and weigh the tomatoes. I use a kitchen scale but for this quantity of produce you can use the bathroom scale. Cut them up whole and put them in a large pot with a little water to prevent scorching and add the onions, garlic, sweet peppers, celery seed, salt and cayenne pepper, cooking them over medium-low heat until they are mushy. While you are waiting on that, put

the black pepper, allspice, mustard seed and cinnamon in a spice bag. Bring the three cups of vinegar to a simmer in a smaller pot, put the spice bag in the vinegar, and allow that to simmer for 20–30 minutes. Remove the spice bag and turn off the heat on that burner.

Once the tomatoes and other ingredients in the pot are mushy, carefully process them through a hand-cranked strainer. Clean out the pot, dry it, and then put the liquid that results from the straining back into the pot. Add the vinegar and sugar. Bring to a simmer for 30 minutes.

After this, you need to either simmer this while stirring for about 12 hours to get rid of the liquid, or put it in a large crock pot. I recommend the crock pot. Once the ketchup has simmered for about 12 hours and become thicker, fill sterilized pint jars leaving ¼ inch of head space and process in a boiling water canner for 30 minutes.

Allow this to set for a couple of weeks before use for full flavor to develop. You'll be amazed at how good this is!

❷ A strainer comes in handy for making large batches of sauce and ketchup for canning.

18

Turnips, Rutabagas and Radishes

Some variants of turnips, rutabagas and radishes have been cultivated for hundreds and even thousands of years for good reason: they are versatile, nutritious and delicious! Both the roots and leaves of all three are edible, and can be cooked in a variety of ways. All three roots are high in vitamin C, folate, thiamine, niacin, and a number of essential minerals including potassium and copper. Their omega-3 to omega-6 fat ratio is 3:1 and they are a substantial source of cardio-protective dietary fiber.

But the good news continues into the leaves of these staple crops. The greens are strongly anti-inflammatory, and a single serving contains 350 percent of the RDA of vitamin A along with a whopping 1,050 percent of the RDA of vitamin K, a quarter of the days supply of vitamin E and calcium and valuable quantities of folate, copper, manganese and more. In essence, just like their closely related cousins broccoli and cabbage, turnips, rutabagas and radishes are a superfood.

Turnips were a staple crop for settling the American West because they keep well in root cellars while supplying vital vitamin C throughout the harsh winters. Turnips, and turnip greens in particular, tend to be more appreciated in the American South than in the rest of the country, but its taste and nutritional properties argue in favor of a place in the garden.

Eaten raw, a small slice of turnip, rutabaga or radish will share a characteristic pungency from the allyl isothiocyanate created by damage to the cells. These isothiocyanate compounds are a defense mechanism to keep herbivores from eating the plants, but in the small quantities normally consumed in food they are perfectly safe. Even better, these isothiocyanates and related compounds induce the production of what are called "phase 2 detoxification enzymes" in the liver that selectively detoxify carcinogens.[16,17] Cooking tends to remove the bite by eliminating an enzymatic precursor to isothiocyanate formation, but studies indicate that this doesn't adversely affect the formation of detoxification enzymes.[18]

All of this means that turnips, rutabagas and radishes are potent cancer preventatives, and if your turnips have a sharp taste when raw, that just means they are good for you.

Variety Selection

Your local agricultural store likely only carries two varieties of turnip at most: Purple Top White Globe and Golden Ball. But if you look in the catalogs of heirloom seed companies, you'll find at least a dozen varieties from which to choose. As there are no particular diseases for which resistant varieties exist, your primary selection criteria is your own interests and tastes.

This same applies to rutabagas. At the agricultural store you'll be lucky to find even one variety, but you'll find at least half a dozen varieties in heirloom seed catalogs. Rutabagas are sweeter than turnips, and if your family hasn't developed a taste yet for this family of root vegetables, rutabagas would be a good place to start. Just look through the catalogs and find a variety that looks tasty.

Radishes are an entirely different proposition! With at least three dozen readily available varieties ranging from white to red to black and ranging in size from the size of your thumb to the size of an apple, you will find a lot of offerings that look nothing at all like the vegetable you associate with the word "radish." Initially, I would recommend trying a very common variety that looks familiar, such as French Breakfast. After that, though, you should branch out to try many different varieties.

⊗ Seeds for Purple Top turnips are readily available and they produce reliably.

16 Keum YS, Jeong WS & Kong AN (2004) Chemoprevention by isothiocyanates and their underlying molecular signaling mechanisms. Mutat Res 555, 191–202.
17 Zhang YS, Yao S & Li J (2006) "Vegetable-derived isothiocyanates: anti-proliferative activity and mechanism of action." *Proc Nutr Soc* 65, 68–75.
18 Rungapamestry, V., Rabot, S., Fuller, Z., Ratcliffe, B., Duncan, A. (2008) "Influence of cooking duration of cabbage and presence of colonic microbiota on the excretion of N-acetylcysteine conjugates of allyl isothiocyanate and bioactivity of phase 2 enzymes in F344 rats." *British Journal of Nutrition* (2008), 99, 773–781.

Starting and Planting

Turnips, rutabagas and radishes are grown from seed placed directly in the ground. Being brassicas they are somewhat cold-hardy and can be planted anytime the average soil temperature is 50 degrees or higher, but it is best to wait for a soil temperature of 55 for best germination. They will sprout in from one to five days depending on soil temperature. The seeds should be planted ½" deep. When planting turnips and rutabagas, the best technique for maximizing harvest is to space at three inches in all directions, and then come back in about forty-five days to harvest every other plant for greens and young roots. Leave the others to grow larger. Radishes can be spaced at two inch intervals though some varieties can grow as large as turnips so you should check the seed packet for the final thinning distance for the particular variety you are planting.

As with all root crops, deeply dug soil free of rocks will encourage the best growth. Plenty of finished compost (at least two cubic feet per thirty-two-square-foot bed) will encourage the proper biological environment. It is important that the compost be finished, however, as turnips, rutabagas and radishes are especially sensitive to the germination inhibitors present in unfinished compost. Maintaining a soil pH between 6 and 7 is optimal for these plants. The soil should have plenty of trace minerals, either from a wide variety of additives of biological origin or supplemented with sea solids. Boron is a key element for proper growth. Boron is contained in borax and constitutes 11.5% of its weight. You need 300-400 milligrams of boron per thirty-two-square-foot bed; 1½ teaspoon of borax will supply just the right amount. (Use a real measuring spoon, don't "eyeball" it.) Borax is toxic to plants in concentrated form, so you should mix it thoroughly with some other powdery additive such as greensand or wood ashes and distribute evenly. The macronutrients should be supplemented as indicated by a soil test.

A higher quality crop with fewer pest problems can be assured by planting for a fall harvest. That is because once temperatures exceed 75 degrees and most certainly when you get 90-degree days, the quality of the roots suffers dramatically. Rutabagas shrink and become stringy, radishes become woody and turnips become just plain unpalatable. Rutabagas and turnips require 60–90 days to reach harvesting size. Even when planting six weeks before last frost in the spring you are in a race against hot weather on the one end while combating root maggots on the other. If, instead, you plant six weeks before your first expected frost, you will get rapid germination, the season for cabbage maggots will be past, and the roots will be maturing during cooler days. You'll appreciate the results.

Radishes mature much more quickly, sometimes in as little as three weeks. So these are a lot easier to plant as a reliable spring crop because you can have them planted and harvested before warm weather.

Weeds, Pests and Diseases

Because of their rapid germination and prolific growth, if planted in a weed-free bed initially, weeds are unlikely to be an issue. What little weeding is required can be done by hand and will mostly be at the outside edges of the beds where the weeds can get light.

Turnips, rutabagas and radishes have good natural protection from predation and generally do not experience problems of economic importance on the scale of a mini farm so long as crop rotation and sanitation are practiced.

The only economically serious disease that is likely is clubroot, a disease that results in stunted roots unable to draw water so the plants wilt and die. This can be avoided by keeping the soil pH above 6 and preferably 6.5. Once clubroot is in the soil of a bed, you can't grow any cabbage family crops there for eight years, so it pays to do a pH test and adjust the pH if needed so this disease doesn't gain a foothold.

Most pests aren't keen on the peppery taste of these plants, but anything that affects broccoli or cabbage can theoretically come after your turnips if sufficiently hungry. If they do, just treat as described in the chapter on cabbage and broccoli. The only pest I have seen in turnips that poses a substantive threat—and it is completely preventable—is cabbage root maggots. Cabbage root maggots are the larvae of a fly that looks like a slightly smaller and more streamlined version of a housefly. They overwinter as pupae in the soil, and emerge at the time you'd usually plant seeds. Once the plants emerge, they lay eggs at the base of the plant that burrow into the soil and then eat the roots voraciously. With root vegetables you may not even know they have been affected until a very disappointing harvest.

Two factors disproportionately attract this pest. The first is rotting organic matter in the soil such as immature compost. The second is planting when the soil temperature is a little too cold. If you avoid immature compost, plant at an average soil temperature of 55 degrees and make sure you don't plant where cabbage-family crops

were grown last year; this pest can be completely prevented by covering your bed with floating row cover once the seeds are planted. Remove the row cover once soil temperatures average 65 degrees and you are home free.

Harvest

You don't want turnips, rutabagas or radishes to wait too long in the ground as they'll get woody and their flavor will suffer. Once soil temperatures are averaging above 75 degrees they need to be harvested even if they are smaller than you'd like. Turnips for "bunching"—to be sold with greens and root together—should be harvested at a diameter of two inches. Those that will be "topped"—meaning that the roots will be sold or used without the greens—should be harvested at a diameter of three inches. If you are like me, you have seen so-called "turnips" in the produce aisle at the grocery store that are a solid five or six inches in diameter. These aren't turnips—they are rutabagas. Rutabagas should be harvested at four inches for optimum quality. The reason they are so large in the supermarket is because they sell on the basis of weight rather than quality.

Radishes can be harvested at practically any stage, so long as you don't let them wait more than a week or so after they have reached the mature size for the variety you are growing. After that, they tend to split and become less tasty.

Saving Seeds

Turnips, rutabagas and radishes are biennials that produce flowers and seed in their second year. Turnips and radishes are outbreeding plants subject to inbreeding depression if too few are grown for seed, and depend upon pollinators such as bees for pollination as they don't usually self-pollinate. Rutabagas are self-fertile and naturally inbreeding, though they will outbreed with the help of bees.

Radishes won't interbreed with other cabbage-family crops with the exception of other radishes. So only grow one variety of radishes for seed in any given year. Grow at least twelve plants for seed.

Turnips will interbreed with other turnips, broccoli rabe and Chinese cabbages. So only grow one variety of turnip (and no Chinese cabbage or broccoli rabe) for seed in a season. You should grow at least six plants for seed, but I would recommend an even dozen.

Rutabagas will interbreed with other rutabagas and with some varieties of turnip that are grown as livestock feed. Rape (a relative of mustard) can also interbreed with rutabagas, as well as Siberian kale. The species classification of rutabagas is a bit confused among various authorities, but they shouldn't interbreed with species of turnips you'll be growing. Again, to maintain genetic diversity, grow at least six plants but preferably a dozen.

Despite these differences, seed saving for all three is the same. In areas with mild winters, you can heavily mulch the roots in the ground to help them survive over the winter. In areas with harsh winters, the roots should be dug, foliage trimmed to two inches, and stored in peat moss at 95 percent humidity and temperatures between 33 and 40 degrees. In the spring, plant them in the ground at their original depth as soon as the soil can be worked.

The bulbs will leaf out and then grow a stalk around three feet tall. This stalk is somewhat delicate and I would recommend staking it. An amazing number of flowers will grow on the stalk and bees will seemingly congregate from miles around to have fun spreading pollen and fertilizing the plants. Harvest the seed pods once they turn brown. As they are fragile, I recommend stripping the pods into a plastic bag. The pods can then be broken up and the seed separated from the chafe through winnowing.

Let the seed set out in an open bowl for a couple of weeks, and then dry over a dessicant for a week before storing in a sealed container for up to five years in a cool, dark place.

Preparation and Preservation

Due to tradition, we think of rutabagas and turnips as something only eaten cooked and radishes as something only eaten raw. The reality is that these are interchangeable. Likewise, we eat turnip greens but neglect radish greens which are just as edible and delicious. Rutabaga greens are likewise edible. The greens, if dry, will keep in a bag in the refrigerator for a week. They can be steam-blanched for four minutes and then chilled in ice water, dried, and frozen in freezer bags from which all air has been excluded. Or they can be dehydrated after blanching and used as an addition to soups, stews, dips and sauces.

The roots store best in peat or sand with the leaves removed at 95 percent humidity and temperatures of 32 to 35 degrees. Summer radishes will keep for a month like this, but turnips, winter radishes and rutabagas will keep for several months this way.

In practice, it is hard to achieve such perfect storage conditions, which is why you will often find turnips and rutabagas in the supermarket to have been waxed. The wax prevents moisture loss for storage in less humid environments, and because the hot wax kills pathogens on the surface, it allows for long-term storage under less perfect conditions. To wax turnips and rutabagas, remove the tops and thoroughly wash and dry them first. (They must be thoroughly dried before immersing in wax or dangerous splatters of wax will occur.) Heat up regular canning wax in a pot on an electric stove or using a double-boiler if you have a gas stove. Using a slotted spoon, dip the vegetable in the wax and make sure it is thoroughly wet with the wax, then set aside on some paper bags for the wax to harden. Don't hold in the wax any longer than necessary to thoroughly coat with wax. Peel the wax and top layer of the vegetable and discard before eating.

Radishes, rutabagas and turnips also freeze well. Cut into uniform ½" chunks, water blanch for four minutes or steam blanch for six minutes, cool thoroughly in ice water for another five minutes, pat dry and then seal in freezer bags excluding air. You could also opt to dehy-drate them for future use in soups or stews by following the directions of the manufacturer of your dehydrator.

There are a lot of ways to eat turnips and rutabagas. They can be boiled and mashed like potatoes, baked, cooked into stews and more. The greens can be eaten raw in salads, steamed, or boiled in the fashion of collard greens. I like to sauté them with olive oil and garlic.

Oven Roasted Radishes

Ingredients:

1 lb radishes, cut uniformly in halves or quartered
1 leek (mild onion can be substituted)
1 Tbsp toasted sesame seed oil
1 Tbsp canola oil
2 Tbsp soy sauce

Procedure:

Preheat oven to 425 degrees. Wash and dry the radishes, and cut into uniform sections so they bake at approximately the same rate. Thoroughly coat the radishes with the toasted sesame seed oil and canola oil by mixing with your hands in a bowl, and pour into a baking dish. Put in the oven and set your timer for 20 minutes. Thinly slice the white portion of the leek, discarding the remainder. When the timer goes off, add the leeks and soy sauce to the radishes and mix thoroughly, then return to the oven for another 7 minutes. You'll never think of radishes as just a salad garnish again!

✪ Oven roasted radishes will have you looking at radishes in a whole new light!

PART II

Tools and Techniques

19

Planting Guides and Seeders

Ah! The joy of planting! Your beds are prepared and ready to accept the seeds that will bring forth an abundant harvest, and the anticipation feels almost electric as you breathe in the smell of soil mingled with the scents of spring. You rush out the door eagerly with packets of seeds in one hand and a map of where everything will go in the other.

About an hour later, after you have painstakingly punched about 200 precisely spaced holes in the soil at two-inch intervals, your back is aching, your knees are dirty and the mosquitoes have come out in force. All you have done is poke holes and you still haven't even planted a seed, but when it comes to that the seeds are so tiny you can barely pick them out of your hand. You know placing the seeds in the holes will take forever.

Intensive agricultural techniques that involve close plant spacings are certainly space efficient, but as you slap another blood sucker off your forearm, you start wondering if it is worth it. The produce aisle at the supermarket is starting to look appealing.

Let's face it—as much as we may enjoy the fruits of our labor, on some days the details of mini-farming are sheer drudgery, and the initial planting of tiny and closely spaced seeds such as mustard and carrot is enough to make you think twice. Whenever I try to handle seeds that small, my fingers feel about six feet thick and as clumsy as an ox. It's frustrating. And how on earth am I supposed to precisely space all of the holes for those seeds? After poking a couple of hundred holes, I want to space them further apart just to make the task end more quickly, and nature doesn't reward shortcuts.

After thinking about these problems a bit, I developed a couple of solutions to making a lot of precisely spaced holes in your seedbed in a hurry, and have some methods for placing these seeds. This will help remove the drudgery and bring back the eager anticipation!

All-Purpose Fixed Planting Guide

Almost all seeds or transplants are spaced at multiples of two or three inches. That is to say plants are spaced at two, three, four, six, eight, nine, twelve or eighteen inches. This means

⊗ Leveling

⊗ Tamping

⊗ Making Holes

that with rare exceptions, **spacing** can be accommodated using fixed measurements of two or three inches.

An easy way to accomplish this is to take a piece of board, mark off two-inch intervals, and drill a long deck screw into each mark, leaving about an inch and a half protruding.

This board can be used to level the soil in a bed. It can also be used to tamp down the soil for a firm seed bed. Once the soil is leveled and tamped down, you can use the board to make hundreds of perfectly spaced seed holes in a hurry. To use it, lay it along the flattened soil in your bed, press the heads of the screws into the soil and wiggle it a bit. Now you have evenly spaced holes every two inches. If your seeds are spaced at four inches, just plant in every other hole. If they are spaced at six inches, then skip two holes after each one that is planted and so forth. So this board will work for spacings that are a multiple of two inches.

On the other edge of the board you can mark spacing at three inches, and this will work for spacings of three, six, nine, twelve inches and so forth. Using these two edges you can easily poke hundreds of perfectly spaced holes for seeds or transplants in just a minute.

Even better, the boards can also be used to make evenly spaced furrows for mesclun mix as well as evening out the soil in beds after mixing in soil amendments. After evening out the soil, you can use the flat side of the boards to pack down the soil a bit to make a picture-perfect seed bed prior to using the edge of the board to make the holes.

For this purpose, I would advise using 2"x4" stock between three and four feet long. Anything else will likely be either too fragile or too unwieldy. Once you have made the board, if you paint it with an exterior latex paint to protect it from the elements it will last for many years with just a touch-up of paint now and then.

Adjustable Planting Guide

The adjustable planting guide is the Rolls Royce approach to this problem. It is more flexible but can easily cost as much as $50, plus is more difficult to make. Nevertheless, I made one and I have to admit is works really well and that the larger head leaves a better hole for seeds. The materials that I have used in this case are just one way of accomplishing this task. Once you see how it works, you can do the same thing using other materials.

Materials:

1   6' length of ½" aluminum "U" channel
24 $\frac{5}{16}$" 18 thread bolts, stainless
48 $\frac{5}{16}$" 18 thread nuts, stainless

Tools:

Hack saw
Drill or drill press
$\frac{21}{64}$ drill bit
Combination square
Measuring tape
Metal scribe or sharp nail
Nail
Hammer

Procedure:

Cut the aluminum U channel to a 4' length, saving the 2' piece for other projects.

Mark a center line along the exact center of the length of the channel using the combination square and a metal scribe or a fine-point magic marker. Using the measuring tape, use the scribe to mark one inch intervals along the center line. Use the hammer and a nail to make a slight indentation at each intersection between the one inch interval and center line.

Drill a ²¹⁄₆₄ inch hole using the drill or drill press at each indentation.

To use the adjustable planting guide, put a nut onto the bolt, leaving an inch of the thread protruding.

Put another nut into the U channel above the hole into which the bolt will be inserted. (The U channel fits the nut perfectly so no wrenches are needed.)

Screw the bolt into the nut through the hole in the U channel. Do this for whatever distance is needed. Adjust the bolts and nuts for proper depth and a snug fit.

To use the planting guide, place the properly spaced bolt heads on leveled earth and press to leave an indentation of the required depth. Then, lift and place the guide a suitable distance from the first row and repeat until done.

Putting Seeds in the Holes

Larger seeds, such as beans, peas, corn and so forth are easily handled and placed in the holes. But smaller seeds such as carrots, onions and lettuce can be challenging. It can be frustrating trying to pick up those seeds and place them in the beds one at a time. Usually, I use my daughter with her small fingers for such chores, but when she isn't around other options are required.

Some seed producers have come up with pelletized seed to help with this. Carrot and lettuce seeds are surrounded by a coating that makes it easy to handle by hand or in automated seeders. The coating dissolves once the seeds are watered. This is a pretty good solution but so far it has unfortunately only been applied to a few vegetables. Luckily, there are some other solutions, though they all require some practice to master.

Seed spoons are tiny spoons formed in bright yellow plastic. You hold the seed in the cup of your hand, and use the other hand to manipulate the spoon. If you pick the right size (it comes with four sizes), every time you push the spoon into the mass of seeds in your hand, you will pull it back out with exactly one seed. Then you can easily put it where you wish. These cost less than a packet of seeds and work well.

⊗ Seed spoon

Another option is a "Dial Seed Sower." This device holds seeds in a reservoir and you regulate the rate at which seeds leave the reservoir to slide down a slick slide by changing the seed size on the dial and lightly shaking the device. Once you get practiced at it, you can put exactly one seed of practically any size exactly where you want it.

Dial Seed Sower

Mini SeedMaster

Yet another option is a plunger-style hand seeder called the Mini-SeedMaster that looks like an oversized syringe. This takes a limited amount of seed into its canal at any given point in time and when held at a 45 degree angle it delivers seed from the reservoir to the soil with a depression of the plunger. I have found this works well with seeds like spinach and turnips, but not as well with the even smaller seeds such as carrot. Still, it allows planting a lot of chard in a hurry.

All of the foregoing devices are inexpensive in that they cost $10 or less. Considering that developing a bit of skill with them would easily repay their cost in time, they are a decent investment. At nearly $25, a vacuum hand seeder is a bit more expensive. This device uses a vacuum bulb with tips sized for the seeds you are planting. It allows you to pick up one seed at a time and deposit the seed where you'd like it. It requires a bit of manual dexterity, but once you get the hang of it you'll start using it for seeding your indoor transplants as well. It's a real time-saver.

HEATED BASE
(Place Water Pan on This Label)

CAUTION: VERY HOT TO TOUCH

Farm Innovators, Inc.
2255 Walter Glaub Drive • Plymouth, IN 46563

1-800-277-8401

120 VAC/1A   125 Watts   **Heated Pan**

"Warning"   Model HP-125

Store indoors after winter use. Inspect cord before using. Do Not Immerse.
Do not use with extension cords. Read All Instructions. Caution Must be grounded.
This unit gets very hot to the touch!

Made in China   2820   SN:

20

Heated Water Platform

Here is the problem: you live in a climate where water freezes outside in the winter. Because your chickens don't appreciate trying to drink ice, you get a heated base and a metal waterer to set on top of it. But then you discover two problems: the base and waterer are too close to the ground so the chickens are slinging water everywhere, and the floor of the coop isn't level so when you put the waterer on the base, the water leaks out all over the floor and bedding material instead of being consumed as needed.

To solve this problem, here is a platform that you set the heated base upon, and then the waterer on top of that. The platform has adjustable legs so that it can be made level on any floor; the height can also be adjusted so that the chickens can still drink, but with minimal waste.

Materials:

1   ½" plywood cut 17"x17"
2   1"x2" stock cut 17" long
2   1"x2" stock cut 15-½" long
4   2"x2" stock cut 5" long
20 1½" deck screws
4   ⅜" nuts
4   ⅜" bolts 4" long
Epoxy
Outdoor latex paint and brush

Tools:

Carpenter or other saw for cutting wood
Drill or drill press (preferred)
⅛" drill bit
⅜" drill bit
⁹⁄₁₆" spade bit
Driver for the deck screws
Combination square
Measuring tape

Procedure:

Cut the lumber to the specified dimensions.

Drill ⅜" holes 3" deep in the center if the four 2"x2" pieces.

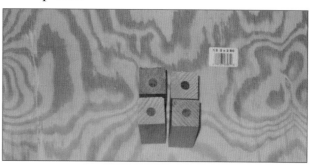

For each of the four 2"x2" pieces, use the spade bit to drill a flat ⁹⁄₁₆" hole ½" deep centered on the previously drilled ⅜" hole.

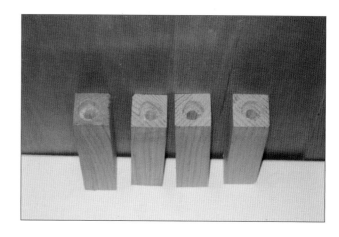

Assemble the frame using the 1"x2" pieces as shown. Use one deck screw on each corner, pre-drilling each hole with the ⅛" drill bit to prevent splitting. The final dimensions of the frame should be 17"x17".

Attach the cut plywood to the frame using one deck screw centered along each side.

Attach the four 2"x2" legs by pre-drilling and using one deck screw. Attach to the 1"x2"x17" piece as shown.

Screw the bolts halfway through the nuts and set into the legs. Carefully apply epoxy to hold the nuts to the legs, taking care to avoid applying the epoxy to the bolts.

Once the epoxy is dry, paint all surfaces of the platform. Once the paint is dry, center the heater and screw four screws into the top as shown to keep the chickens from pushing the heater off the platform.

21

Easy Trellising

Maximizing your productivity per unit area depends on making the best possible use of the space available. For many crops, including pole beans, indeterminate tomatoes, cucumbers, peas and vining squash, this means using a trellis. The problem with trellising on a mini-farm is that because of crop rotation, you might need a trellis for a particular bed one year but not for the next three. Because of this, portability and easy setup/take-down are important factors.

In a prior book, I discussed using electrical conduit cut into designated lengths for this task. And that certainly works well, except that the conduit can be difficult to cut, tends to rust where it contacts the ground, and requires a screwdriver for assembly. That system is good and if you are already using it, that's great! If you aren't already using electrical conduit, or just need to expand your trellising, you might consider the PVC pipe method I describe here.

PVC pipe is UV-stabilized so it handles the elements well. It doesn't rust, and the pipe fits tightly into the fittings without need for tools. Assembly and disassembly are as easy as using Tinker Toys™, only the parts are larger. In comparing PVC pipe to galvanized electrical conduit, the conduit bears weight better but the PVC is considerably less expensive. Comparing the two, even though PVC pipe would need support in more places, it is still less expensive.

To start with this system, buy ten pieces of 10'-long ¾" schedule 40 PVC pipe. The first six pieces are cut into two pieces, one six feet long and the other four feet long. This gives you twelve uprights total: six that are six feet tall and six that are four feet tall. The remaining four pieces of pipe are each cut into two pieces 46¾" long and one piece 22¾" long. This will give you eight long cross-pieces and four short cross-pieces. You will also need a collection of fittings.

⊗ **Re-bar hammered into the ground**

You will need elbows for connecting the cross-pieces to the uprights at the ends of the bed, tees for connecting cross-pieces together and allowing for additional supports and side outlet elbows for running trellises around corners. You can get started with six of each. You can expand this system as needed by getting more PVC pipe and fittings, and cutting the PVC to the specified lengths.

Just as with the system based on electrical conduit, the pipe slides down over 18" pieces of re-bar you have hammered straight into the ground at the ends of the bed and at four-foot intervals.

Four-foot intervals are required for most plants because PVC isn't as strong as electrical conduit. But if you decide to grow something extremely heavy, you can use the shorter cross-pieces and put more vertical supports using tees.

Place deck screws along the trellised side of the bed spaced every six or twelve inches as needed, and use these to anchor string or wire running between the bed and the cross-piece.

❂ Deck screws along the trellised side of the bed.

22

Weed Control Techniques

In general, weed control is easy using the methods I spelled out in *Mini Farming* because the beds are always growing something useful. During the growing season you have crops growing so densely as to shade weeds and off-season cover crops crowd them out. So theoretically weeds just have no chance.

But theory runs smack into reality when time constraints prevent planting a cover crop, weeds grow unnoticed along the edge of a bed then go to seed, or weeds manage to find sufficient light despite dense plantings. Another source of weeds is from the surrounding yard grass growing into your beds, and if you established your beds on previous grass, some of that may eventually grow through as well creating a weed problem.

Then again is the problem of self-seeding that is common with mustards and tomatoes that are allowed to go to seed. They can create dense stands of thousands of little plants in a bed that will be growing something else the next season.

Once upon a time I created a serious weed nightmare for myself by throwing some free fresh horse manure on one of my beds. I didn't realize how many weed seeds were in fresh horse manure that hadn't been composted; it took three seasons to finally get the resulting weeds in that bed under control. Now manures get composted before going on my beds!

So it's just a matter of time before you start having to deal with weeds. Sooner or later you will look at a bed in the spring with dismay realizing thousands of unwanted plants are growing where you intend to plant something else entirely, and I want to share some strategies for dealing with that problem or preventing it altogether.

Pre-Sprouting Weeds

This technique is very useful in beds that will be used for crops such as tomatoes or squash that are very susceptible to frost. The idea is to prepare the bed in early spring with any soil amendments or tilling that might be needed, and then just let it sit while all the weed seeds sprout. You can accelerate the sprouting of weeds by putting some clear plastic over the bed to trap heat for a week or so. Once they have sprouted, they can be pulled by hand or eliminated with either a hoe or a cultivator.

Use of a Stirrup Hoe

Stirrup hoes come in a number of configurations, but the one I use is shown here. Stirrup hoes are designed to travel just barely under the surface of the soil, anywhere from a quarter to half an inch, so they will sever weeds with their cutting edge as the hoe is drawn toward you. As you push the hoe away from you, it rides on top of the soil. This way, it gets weeds but doesn't disturb more deeply rooted plants that aren't

desired. In plantings that aren't very dense, such as tomatoes or corn, you can easily fit this between the desired plants with a bit of care. My daughter was amazed that using just this simple hand tool I was able to completely weed a bed in under a minute. Once you get the feel for a stirrup hoe, it is an exceptionally efficient device for controlling weeds.

The Manual Rotary Cultivator

The manual rotary cultivator is useful for controlling young weeds less than two inches high. It uses a series of interlocking rotating tines to grab the roots of weeds and pull them out. They can

be made as narrow as two inches for getting into tight places. In addition, they can be used to incorporate amendments into the soil to a depth of one and a half inches. If you put some elbow grease into it, it will go even deeper.

This device is moved back and forth across the area to be weeded with slight downward pressure. If the tines stop moving, it is because either a long root has become entangled or a stone has jammed the mechanism. Remove the obstruction and continue. Though this isn't quite as fast as a stirrup hoe, it is more flexible for tight spaces and works extremely well.

The Flame Weeder

These come in a number of styles from a couple of different manufacturers. I have a simple unit that accepts a standard propane tank, but there are larger models that require you to drag around a large cannister of fuel. For a mini farm something that size is overkill.

Flame weeding is very prevalent in organic agriculture for the obvious reason that it kills weeds without the use of poisonous chemicals. It also has the advantage of leaving the soil undisturbed. Often what happens with manual

methods of weed control such as hand-weeding, using a hoe or a cultivator is that more seeds are brought into a zone where they will sprout. Flame weeding leaves the soil untouched.

Even better, flame weeding can prevent weeds from sprouting by killing weed seeds in the top quarter inch of soil. This is very useful when preparing a bed for crops that are very susceptible to weeds like carrots or onions.

A flame weeder is like a giant propane torch. In daylight, the flame is invisible so exercise extreme caution. This device is a propane torch on steroids and it can cause severe injuries in addition to starting fires. Also, because the heat can be deceptive, do not use this in a bed containing live crops or you'll have a lot of unexpected dead crops the next day.

In spite of the fact it is called a flame weeder, you do not use this to incinerate weeds. All you do is aim at the weed from the distance specified by the manufacturer until the weed starts to wilt. That's all. That wilting is caused by the bursting of the internal cells of the plant and it's effectively dead. I have found that a lateral movement of about one foot per second allows sufficient time with my particular flame weeder, but you should follow the directions that come with your unit over mine.

Even with no weeds visible in a bed, you can use the flame weeder to sterilize the top bit of soil and delay weeds so delicate plants can get a head start. I go over the soil in the bed slowly from about a foot away until all of the soil has been covered.

Chickens Wreak Havoc on Weeds

They also wreak havoc on crops, so don't let them run loose in your garden at random or you'll have the most expensive eggs in town! But on a controlled basis, turning chickens loose in beds that need some weeding prior to the start of the season is a real winner. Chickens turn anyplace they run into a desolate moonscape devoid of living matter in no time flat, and they'll do the same for your beds. This sort of free labor helps them earn their keep, especially if you have a grouchy rooster like I have who is the terror of the county.

Solarization

Though not practical for large-scale operations, **solarization** is perfectly suited for **mini-farming** because it applies very easily to raised beds. The technique is straightforward. Weed the bed as well as you can, even out the soil, and then water it thoroughly with the equivalent of an inch or more of rain. Then put clear plastic over the bed, making as close contact as possible between the plastic and the soil. As the sun shines in through the plastic, the heat will be trapped in the soil of the bed, raising temperatures as high as 160 degrees. Temperatures this high will not only kill most weed seeds, but a great many **pathogen**s as well.

If you leave the plastic in place for a couple of months, the top couple of inches of soil will be effectively sterilized. This is good in that it will kill pathogens and weed seeds, but bad in that beneficial organisms will be harmed as well. But because soil is a good insulator, organisms more than a couple of inches below the soil will survive just fine. If your bed has received generous compost all along, once the plastic comes off just a light tilling with a three-tined cultivator will be sufficient to bring the soil back to life.

PART III
Greater Food Self-Sufficiency

23

Making Your Own Country Wines

Wine making is one of the oldest methods of food preservation. Like preserving cabbage through the lactic acid fermentation process that results in sauerkraut, the juice that is made into wine is preserved through the byproducts of a controlled fermentation. In wine the levels of sugar in the original juice are reduced to make the juice unattractive to organisms that require sugar for growth, and the sugar is replaced with alcohol that makes the juice an inhospitable environment for most spoilage organisms. Meanwhile, many of the beneficial nutrients in the original juice are preserved, including vitamins and antioxidants. The yeast used to convert the sugar to alcohol also imparts a number of B vitamins to the mix.

Later, wine became an end in itself for which fruits were grown, and an entire culture and mythology have grown up around grapes, wine making and wine. What started as a method of preserving the essential nutrients of grapes in an era when aseptic packaging and refrigeration did not exist has now grown into a multi-billion-dollar global industry, and there are bottles of wine that can only be had for a cost exceeding that of a new car.

The term wine, in the purest sense of the term, applies only to the results of fermenting the juice of European vitis vinifera grapes. These are a species that is distinct from the grapes indigenous to North America, and only vitis vinifera grapes—and no other grape or fruit—have the right levels of sugar, tannin, acidity and nutrients to produce wine without adding anything. Grapes grown in particular regions lend their unique flavors to wines named after them, such as Champagne, and wines produced by some wineries have even become status symbols, such as those produced by Château Lafite Rothschild.

Anyone who has seen a wine critic on television can be a bit intimidated by the prospect of trying to make a wine that is even drinkable, much less enjoyable. Fortunately, Frederic Brochet conducted two studies using 57 wine experts at the University of Bordeaux in 2001 that will forever put the wine experts into perspective.[1]

In the first study, the experts were given two glasses of wine to describe, one being a white wine and the other a red wine. Unknown to the experts, both glasses were a white wine but the wine in one of the glasses had been dyed red. Not even one of the fifty-seven experts at the University of Bordeaux could distinguish that the red wine was really white, and they even went on to describe the fake red wine as having characteristics associated with red wines such as "tannic notes."

In the second study, a cheap wine was put into bottles denoting both a cheap and an expensive wine. Same wine, different bottles. The experts described the wine in the expensive bottles as "woody, complex and round" while describing the exact same wine in the cheap bottles as "short, light and faulty."

What this means is that you need not be intimidated by wine snobbery. All you need to do is make a sound product using good ingredients and proper methods, and as long as you put it in a nice bottle with a nice label and serve it in a nice glass it will be fully appreciated. Details really matter when you want to make an impression and present your wine, so even if you performed your primary fermentation in a plastic bucket, don't you dare serve it in a plastic cup!

In this chapter I am going to provide an overview, a description of the necessary equipment and ingredients, sanitation and cleaning procedures, a step-by-step process for wine making and a table to use as a basis for making wine out of common fruits. Don't gloss over the descriptions of the equipment and ingredients, because the descriptions also cover important procedural details and information that will help you make good wine.

⊗ Always display your wines for best effect. Just say no to plastic cups!

1   Downey, R. (2002), "Wine Snob Scandal," *Seattle Weekly*, Feb. 20, 2002.

An Overview of Country Wine Making

What I describe in this chapter is the manufacture of so-called country wines. As described earlier, only the results of fermenting vitis vinifera grapes can be properly termed wine, so the fermented results of other fruits with an alcohol content and keeping qualities similar to wine are termed country wines. These are in no way inferior, and in fact being free of the constraints of traditional wine making leaves you open to experiment broadly and create delightfully unique wines that are forever beyond the reach of traditional wineries. Home wine making of up to 200 gallons annually is legal in the United States so long as you don't try to sell it. (If you try to sell it you will run afoul of the infamous "revenuers" who always get the culprit in the end.)

Americans drink nearly two gallons of wine per capita annually, meaning the consumption for a standard household is just shy of eight gallons. That's forty bottles of wine. If you figure $12/bottle, that's nearly $500 per year. At that rate, and using fruit you either get inexpensively in season or free in your back yard, you will quickly recoup your investment in materials and supplies. In addition, homemade wines make excellent personal gifts; every year I give bottles to friends and business associates for holiday presents. The wine is always appreciated.

The business of making wine is conceptually straightforward. The juice (and sometimes solids) of a fruit are purified of stray microbes and supplemented with sugar, acid and other nutrients to make a must, inoculated with an appropriate strain of yeast, and fermented. The fermentation takes place in two distinct phases. The first phase, known as the primary fermentation, is very fast and lasts only a couple of weeks. The wine is then siphoned (a process called racking) into a new vessel and fitted with an airlock where it may continue its secondary fermentation for several months with a racking again after the first couple of months or anytime substantial sediment has formed.

I'll explain the specifics of the equipment, techniques and terminology throughout this chapter, along with some of the nuances. For now, I want to convey that if you normally consume wine or would give wine as a gift, making your own quality wines is inexpensive, fun, and easier than most would believe.

There are places where you will be tempted to skimp or make-do on the list of ingredients and equipment I am about to present, but let me encourage you to get everything on the list. Because the techniques I describe rely on natural ingredients whose constituents will vary, all of the testing equipment is necessary. The other equipment and ingredients are necessary to maintain sanitary conditions or make a quality wine. If you don't live near a store for wine hobbyists, there are a number of excellent sources on the Internet that can be located via a web search. To save on shipping, I'd recommend getting as much from one store as possible.

Primary Fermenter

The primary fermenter is a large plastic bucket made of food-grade plastic. It is sized at least 20 percent larger than the largest batch of wine you plan to make in order to keep the constituents of the vigorous primary fermentation from spilling out of the fermenter and making a mess you will not soon forget. The bucket should be equipped with a lid and gasket, and also have provisions for fitting an airlock. These are available in various sizes from beer and wine hobby suppliers. I'd recommend a two gallon and a six gallon bucket. Even though it is possible to get these buckets for free from restaurants, I would advise against it as most were used to hold something that was previously been pickled using vinegar. You don't want vinegar organisms in your wine.

In general, the primary fermentation evolves carbon dioxide so rapidly that an airlock isn't strictly necessary. Furthermore, the first stages of fermentation require oxygen until the yeast cells multiply enough to reach a critical mass before the start of fermentation. Just plugging the hole in the lid with a clean cotton ball that allows air movement but blocks dirt, dust and insects will suffice. (Replace the cotton ball if it becomes saturated with must.) Even so, I usually use an airlock after the first week.

It is possible for the smells and tastes of plastic to become infused into wine. This is not a concern for the primary fermentation because the wine is only in contact with the container for a couple of weeks, the container is food-grade plastic selected for its low diffusion, and you cleaned it thoroughly prior to use.

Secondary Fermenter

Because the wine stays in contact with the secondary fermenter for months or even years, this is best made of glass. You can also use specially made oak casks for a long secondary fermentation, but these are very expensive and need special care and maintenance. So for now, I would skip the oak casks.

The glass vessels come in various sizes from one gallon up to five gallons. The smaller one gallon vessels are just one gallon jugs, and the larger three or five gallon vessels are glass carboys used on water coolers.

You will also see some plastic carboys available in wine making magazines and from various suppliers. These are advertised as being made in a way that makes them impervious to the diffusion of the plastic into the wine, and they offer the advantage of being much lighter than glass so the shipping costs are lower. Nevertheless, plastic is harder to clean than glass, so I would not recommend these if glass can be obtained instead.

You will also need to get a special brush for cleaning your jug or carboy because the opening is too small for even the smallest hands and a regular bottle brush is too short and isn't bent for cleaning around the edges.

The fermentation that takes place in the secondary fermenter is long and slow. As the carbon dioxide is evolved more slowly, it is possible for air

❽ Common primary and secondary fermentation vessels for one and five gallon batches. The secondary fermenters are glass.

to be drawn into the vessel, especially if temperatures change. During secondary fermentation, you want to prevent oxygen from coming into contact with the wine, because oxygen adversely affects the quality of the wine by changing the character of some of the evolved organic compounds.

By fitting the hole in the fermenter with a stopper and an airlock, you will allow a protective blanket of carbon dioxide to cover the surface of your wine. You will need rubber stoppers with one hole in them that are sized correctly for your secondary fermenter. The airlock is prepared, put into the hole in the stopper, and then the stopper is placed in the hole at the top of the fermenter.

Because you will be racking your wine from one secondary fermenter into another, you need two secondary fermentation vessels.

One thing that people often overlook is a carrying handle. If you are making wine in batches larger than a gallon, those carboys are extremely heavy and difficult to handle. The handle that you order can be installed on a carboy and then removed to be used on another, so you only need one. They cost about $10 at the time of this writing and are well worth it as they make the task of handling carboys a great deal easier.

Airlocks

Airlocks are devices installed on a fermenter that allow gas to escape, but do not allow air to leak back in. They come in a variety of configurations, but all are filled with water or a solution of potassium metabisulfite". The airlock is filled to the level specified on the device, inserted in a one-hole rubber stopper and then attached to the fermenter. You should have at least two of these. The style you choose doesn't matter.

Racking Tube

A racking tube is a long two-part tube that is inserted into the wine and pumped to start a siphoning action in order to transfer the wine from one container into another. It has a knob at the bottom that directs the flow of fluid in such a way as to minimize the amount of sediment transferred in the process. You will also need five feet of plastic tubing to go with it. A stop-cock, which is a plastic clip that can be used to stop the flow temporarily, will come in handy when using the racking tube to transfer wine into final wine bottles for corking.

Racking tubes come in two sizes: one that is smaller and will fit into a gallon jug and one that is larger and will not. Get the smaller one initially as it will work for both gallon jugs and five gallon carboys.

Always clean your racking tube and plastic tubing before and after use, and run a gallon of sulphite solution through it to sterilize the components. Otherwise, it will accumulate debris attractive to fruit flies that carry vinegar bacteria and you will unwittingly start manufacturing vinegar instead of wine. The tubing is inexpensive and it is best to replace it after several uses.

Corker

Corkers are used to insert corks into wine bottles. As you've discovered if you have ever tried to put a cork back into a wine bottle, corks are slightly larger than the holes they are intended to fit. A corker compresses the cork enough for it to slip inside the bottle. Corkers come in many sizes and styles, but I would recommend a metal two-armed lever model which, although somewhat more expensive than the plastic models, does a better job and will serve you well for your lifetime.

Corks need to be soaked before insertion. You don't want to inadvertently transfer a spoilage organism on the corks, so I recommend boiling the corks for twenty minutes and then allowing them to sit in the boiled water for another ten minutes before corking. This will make the corks pliable without contaminating them.

Another problem you may encounter is the cork backing out of the bottle after it was inserted. This is caused by the fact that the cork fits so tightly that the air in the bottle is compressed as it is inserted. The compressed air forces the cork back out of the bottle. You can solve this problem with a bent sterilized paper clip. Straighten the paper clip except for a hook that you leave for it to hang on the edge of the bottle's mouth. Insert the straight part into the bottle mouth and leave it hooked in the edge. Insert the cork as usual. The paper clip has allowed room for compressed gases to escape. Pull the paper clip out and you are done.

Wine Thief, Hydrometer and Acid Test Kit

A wine thief is a long tube with a special valve on the end that allows you to remove wine from a container very easily. Clean and sanitize it before and after use. It is generally recommend that wine removed not be returned to the container to avoid contamination. However, unless you have added an adulterant to the wine (such as sodium hydroxide for testing acidity), as long as the wine thief and any equipment used are cleaned and sanitized, I have never had a prob-

lem from putting the wine back in to the same container.

The biggest reason why you would want to "steal" wine in this fashion is so it can be tested for specific gravity and acidity, and that is what the hydrometer and acid test kit are for.

A hydrometer looks like a strange thermometer with a bunch of tiny weights in a large bulb at the bottom. The specific gravity, or the density of the liquid, determines how deeply the hydrometer sinks into the liquid, and this is read on the scale.

The density of a liquid varies with temperature, so I would encourage you to kill two birds with one stone and get one of the hydrometers that also has a thermometer built into it. This will allow you to easily apply temperature corrections to the hydrometer reading.

The reason why specific gravity is important is because it tells you how much sugar is in the

❷ The hydrometer and acid testing kit are crucial tools for making country wines based on real-world fruit rather than idealized recipes.

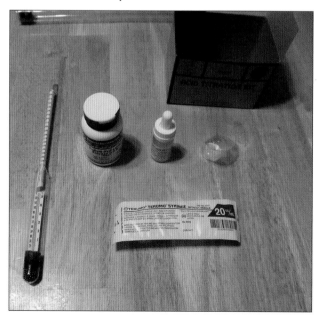

must or wine, thus allowing you to gage how much more sugar should be added or when a fermentation has completed.

Acidity is an important characteristic of wine that has an effect even upon the more complex products of fermentation, so it can profoundly affect the flavors of a wine. Most juices used to make country wines will not have an ideal level of acidity, and an acid test kit will allow you to easily assess whether the acidity of your wine should be increased or decreased and by how much.

Nylon Straining Bags

These are fine-meshed nylon bags with zippered closures used to hold fruit for crushing in a fashion that allows you to remove the solids later with minimal mess. The bags can be cleaned, sterilized and reused many times. These come in very handy when making wines from crushed blueberries, cherries and similar fruits. They come in various sizes in order to accommodate different sized batches of fruits and **wine**.

Wine Bottles

You will need wine bottles. Usually, light-colored wines are bottled in clear bottles and dark colored wine in green or brown bottles. This is predominantly a social convention, though the darker glass serves the purpose of protecting the coloring matter in the wine from being bleached out by ultraviolet light and sunshine. Your wine should be stored well away from sunshine anyway.

Either way, you will certainly want to use real wine bottles that require a cork. Real wine bottles usually have a concave section at the bottom that allows for solid sediments to remain separate from the wine and have a top made to facilitate a perfect seal with a cork.

There is debate among experts (remember the experts from earlier in the chapter?) over the use of plastic, screw-top caps or genuine cork, and whether this has an effect on the long-term taste and quality of wine. In my opinion corks are best simply because they are easiest. Corks are inexpensive in quantity, easily inserted for a perfect seal using simple equipment and will literally last forever if a bottle is stored on its side to keep it wet. Unlike the experts, I can't tell the difference between a wine stored in a corked bottle as opposed to one using a screw closure, but I recommend corking because it is easier and cheaper in the long run. Also, it just looks better, and the presentation of your wine is as important as any of its other qualities in terms of the reception it receives.

If you decide to make a sparkling wine, you will need to get bottles specifically for that purpose because ordinary wine bottles aren't rated for that pressure. You will also need special plastic corks and wire closures that will hold the corks in place on the bottle.

Wine bottles come in 375 ml and 750 ml sizes. You will need five of the 750 ml bottles or ten of the 375 ml bottles for each gallon of wine that you are bottling.

Consolidated Equipment List

The following list will make it easy to get everything you will need for the foreseeable future in one shopping trip. I priced this out with a well-known Internet beer and wine hobby shop for $228.60 plus $63.22 for shipping. At that price for shipping, if you can find the gear locally it is worth the trip. You could also save some money by only getting the equipment needed to make one-gallon batches, and the equipment would only cost $134.75 plus $25.95 for shipping. These costs also don't take into account that it is often easy to get wine bottles for free. I get mine from a co-worker who works part-time at a bar. He brings me a few dozen empty bottles and I give him a couple bottles of wine yearly.

1 Five-or six-gallon plastic fermenter with sealing plastic lid and grommet

1 Two-gallon plastic fermenter with sealing plastic lid and grommet

2 Five gallon secondary fermenters, preferably glass

1 Carboy handle

2 #6.5 universal rubber stoppers with one hole

2 One-gallon secondary fermenters, glass

2 #6 rubber stoppers with one hole

4 Airlocks

1 Racking tube, sized to fit the one gallon secondary fermenters, but will work with both

5 ft ⅜" plastic tubing

1 Hose clamp, ⅜

1 Wine thief

2 Nylon straining bags

1 Hydrometer with Specific Gravity scale and built-in thermometer

1 Testing jar for the hydrometer (optional, I clean my hydrometer thoroughly and put it in the wine thief)

1 Acid test kit

1 Two-handed corker

36 Wine bottles

50 Corks

In addition to equipment, making country wines requires a variety of innocuous but nevertheless important additives. All fruits other than European grapes will require additional sugar in the form of either sugar or honey. Most fruits will either be too acidic, or (most often), they won't contain enough acid. Likewise, most won't have sufficient tannin to give a properly wine-like mouth-feel. Of course, yeast will need to be added, and the fruits don't have sufficient nutrients on their own to sustain a healthy fermentation to completion, so nutrients will need to be added for the yeast.

Citric, Malic and Tartaric Acids

Though most fruits contain more than one of these acids, citric acid is usually associated with citrus fruits, malic acid with apples and tartaric acid with grapes. You can buy these mixed together as a so-called "acid blend," but they are inexpensive and I recommend buying them sepa-

◉ Airlocks, wine thief, racking tube, stoppers, corkers and other gear. These will give many years of faithful service if given proper care.

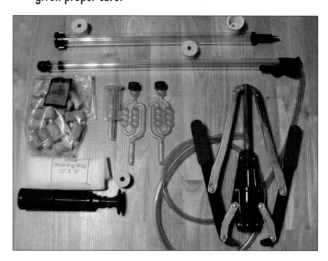

rately. This way, you can use the right acid for the fruit you are using or the character you want your wine to have and you aren't locked in to the formula of a given manufacturer. If you are using a recipe that requires "acid blend" you can make it yourself by thoroughly mixing an equal quantity of each of the three acids together.

The acidity of your must should be checked prior to the beginning of fermentation with your acid test kit. Most often, acid will need to be added.

The instructions in your acid test kit will tell you how much of these acids are required to bring your must to a suitable starting level. Acid levels are measured as equivalent to a certain percentage of tartaric acid, without regard to which acids are actually present. When making country wines, you want the acidity of your must to fall between 0.55 percent and 0.65 percent tartaric. For white grape wines, 0.65 percent to 0.75 percent usually gives the best flavor. Red grape wines do best in the narrow range of 0.60 percent to 0.65 percent.

One level (measuring) teaspoon of citric acid, malic acid, tartaric acid or acid blend will raise the acidity of one gallon of must by 0.15 percent.

Measurements of real world phenomena seldom make for convenient word problems with answers in nice round whole numbers. If you have five and a half gallons of must that measures 0.48 percent tartaric, how much acid do you add?

First, look at the range. Anything between 0.55 percent and 0.65 percent will work, though closer to the low end of that range is usually better. But we'll pick 0.60 percent as our target.

Subtract your measured percentage of 0.48 percent from your target percentage of 0.60 per-

cent. The answer, 0.12 percent, is the amount of acid that needs to be added.

We know that one teaspoon added to one gallon equals 0.15 percent, so if we divide the answer (0.12 percent) by 0.15 percent, we will get the number of teaspoons needed per gallon. The answer is 0.8 teaspoons. Since we have 5.5 gallons of must, if we multiply 0.8 x 5.5 we will get 4.4 teaspoons total.

They don't make measuring spoons in increments of .4, so just eyeball it. .4 is just shy of one half, so add four teaspoons plus a not-quite-full half teaspoon and you're done.

If the acid level is too high, though it is possible to lower the acidity by the addition of a base such as potassium bicarbonate, I would recommend lowering the acidity by diluting the must with water. This is because the addition of a base to an acid neutralizes the acid by creating a salt. Sometimes the salt will precipitate out, but sometimes it will not and the results will adversely affect the taste of the wine.

One note: acid test kits usually contain a standardized sodium hydroxide solution. Sodium hydroxide is used to clean out drains, turn fat into soap and has even been used as a weapon to blind and maim. Even though the standardized solution they use is quite weak, please wear latex gloves and safety glasses while using it.

Grape Tannin

Tannins are responsible for the astringent taste of a wine. They are present in the skin and seeds of grapes, and so wines that result from conducting the primary fermentation with the skins and seeds will tend to have more tannin and have more astringency. White wines derived from pressed juice are therefore less astringent than red wines derived from fermenting with the skins.

Ingredients other than grapes can have more or less tannin content, and that content will vary based upon the amount of time whole fruit is left in the primary fermenter as well.

Unfortunately, assessing the tannin content of a must is a devilishly complex exercise in experimental chemistry. If you are curious, please see *New Tannin Assay for Winemakers* by Moris L. Silber and John K. Fellman for the most accurate method using protein dye markers or the older (and more controversial) precipitation technique published by Hagerman and Butler in the *Journal of Agricultural Food Chemistry* in 1978.

Unless you are a pretty ambitious amateur (or professional) chemist, you will determine how much tannin needs to be added to a must based upon the primary ingredient in the must and the table at the end of the chapter. This will get you close enough for all practical purposes.

Pectic Enzyme

Pectins are long chains of carbohydrates composed of various sugars that form the cell walls of the fruits used to make wine. Pectins are responsible for turning the juices of some fruits into jelly. European grapes contain enough pectic enzyme—an enzyme that destroys pectin—to destroy that pectin so you end up with a clear fluid wine rather than a semi-solid gelatinous mass. Other fruits don't usually have enough of this enzyme naturally, which makes them excellent for making jelly but suboptimal for wine.

Pectic enzyme purchased from the wine making store is used in small amounts to supplement the natural pectic enzymes in the must.

Over time, this degrades the pectin and thereby either makes its sugars available for fermentation or precipitates the leavings into the bottom of the fermenter so they are left behind at the next racking. Therefore, pectic enzyme helps to produce clear wines.

You may recall that one reason most fruits and vegetables are blanched before freezing or dehydrating is that the high temperature of blanching inactivates the enzymes that cause the produce to degrade over time. The same will occur with pectic enzyme, so pectic enzyme should only be added to a must with a temperature under 80 degrees and the must cannot be reheated thereafter.

It is common in wine making to heat certain ingredients in order to assure their sterility, such as honey and sugar mixed with water. These ingredients should be added to the must and the temperature of the must allowed to drop adequately before pectic enzyme is added. The container of pectic enzyme has instructions printed on the label for how much to add to your must.

Fermentation Inhibitor

It can be difficult to judge when fermentation is completed. Early in wine making it is also common for the home wine maker to be a bit impatient (and justifiably so!) for the finished product. The unfortunate side effect of bottling a bit too early is a wine bottle with a popped cork (and corresponding mess) or even a shattered bottle. Sometimes you can get lucky and just end up with a barely perceptible sediment and a lightly sparkling wine. In wine judgings, this is considered a defect in a still wine, but for home use it is a delightful thing. Still, if you want to make sparkling wines it is better to make them on purpose rather than accidentally, because their accidental manufacture is attended by some risk.

Potassium sorbate, a semi-synthetic preservative that inhibits fermentation, is added to wines as a stabilizer to prevent further fermentation. It is used in two instances. First, to absolutely guarantee an end of fermentation in wines that are bottled young. Second, to stop fermentation in wines that are intentionally sweet and the only thing inhibiting the yeast is the high alcohol content.

The positive is that potassium sorbate works well, is generally accepted as safe and will give you good insurance against exploding bottles. It is seldom noticeable at all when used for young wines and white wines. The downside is that it can develop off smells in some wines over a period of years. So if you are making a wine that you plan to keep for many years, rather than using potassium sorbate" I would recommend bulk aging it for at least a year in a secondary fermenter to assure the end of fermentation prior to bottling.

Another method of ending fermentation is to add supplemental alcohol to the wine in the form of brandy (which is distilled from wine). This process is called fortification. Raising the alcohol level in the wine above the alcohol tolerance of the yeast (usually 20 percent) assures its dormancy. Fortification is used in the manufacture of port wines. Port wines are typically sweet and dark, though some dry and white ports exist. These sweet wines were stabilized for shipping purposes by racking them into a secondary fermenter that already contained enough brandy (about ¼ of the volume of the wine) to raise the alcohol level to 18 percent to 20 percent. This brought about a quick end to fermentation while retaining as much as 10 percent residual sugar. The stability of port wines can allow them to keep for decades.

Yeast Nutrient, Yeast Energizer, Thiamine and Lipid Supply

During the reproductive phase of yeast in the must, the sheer volume of yeast that is created from a tiny packet is impressive. There will literally be millions of yeast cells per milliliter of must. All of this cellular budding and division requires core building blocks for protein and the other parts of a yeast cell. As with many important factors, though these are usually present in European grapes to a sufficient degree, they are lacking in practically all other primary ingredients for wine making.

A wine can be made successfully in some cases without the addition of nutritional building blocks for the yeast, but adding those building blocks will go a long way toward stacking the deck in favor of a successful outcome.

You will see wine supply stores selling many supplements for yeast with names such as yeast nutrient and yeast energizer. There is no universal standard, and so the precise ingredients will vary with the supplier. In general, they will contain purified sources of nitrogen and phosphorus at a minimum, though many will also contain a variety of B-vitamins. Yeast nutrient usually contains only food grade ammonium phosphate, whereas yeast energizer will contain this along with magnesium sulfate, killed yeast and the entire vitamin B complex, of which thiamine (vitamin B1) is the most important. Sometimes you may see urea as an ingredient. If you do, don't worry. This is purified food-grade urea that supplies nitrogen for building proteins and it is perfectly safe.

I would recommend using yeast energizer in preference to yeast nutrient. But if you use yeast nutrient instead, at least add a 100 percent RDA thiamine tablet and a pinch of Epsom salt in addition for each gallon of must.

The cell walls of yeast also require lipids (fats), and such fats are in short supply in some wine musts—especially meads made predominantly from honey with little or no fruit. In such cases, you can use yeast hulls as an additive or a specialized additive that contains essential fatty acids such as FermaidK or Ghostex.

Sulfite

Some people who get headaches from drinking wine believe themselves to be sensitive to sulfites. Usually, however, they get headaches from red wine but not from white wine, both of which contain sulfites. So sulfites are not the issue.[2] This headache is called "wine headache," and experts disagree widely on its true cause. Less than 1 percent of people are truly sensitive to sulfites which are found ubiquitously in lunch meats, dried fruits and even white grape juice from the supermarket. Obviously, if you are truly sensitive to sulfites you should avoid them at all costs.

Sulfite is used so pervasively in wine making and considered so essential that its use is even permitted in wines labeled as USDA Organic. Though it is possible to make wines without the use of sulfites and I have successfully done so, the odds of success for a beginner are greatly enhanced by using sulfites, especially if using fresh fruits in the must.

Sulfite is used in wine making as a sanitizer to kill or inhibit wild yeasts and bacteria so you end up making wine instead of vinegar. It is also used to help clear wines during racking to arrest fermentation and to help prevent oxidation and consequent degradation of flavor.

Sulfite comes in many forms, but for our purposes two forms are important. The first is potassium metabisulfite in the form of Campden tablets. Campden tablets are sized with the idea in mind of accurate dosing of wine and musts to purify must prior to initiating fermentation and help clear and preserve the wine later. To use Campden tablets, do not just plunk them into the wine or must. Instead, use a cleaned and sanitized wine thief to remove four to eight ounces of must or wine and put it into a sanitized glass. Thoroughly crush the requisite number of tablets, and add the powder to the must or wine. Stir to dissolve. Once the tablets are dissolved, add the must or wine back to the original container. For the initial sanitizing of a must, use two tablets per gallon of must. For protecting wine from spoilage and oxidation, add one tablet per gallon before racking.

The second is powdered potassium metabisulfite. In powdered form it is used to make sterilizing solutions for sterilizing equipment.

Make a gallon jug (a clean empty plastic water jug is fine) of sanitizing solution. To make the sanitizing solution, dissolve a measuring teaspoon of potassium metabisulfite powder in a gallon of water. You can use this solution repeatedly, and pour it back in the bottle after each use until it loses its potency or becomes obviously dirty. If you keep the container tightly sealed

2   K. MacNeil, (2001) *The Wine Bible.*

when not in use, it will stay effective for a very long time. You can tell if it is potent by sniffing the solution. If you sniff it and believe you have just endured a World War I gas attack, then it's good. If it just barely tickles your nose, it needs to be replaced.

There are other sanitizers available and when you have become more experienced and confident, you can branch out and start experimenting. But sulfites are the easiest to use not only for the beginner, but also for the most prestigious of professional wineries.

Yeast

Yeast is the star of the show. Wild yeast naturally colonizes the surfaces of fruits, so sometimes crushed fruit, left to its own devices and protected from other organisms, will ferment all by itself. In fact, this is the case in certain famous wine regions where the wild yeasts inhabiting the area have co-evolved with the wine grapes. Though most wine yeasts are of the species *saccharomyces cerevisiae*, there are hundreds if not thousands of variations of this species, some with dramatically different properties. The genome of wine yeast has over twelve million base pairs, making for substantial possibilities for variation.

In practice, wine makers do not rely on wild yeasts because the unpredictability can often result in serious failures or faults in the finished product. Instead, wine makers usually purify the musts of wild yeasts and bacteria by adding sulfite. Once the sulfite has been added, the must is stirred thoroughly and then allowed to sit for a day before a cultured wine yeast of known character is added.

Adding yeast to the must is known as pitching the yeast, though in reality little real pitching occurs because one and five gallon batches are relatively small. In batches of this size, the packet of yeast is just sprinkled as evenly as possible on top of the must in the primary fermenter. Do not stir. If you stir, it will take the yeast far longer to build up a head of steam and because it is added after the sulfite has dissipated, you expose your must to a risk of spoilage by delaying the onset of production of alcohol.

Because yeast needs oxygen in its initial replication stage before fermentation begins, you should aerate the must by stirring it vigorously before pitching the yeast. Some wine makers put a sanitized fish tank aerator connected to an air pump into the must for an hour or so before pitching the yeast, but I have found a good vig-

Modern dry wine yeasts are inexpensive and work very well. Don't try to use bread yeast. It will work, but your wine will be very sweet and taste like bread.

orous stirring (carefully so as not to make a mess) to be sufficient.

Yeast comes powdered in packets, in liquid in vials and in many other forms. As you become a more advanced wine maker, you might decide to use some of these other yeasts. But your initial use should be of powdered dry yeast in individual foil packets. These are very well characterized and foolproof. Just open the packet and sprinkle on top of the must—and it works. Don't be fooled by the simplicity of use or the fact these yeasts are inexpensive. These are a very high quality product and I have used them successfully for years. If you skimp and use bread or beer yeast to make your wine, don't complain if your wine tastes like bread or is syrupy-sweet because the alcohol tolerance was too low.

I can't cover all the possible yeasts you might be able to find. Instead, I want to cover some common yeasts that will be most generally useful for practically anything you'd like to try to turn into wine.

Red Star Pasteur Champagne

This is an excellent all-around yeast for making dry wines. It produces glycerol as well as alcohol, and this gives wines a nice mouth-feel. I particularly like using this yeast in wines containing apple, pear and flower ingredients because it produces fresh aromas that match these ingredients. It works well at lower temperatures, even as low as 55 degrees, and tolerates up to 16 percent alcohol.

Red Star Montrachet Yeast

If you don't have much control of the ambient temperature of your must, this yeast is a good choice. It can work at temperatures ranging from 55 to 95 (though it does less well at the extremes than it does in the middle of that range), and produces less acetaldehyde than most yeasts. The aromas are nice, and with an alcohol tolerance of 15 percent, this yeast is well adapted to making sweet port-style wines.

Lalvin D-47

If you'd like to make a dry white wine starting from apples or pears, this is an excellent choice. It's temperature range is narrow—only 58 to 68—but that makes it perfect for fermentations that proceed in the house during the winter when homes are usually maintained precisely in that range. The sediment formed by D-47 is compact, a fact that makes racking easier.

Lalvin ICV-D254

With an alcohol tolerance of 18 percent, ICV-D254 will ferment any practical must to dryness. This yeast ferments quickly, so you'll want to keep the temperature under 80 degrees to avoid foaming. You might want to keep the temperature even lower to preserve volatile flavor components because ICV-D254 creates a very complex and fruity flavor profile that really enhances the fruit character of a wine. This would be a good choice for blueberry wine.

Wyeast 4632 Dry Mead Yeast

Meads, also known as honey wines, are enjoying a resurgence in popularity. Many yeasts will work to make mead, but this yeast in particular creates flavor notes that have resulted in many award-winning meads. The temperature range is 55 to 75, but you'll want to stay as close to 65 as you can to maximize flavor production. Wyeast 4632 has an alcohol tolerance of 18 percent and will result in a very dry mead.

Consolidated Ingredient List

The following ingredient list will allow you to make many successful gallons of wine. As your experience expands, you may wish to adopt different materials and techniques, but most home wine makers find that this list is more than sufficient for their needs. In compiling this list, I went to two well-known online retailers of wine making supplies, and in both cases the total cost was under $40. You can save $7 by omitting the Wyeast #4632 from the list.

4 oz.	Citric acid
4 oz	Malic acid
4 oz	Tartaric acid
2 oz	Liquid tannin
½ oz	Pectic enzyme liquid
2 oz	Yeast energizer
1 oz	Potassium sorbate
100	Campden tablets
4 oz	Powdered potassium metabisulfite"
2 pkt	Red Star Pasteur Champagne yeast
2 pkt	Red Star Montrachet yeast
2 pkt	Lalvin D-47 yeast
2 pkt	Lalvin ICV-D254 yeast
1 pkt	Wyeast #4632 Dry Mead yeast

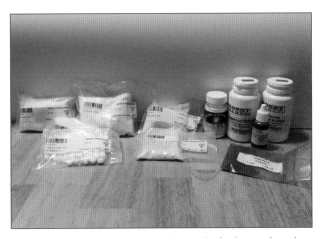

It looks like a chemistry set, but works far better than the old formulas requiring lemon and tea.

Sources of Sugar

All of your wine musts will contain less sugar than is needed to make a self-preserving wine. The sugar content of common fruits (other than wine grapes) is insufficient. In order for a wine to be self-preserving without need for pasteurization or the addition of preservatives, it needs an alcohol content of at least 9 percent. From the perspective of chemistry, because the yeast contains enzymes to turn many forms of sugar into a sort more easily used, any common source of sugar will have the same result in terms of alcohol production. You can use granulated sugar, dextrose, glucose, fructose, honey, molasses, brown sugar, dried fruits, concentrated fruit juices and more.

Though the source doesn't matter in terms of creating alcohol, it can make a big difference in terms of taste because many of the chemical compounds that make honey or brown sugar have a distinctive taste and aroma will be preserved in wines that include them. For this reason, I would recommend against using brown sugar or molasses.

Glucose, dextrose, fructose and sucrose (table sugar) are all treated identically by yeast. Nothing is gained by using the more expensive fructose from a health food store over an inexpensive bag of granulated sugar from the grocery store. None of these contribute flavor to the wine, and simply serve as a source of sweetness or alcohol. They are a good choice for wines in which you want the tastes and aromas of the primary fruit to dominate their character.

Containing a wide array of minerals, amino acids and vitamins, honey is a worthy addition to many wines. A number of cultural traditions have grown up around honey wines. Strictly speaking, a wine made from honey alone is called mead. Wine that combines honey with apples is called cyser, whereas wine made from honey and any other (non-grape) fruit is called melomel. Wine made from honey with added herbs is called metheglin, and wine made from honey and grapes is pyment.

When making mead variants, the source and quality of the honey you use makes a difference in the taste of the finished product. The generic blended honeys in the supermarket are fine when the honey is primarily used as a source of sugar; if the tastes and aromas of the honey will be important to the end product, you will want a single-source honey from a bee keeper. The nectar that the bees collect affects the mineral content and flavor of mead. In general, darker honeys impart stronger flavors. Clover, alfalfa, orange blossom, wild flower, mesquite and many others are available.

Bottled juices and juice concentrates can also be used as a source of sugar, especially given that sugar is their primary solid constituent. Bottled juices and juice blends from the natural food section of the grocery store are often 100 percent juice from the described fruit. These have been specifically formulated to retain the distinctive flavor of the fruit, and can be easily used as an addition to wines. You might want to be sparing in their use, though, as they often cost as much as $10/quart.

Grape juice concentrates can help add "vinous" quality to a country wine, making its mouth-feel resemble that of traditional wines. These are special concentrates purchased from wine making stores that have had the water removed under vacuum and have been preserved with sulfites rather than through heat, and they therefore preserve a distinctive grape character. They are expensive at roughly $16/quart, but good additions as part of a must. They come in white and red varieties.

Dried fruits contain a lot of sugar. Most have also been sulfited to preserve their color. When they are chopped up and added to a must, a portion of the sugar they contain is leeched into the must. Raisins, dried apricots and dried currants are very popular additives in small quantities and can lend country wines a sherry-like taste. In general, one cup of minced dried fruit will impart three ounces of sugar to the must though this rule of thumb is no substitute for measuring with a hydrometer. Do keep in mind that making wine out of a dried fruit can concentrate the effects of that fruit, as I found to my chagrin with some prune wine I made.

Adjusting Sugar Levels Using a Hydrometer

Many wine making books and pamphlets are full of recipes that specify a certain fixed amount of sugar for a given fruit. Such recipes rely upon the false assumption that the sugar content of a given fruit is the same no matter how close to ripeness it was when harvested, how long it has been stored, or even the variety of the fruit in question.

The key to getting the sugar right is using a hydrometer. The hydrometer was discussed briefly earlier. As stated, it looks a lot like a thermometer with a big bulb on the end. It measures the amount of dissolved solids in a solution by how far it sinks. There is a long stem and a scale, and the specific gravity is read where the liquid touches the glass. This is important because the surface tension of the liquid will give a false reading anywhere else, so be sure to read the value where the liquid is touching the glass.

I use a wine thief that doubles as a hydrometer jar. So I clean and sanitize the wine thief and hydrometer, and then give the hydrometer a spin as I put it into the liquid. Giving the hydrometer a spin is necessary because otherwise air bubbles could cling to it and give it false buoyancy that would give inaccurate readings.

Once you have your reading, you will need to correct it to compensate for the temperature of the must, because hydrometers are calibrated for 60 degrees. If the temperature is between 40 and 50 degrees, subtract 0.002 from the reading. If the temperature is between 50 and 55 degrees, subtract 0.001. If the temperature is between 65 and 75, add 0.001, and if the temperature is between 75 and 80, add 0.002. If the temperature is over 80, let it cool before measuring.

Specific Gravity Correction

Temperature	Specific Gravity Correction
40	- .002
50	- .001
60	0
70	+ .001
80	+ .002

Even though a particular strain of yeast might have a theoretical alcohol tolerance exceeding 20 percent, such yeasts will not thrive in musts containing enough sugar to make that much alcohol. Higher levels of alcohol like that are achieved by adding small amounts of sterile sugar syrup as existing sugars in the must are depleted or by fortification. That sort of technique is beyond the scope of this chapter, except to note that in order to avoid a fermentation failing due to excessive sugar levels, you should limit the initial specific gravity of your musts to no greater than 1.100, which corresponds to 13.6 percent alcohol. Likewise, you want your wines to have enough alcohol in them to preserve them. Because water may be added to the wine at some rackings—thereby diluting the alcohol—you should also aim for a starting specific gravity that exceeds 1.080, corresponding to 10.6 percent alcohol.

Almost all of your musts made from pressed or juiced fruits will contain insufficient levels of sugar to reach the minimum necessary alcohol content. As a result, sugar will need to be added. You can determine how much by using the following equation. In practice, the volume of the must will be increased slightly by the addition of the sugar, so the results won't be perfect, but they will certainly be better than a one-size-fits-all-fruits recipe.

Ounces of Sugar = (Desired S.G.—Measured S.G) x 360

If you decide to add honey rather than sugar, then multiply the amount of sugar needed by 1.3 to make up for the moisture content of honey. Ideally, you would use a scale for measuring sugar to be added, but if you don't have one, you can use measuring cups and allow for seven ounces of granulated sugar per cup.

For example, if you are making cyser from juiced apples and the measured S.G. Of your must is 1.040 but you want a starting S.G. Of 1.090, you first determine how much sugar is needed:

(1.090—1.040) x 360 = 18 ounces

Because you will be using honey instead of sugar, you'll multiply that by 1.3 to compensate for the moisture content of the honey: 18 x 1.3 = 23.4 ounces

Cleanliness and Sanitation

Before I get into the details of making wine, I want to delve a bit into cleanliness and sanitation, as these are crucial for a successful outcome. You don't need a laboratory clean room or a level 3 hazmat facility to make wine. You can do it in your kitchen and dining room. But you need to be attentive to detail. Everything that touches your must, wine or wine-in-progress must be clean and sanitized.

"Clean" simply means "free of visible dirt or contamination." Dish soap and water are adequate cleansers. Wine bottles, fermentation vessels, your wine thief, plastic tubing, your hydrometer and all utensils that touch your wine need to be cleaned. Sometimes, all that is needed is to add some soapy water and shake. Other times, as with

carboys, you may need to use a special brush. For subsequent sanitation procedures to work, the surfaces must first be clean. Once they have been cleaned, they should be thoroughly rinsed.

To sanitize the equipment, all surfaces that will touch the must or wine should be rinsed or wiped down with a sanitizing sulfite solution. Don't rinse afterwards. For bottles, vessels and carboys you can add a portion of the solution and swish it around thoroughly so that it contacts all surfaces, and then pour it back into your container of solution. For other utensils, soak paper towels in sanitizing solution and use those towels to wipe them down immediately before use.

Your hand siphon and tubing might look to pose a problem at first, but there is an easy technique for keeping them clean. For this technique, you need two clean plastic gallon jugs that were previously used for water. Put one with soapy water on your counter and the empty one on the floor. Now, use your siphon to pump the soapy water all the way up into the tube and through the tubing into the empty container on the floor. Then, switch the containers and repeat the process until the equipment is clean. Empty out the containers and rinse them thoroughly. After this, use the sanitizing solution on the counter, and siphon that into the empty container on the floor. Make sure to wipe down the outside of the equipment and tubing as well, as these may contact the wine.

Making the Juice for Wine Must

Wine grapes are the perfect fruit for making wine. All you need to do is crush them and they make the perfect amount of juice with the perfect levels of acidity and sugar. Every other fruit is imperfect in some way; either it is so acidic it will require dilution and then won't have enough sugar, or even at full strength it lacks sugar, acidity or both.

Juice for country wines is primarily obtained using only one technique. In this technique, the fruit is placed in a clean nylon straining bag in the bottom of the primary fermenter, crushed with cleaned/sanitized hands, and the difference in volume is made up by adding water. The water helps to extract the dissolved sugars and flavor compounds, and as fermentation begins, the alcohol created helps to extract the color. This technique is best suited to softer fruits that are easily crushed by hand, though it is used for practically all fruits for the overwhelming preponderance of country wines.[3]

As an alternative, especially for harder fruits such as apples, I recommend using a high-quality juice machine such as the one pictured. Both Juiceman™ and Champion™ make high-quality durable juicers, and I'm sure there are others. I've had mine since 1994. With these machines, the expressed juice goes into one container and the pulp goes into another. For darker fruits from which you want to extract color, such as cherries or blueberries, scoop the pulp from the pulp container into a nylon straining bag that you put in the bottom of the primary fermenter. (Note: exclude the pits from stone fruits as they contain a cyanogenic glycoside that is poisonous.)

You can also add bottled juices. I don't recommend the regular bottled juices from the supermarket shelves as they are too diluted, often have other juices added, and have been overly

⊗ The juice machine makes suitable juice for wine must in short order. Anything that can be juiced can be turned into wine.

processed to create a homogenized drinking product. Instead, get the juices from the natural food section that are labeled as being composed 100 percent of the listed fruit. Though they are expensive, they make a worthy adjunct to fresh fruit. Wine grape concentrate has already been mentioned, but natural concord grape juice can be added as well to convey a vinous quality to the finished wine. (If you grow your own table grapes as I do, adding some of these will add a unique character to your wines.)

Some fruits are either highly acidic or highly tannic to such an extent that you wouldn't want to use a juice composed exclusively of the extracted juice in order to make wine because the results would be too sour or bitter. In those cases, only a portion of the must is made from that fruit, and the rest is made up from water or other juices.

What follows is a recipe table that indicates how many pounds of a given fruit to use in making a gallon of wine from that fruit, how much tannin to add to that wine per gallon, and any other adjuncts that I'd recommend. Any deficit in juice to make a gallon is made up with water.

---

3   If you are using purchased fruits, please make sure they are unwaxed. The wax that purveyors use to make fruits look pretty will turn your intended wine into a useless mess.

General Recipes for Making Wine from Common Fruits and Flowers

	Pounds	Fruit Preparation	Adjuncts	Pectic Enzyme	Tannin	Yeast Variety	Notes
Apple	10 lbs	Juice machine	½ lb raisins in straining bag	Double specified on container	¼ tsp	Red Star Pasteur Champagne	Use the juice but not the pulp
Blackberry	4 lbs	Crushed in straining bag	½ lb raisins in straining bag	As specified	None	Red Star Montrachet	
Blueberry	8 lbs	4 lbs juiced, 4 lbs crushed in straining bag	½ tsp vanilla and one stick cinnamon in bag	As specified	None	Lalvin ICV-D254	
Cherry, Sweet	4 lbs	Juice machine, add pulp to straining bag	1 quart bottled cherry juice	As specified	None	Red Star Montrachet	Exclude the pits
Dandelion	5 cups flower heads	Put the flower petals (only!) in straining bag	1 lb raisins in straining bag	None	¼ tsp	Lalvin D47	Ferment at under 70 degrees
Nectarine	3 lbs	Pitted and juiced in machine	½ lb raisins in straining bag	As specified	¼ tsp	Red Star Pasteur Champagne	
Peach	3 lbs	Pitted and juiced in machine	None	As specified	¼ tsp	Lalvin D47	
Pear	10 lbs	Juice machine	½ lb raisins in straining bag	Double specified on container	¼ tsp	Red Star Pasteur Champagne	Add one stick cinnamon to straining bag

	Pounds	Fruit Preparation	Adjuncts	Pectic Enzyme	Tannin	Yeast Variety	Notes
Plum	5 lbs	Pitted and crushed in straining bag	1 lb raisins in straining bag	As specified	None	Red Star Montrachet	
Raspberry	4 lbs	Crushed in straining bag	None	As specified	None	Red Star Montrachet	
Rhubarb	4 lbs	Crushed in straining bag	1 lb strawberry in straining bag	As specified	¼ tsp	Red Star Pasteur Champagne	
Strawberry	4 lbs	Crushed in straining bag	½ lb raisins in straining bag	Double specified on container	¼ tsp	Lalvin ICV-D254	Comes out straw-colored rather than red
Watermelon	10 lbs	Juice machine	1 lb raisins in straining bag	As specified	¼ tsp	Lalvin D47	Peel the outer skin off, and juice the rind

The Primary Fermentation: Step-by-Step

1. Start with fruit juice obtained as described earlier in this chapter.

2. If needed, add enough water to the fruit juice to equal the amount of wine you wish to make. (It is helpful to add previously measured amounts of water to your primary fermenter in advance and use a magic marker to mark gallons and quarts on the outside of the vessel for easy reference.) I use bottled water because my well water is sub-optimal, but if you have good water where you live, tap water is fine. Don't worry about whether or not your water is chlorinated, because the Campden tablets we'll be adding later serve to remove chlorine from the water.

3. Use your hydrometer to measure the specific gravity (SG) of the must. You are aiming for an SG of between 1.085 and 1.110, but in all likelihood your must measures much lower. Add the required amount of sugar or honey to your must. This will slightly increase the volume of your must, but that's fine.

4. Use your acid testing kit to test the acidity of your must. If needed, add acid. Try to use the specific acid (or acid blend) that will

best enhance the character of the fruit. For xample, malic acid will enhance apples and pears whereas citric acid will enhance watermelons and tartaric acid will enhance grapes. If you are in doubt, use an acid blend made up of equal parts of the three acids.

5. Add one teaspoon of yeast energizer for each gallon of must.

6. Add pectic enzyme as directed on the container, or double the amount if the recipe table specifies doing so.

7. Add tannin as appropriate for the fruit being used. (This is described in the accompanying recipe table.)

8. Crush and add one Campden tablet dissolved in a bit of juice per gallon of must. Vigorously stir the must.

9. Cover your primary fermenter, and plug the hole with a bit of cotton ball to keep foreign objects out. Wait twenty-four hours.

10. Vigorously stir the must to oxygenate. Once movement ceases, sprinkle yeast from the packet over the surface of the must. Do not stir.

11. Place the cover on the fermenter, and plug the hole loosely with a bit of cotton ball.

12. Allow to sit for a week. During this time, you should smell the fermentation. Also, it may foam heavily and come out through the hole in the lid. If it does, clean up on the outside and insert a new cotton ball. After the week, replace the cotton ball with an airlock filled with sanitizing solution.

13. Allow to sit for another week or two, until the airlock only "bloops" once every few seconds. This marks the end of the primary fermentation phase. Don't let it set more than a couple of days now before racking, or else the dregs

at the bottom (known as lees) will impart bad flavors to your wine.

Your First Racking: Step-by-Step

1. A day before you plan to rack, move your primary fermenter to a table or counter top. By doing it a day in advance, you give any sludge stirred up by movement a chance to settle. Put a wedge, book, block of wood or something else from 1" to 2" high underneath the fermenter on the edge that is away from you. This will allow you to sacrifice the smallest amount of wine possible with the lees.

2. Clean and sanitize your racking tube, tubing, and your secondary fermenter. Get your rubber stopper and fresh airlock ready. Put your secondary fermenter on the floor in front of the primary fermenter, and then carefully remove the lid from the primary fermenter, creating as little disturbance as possible. Put a bit of the wine in a sanitized glass, and dissolve one crushed Campden tablet per gallon, then add it back to the wine.

3. Put the plastic tubing from your racking setup in the secondary fermenter and the racking tube in the primary fermenter. Keeping the racking tube well above the sediment, pump it gently to get it started. It may take a couple of tries. Gently lower the racking tube as the liquid level diminishes. Watch the liquid in the tube very carefully. The second it starts sucking sediment, raise the racking tube" up to break the suction.

4. Place the rubber stopper with an airlock filled with sanitizing solution in the secondary fermenter. Using a carboy handle if necessary,

move the secondary fermenter to a location out of sunlight where even temperatures are maintained.

5. Immediately clean and sanitize your primary fermenter, racking tube and tubing and stow them away. If you don't clean them immediately they will likely be ruined.

With practice you can rack on your own, but don't be afraid to ask for some help.

The Secondary Fermentation: Step-by-Step

1. Wait. And wait. Then wait some more. Patience, I have been told, is a virtue. After your first racking from the primary to secondary fermenter, the yeast will lag for a couple of days while it tries to catch up. Allow the secondary fermenter to sit unmolested until the wine starts to become clear, you have more than just a dusting of sediment at the bottom of the container, or the air lock only operates once every couple of minutes. This will likely take about a month. Because the secondary fermenter sits for so long, don't forget to check the airlock peri-

The secondary fermentation in this vessel is almost complete.

odically and top up the sanitizing solution in it so it doesn't evaporate and leave your wine vulnerable.

2. The day before racking, sit the secondary fermenter up on a table or counter, and tilt it using a book or other wedge, just as before.

3. Boil some water in a pot on the stove and allow it to cool to room temperature while covered. Clean and sanitize another fermentation vessel as well as the racking tube and tubing. Place the sanitized vessel on the floor in front of the secondary fermenter, put the plastic tubing in the vessel, and put the racking tube in the secondary fermenter. Operate the racking tube and transfer the wine from the old vessel to the new. Add one Campden tablet dissolved in wine for each gallon of wine.

4. Likely, there is an air space between the wine and the top of the new vessel. This is not a good thing as it exposes too much surface area of the wine to oxygen and potential infections. Pour in the sterilized water until the wine is just up to the neck.

5. Clean the rubber stopper and airlock, sanitize them, refill the airlock with sanitizing solution, and install them on the new secondary fermenter. Put the secondary fermenter in a location without sunlight and with even temperature.

6. Thoroughly clean and sanitize the empty secondary fermenter, the racking tube and the tubing.

7. Now it is a waiting game. Over weeks and months your wine will ultimately cease to ferment, and the haze within the wine will settle onto the bottom of the container. Keep an eye

on the wine. Anytime a substantial sediment develops, rack the wine again and top up with sterilized water. Make sure the airlock doesn't go dry and permit foreign organisms to enter.

8. Once the wine has gone at least three months without requiring racking and is crystal clear, it is ready for bottling. You can allow it to age in the fermenter as long as you'd like—even several years. But as fermenters are expensive, you will probably want to bottle the wine and re-use the secondary fermenter on another project.

Bottling Your Wine: Step by Step

1. Make some labels. Gather, clean and sanitize the bottles that will be accepting the wine. You will need five bottles per gallon of wine. Boil an equal number of corks for fifteen minutes, and then allow to sit in a covered pot. Clean and sanitize your corker.

2. Rack the wine, but do not add water to top off on this final racking. Add one Campden tablet per gallon by crushing the tablet and dissolving in a bit of wine and then adding that wine into the new vessel.

3. If you want to add potassium sorbate to prevent re-fermentation, dissolve that also in the wine and add back into the new vessel. Use ¼ teaspoon per gallon of wine.

4. Place the secondary fermenter holding the wine on a table or counter top, tilting as before.

5. Arrange the bottles on a towel on the floor in front of the fermenter and install the plastic hose clamp on the plastic tubing so you can

turn off the flow of wine when switching from bottle to bottle.

6. Put the plastic tubing in a bottle and the racking tube in the wine, pump the racking tube and start the flow of wine, pulling the tube higher in the bottle as the level of the wine increases. Stop the flow of wine when it is about half an inch into the bottom of the neck of the wine bottle, then put the tube in the next bottle and repeat the process until you run out of wine or there are no more bottles to fill.

7. One at a time, place the bottles on solid floor, and use your corker to install one of the sterilized corks. Only work with one bottle at a time. As each bottle is corked, set it out of the way and apply the label. Repeat until all of the bottles are corked.

8. Clean and sanitize your fermenting vessels, racking tube and plastic tubing.

9. Enjoy at your leisure or give as a gift.

Making Wine Without Sulfites

Throughout this chapter I have oriented procedures around the use of sulfites, and I believe its obvious that the reason I have done so is because use of sulfites makes it easier to produce a solid product. Even before modern times, sulfites were employed by burning sulfur to create sulfur dioxide gas to purify musts.

However, there is a small percentage of the population that is genuinely sensitive to sulfites, and some people simply don't want them in their wine. I have successfully made many batches of wine without sulfites, and here are some tips that will allow you to do the same.

- Clean all equipment using scalding (140+ degree) water. Water this hot is, in fact, scalding, so use caution.

- Though it decreases the quality of the result somewhat, you can also pasteurize your must by heating to 150 degrees and holding it there for ½ hour before putting it in your primary fermenter. You can then add bottled water to make up any difference in volume. Make sure the temperature has dropped below 80 before adding pectic enzyme. Musts that have been pasteurized often create very hazy wines. If you do this, do it with fruits that, in the recipe

⊗ Your bottled wines will be prized and appreciated as gifts.

table, require no pectic enzyme and you'll have better results.

- If you don't want to pasteurize your must (and I recommend against pasteurizing your must), you can instead clean your starting fruit very, very thoroughly.

- When using unpasteurized must, your yeast must out-compete all other yeasts and bacteria. So instead of sprinkling the yeast on top of the must, get your yeast ready two days in advance by sprinkling the yeast into a pint jar containing bottled apple juice mixed with a pinch of yeast energizer and then cap it with several layers of cheesecloth. Set it in a dark place at 60-70 degrees. When you add this yeast to your must, just pour it in smoothly. Now your yeast has a head start so it can out-compete the wild yeasts and bacteria on the fruit.

- Observe scrupulous cleanliness.

Your Wine Making Log

Just like cooking, wine making is a bit science, and a bit art. The techniques I have provided are primarily science. Science will give you a drinkable wine, but it takes art to make a truly great wine. Science can tell you how much sugar and acid to add to a must composed of apple juice, but art will tell you that a mix of McIntosh and Golden Delicious apples produces a better wine than a mix of Red Delicious and Granny Smith.

The only way to get really good at wine making is to actually make wine, and keep a log so you can benefit from your experiences over time. I am writing this in 2011. Illustrated is a page in my wine log from 2004. The wines I made in 2010 are superior to those I made in 2003 or 2005; not because the science has changed but because I have learned a hundred nuances. I have learned that grape tannin makes for better wine than a tablespoon of strong tea, that cherries have a lot of natural tannin and that strawberries have so much pectin that a double dose of pectic enzyme is needed to get a clear wine. I have learned which juices enhance each other in a must, and much much more.

One thing I have also learned is not to judge one of your wines harshly too soon. Time really does make a difference. A wine might taste great immediately after being made, not so great three months later, and fantastic another year down the road.

In my wine log, I record specific ingredients, quantities, sources, temperatures, procedures, dates of rackings, and just about anything of potential relevance. I would urge you to do the same. I picked up a blank journal at a bookstore for $5 eight years ago, and it has paid for itself many times over.

One other thing I have learned is that there are a lot of companies out there wanting you to spend untold thousands of dollars on wine making. Unless you decide to get a federal license and go into business, this makes no sense and usually the return you get in quality for the dollars spent is minimal.

For example, you could spend several hundred dollars on a genuine oak cask for aging your wine. Or, you could buy some oak chips for $2, soak them in sulfite solution to sanitize them, and add them to your secondary fermenter. Given the

1/17/2004

Prune Wine

Ingredients
32 oz organic prune juice (64g sugar)
16 oz organic grape juice (56g sugar)
894 g sugar (sucrose) (1014g total sugar)
2.5 tsp citric/tartaric/malic acid blend
8 drops pectic enzyme
½ packet montrachet yeast
Water to make 1 gal
1 tbsp strong tea

Measurements
Acid titration shows 0.25% tartaric
After addition of acid: 0.625% tartaric
Calculated sugar 1014g 11.35% PA
Initial S.G. 1.106 @80° or 1.1085 corrected
or 14.52% PA

I've learned a lot since this log was written, and keeping logs was the key to improvement!

study that I talked about at the beginning of this chapter, I am a bit dubious as to whether even an expert could tell the difference.

You will make far greater improvements in your wine by investing in top-quality home-grown or organic ingredients and fine-tuning your techniques than from fancy gadgets. Thus your $5 log book is your greatest wine making asset.

24

Making Your Own Vinegar

There is vinegar, and then there is vinegar. Most often, we buy vinegar as a commodity product without giving much thought as to quality. The gallon jugs of distilled vinegar in the supermarket are indistinguishable. There is no point in making your own vinegar when you can buy it for $1/gallon in bulk, so this chapter is not about making that kind of commodity product.

Really good vinegar is a complex taste sensation to be savored and appreciated. It takes on the character of the malt, cider or wine from which it is derived, and can also be improved by aging as the complex flavor and aroma compounds meld, recombine and change. It is truly a gourmet product, and handcrafted examples can only rarely be found at less than $20/pint.

Vinegar in general is a healthy condiment. Vinegar increases satiety,[4] thereby reducing caloric intake, reduces the glycemic index

---

4   Östman, E; Granfeldt, Y; Persson, L; Björck, I (2005). "Vinegar supplementation lowers glucose and insulin responses and increases satiety after a bread meal in healthy subjects." *European Journal of Clinical Nutrition* 59 (9): 983–8.

of foods with which it is consumed,[5] and may reduce the risks of certain types of heart disease.[6] And just as wine preserves many of the vitamins and antioxidants in the original fruit, homemade vinegars made from those wines will likewise preserve vitamins and antioxidants, thereby making it even more healthy than the commodity vinegars used in the studies.

So this chapter is not about duplicating commodity products that are cheaper to buy than they are to make. Rather, it is about making a uniquely healthful product with gourmet qualities that will enhance your salads, greens, dressings and anything else you make with vinegar.

Because the prior chapter is about making wine, you will already have the raw materials at hand allowing you to make vinegar inexpensively. So I will focus on using wine as the starting material in this chapter, even though vinegar can also be made using similar techniques if you use beer, hard cider, sake or practically any other product containing alcohol.

Speaking of Wine

I really enjoy making wine. I enjoy every aspect of the process, and I especially enjoy sharing my wine with someone who will appreciate the results of my efforts. But sometimes wine making efforts result in a less-than-stellar product. The wine I made from bottled blueberry juice and brown sugar comes to mind. What on earth was I thinking? You will likely have some learning experiences of your own that will serve as excellent raw material.

Some commercial wines are pretty poor too. Or, even if they are pretty good, maybe they have sat in the refrigerator too long with the cork halfway out and they have started to oxidize. Rather than dump that effort or money down the drain, you might consider using it to make your own vinegar.

Wine that you use to make vinegar can be normally sulfited or it can be non-sulfited, but it cannot have been preserved using potassium sorbate or sodium benzoate. The wine can be white or red, sweet or dry, and made from any conceivable edible fruit. And even though you will likely choose wines for this process that were not optimal for drinking as wine, it is very important that the wine you choose be sound.

Any sound wine that you use, even if it isn't very good for drinking, will still yield a product far superior to the "wine vinegar" you will find at the supermarket. The "wine" they use as a starting product was never intended for drinking in the first place, whereas yours was planned with drinking quality in mind and is hence a better material from which to make vinegar.

What is Vinegar?

Vinegar is a dilute form of acetic acid, ranging in strength from 4 percent to 8 percent. It is made by the oxidation of ethyl alcohol into acetic acid through a fermentation process undertaken by acetic acid bacteria (AAB). Just as the yeast in wine derives its energy from sugar and produces alcohol as a waste product, AAB derive their energy from alcohol and produce acetic acid as a waste product. And just as the alcohol in wine acts

5   Johnston, C. S.; Kim, C. M.; Buller, A. J. (2004). "Vinegar Improves Insulin Sensitivity to a High-Carbohydrate Meal in Subjects With Insulin Resistance or Type 2 Diabetes." *Diabetes Care* 27 (1): 281–2.
6   Johnston, Carol S.; Gaas, Cindy A. (2006). "Vinegar: medicinal uses and antiglycemic effect." *MedGenMed* 8 (2): 61.

as a preservative against organisms that cannot tolerate alcohol, acetic acid acts as a preservative against organisms that cannot tolerate the low pH created by acetic acid. This is how pickling foods in vinegar keeps them from spoiling.

Acetic Acid Bacteria

There are a great many specific strains of AAB. They are present on the surface of both healthy and damaged fruit as well as the nectar of flowers, but they are also commonly transferred by the fruit flies you likely noticed were attracted to your wine.

Wine is produced in anaerobic conditions, meaning that oxygen is excluded. Vinegar, on the other hand, is produced under aerobic conditions as the AAB require oxygen to work. In the absence of oxygen, the bacteria go dormant.

Various strains of AAB[7] are present in wine must from the very beginning and remain in the wine even when it is finally bottled.[8] The primary factor that keeps it suppressed in wine is lack of oxygen and alcohol levels that are too high for the bacteria to process. So especially with newly made wines, all that is theoretically necessary to turn wine into vinegar is to permit the entry of oxygen. In the presence of oxygen the bacteria would quickly proliferate as a film on the surface of the wine and turn the alcohol to acetic acid, especially if the alcohol level is under 10 percent.

But acetic acid bacteria are not the only bacteria that can take hold in wine, and leaving the

results to chance can result in a product that is not only unusable, but thoroughly rotten. So for our purposes, just as a specific strain of yeast is used to make wine, a specific strain of bacteria is used to make vinegar. Acetic acid bacteria are commercially available in a form called vinegar *mother*. Vinegar mother, also known as mycoderma aceti, is a gelatinous substance containing the AAB that forms on the surface of vinegar. Though vinegar could certainly be made from gluconobacter oxydans or acetobacter pasteurianus among many other possibilities, all of the commercially available vinegar mothers are acetobacter aceti.

Acetobacter aceti needs to float on top of the wine you will be making into vinegar so that it has access to oxygen at all times. Without access to oxygen, it will go dormant. The vinegar mother you obtain may look like crude vinegar, or it may look like jelly. If it looks like jelly, it is very likely that when you put it in your vinegar crock, it will sink and thereby go dormant for lack of oxygen. To prevent this, a piece of thin wood about the size of a playing card is floated on top of the wine, and the vinegar mother is placed on it. This piece of wood is usually made of oak and is called a vinegar *raft*.

Vinegar mothers are available as white wine, red wine and cider. All of them have the same acetic acid bacteria, and the only difference is the carrier. In small batches of vinegar—say less than a gallon—the carrier makes a difference in the flavor, but in larger batches of vinegar the carrier doesn't matter.

Some strains of acetic acid bacteria, such as gluconobacter oxydans will go dormant once all of the ethyl alcohol has been consumed. But the acetobacter aceti that you'll be using does

---

7   Acetobacter aceti, gluconobacter oxydans and acetobacter pasteurianus predominate.
8   A. Joyeux, S. Lafon-Lafourcade, and P. Ribéreau-Gayon (1984), "Evolution of Acetic Acid Bacteria During Fermentation and Storage of Wine," *Appl Environ Microbiol.* 1984 July; 48(1): 153–156.

not go dormant once all of the ethyl alcohol is used. Instead, it starts consuming the acetic acid that it produced, with the end result being just carbon dioxide. So vinegar conversions using a commercial vinegar mother must be arrested once the conversion has completed or you'll end up with no vinegar at all.

The conversion process can be stopped in two ways. For purposes of aging the vinegar, it can be placed in a canning jar with a tight-fitting lid that excludes oxygen. This leaves the vinegar alive, but dormant. For purposes of long-term storage or use in an environment where oxygen might be admitted, the vinegar is pasteurized. Vinegar is pasteurized by heating it to 150 degrees for thirty minutes with the lid on tight (except for when a candy thermometer is used for testing) to prevent evaporation. Once it has been pasteurized, it can be stored in any clean container for a nearly indefinite period of time.

Equipment and Ingredients

Making vinegar is easier than making wine and requires minimal equipment or ingredients. Other than a vinegar crock and the wine you'll be using, you can get everything else you need for under $30.

Vinegar Crock

Vinegar can theoretically be made in any sort of container. Traditionally, it is made in oak barrels called vinegar casks or in ceramic urns known as vinegar crocks.

There are three important features in a container used to make vinegar. The container should have a mouth wide enough that you can insert your vinegar raft and preferably your whole hand. It should have a tap, spout or spigot near the bottom, but far enough from the bottom that it doesn't pick up sediment. Finally, it should be made of a material that will not react with the vinegar. Vinegar is a dilute acid, so it will react with most metals given time.

Given these features, you are not constrained to only use products officially sold as vinegar crocks. Anything officially sold as a vinegar crock will quite frankly be seriously overpriced. I looked on the Internet recently and found many of them priced at nearly $100!

I use two containers to make vinegar. One is a miniature ceramic water crock that holds a half gallon. It costs $24. The other is a one-gallon plastic beverage dispenser I picked up at a department store for $4. Both of these containers have the essential features, including the spigot. Normal ceramic water crocks hold 2½ gallons, an amount which may far exceed the amount of vinegar you plan to make. That's why I got a miniature half-gallon crock.

You could go all out and get an oak vinegar cask, but that will set you back at least $80. If you want your vinegar to be oak-aged, you can just put oak cubes in the sealed pint or quart jar that you are using to age your vinegar.

Cheesecloth and Rubber Bands

You put these over the mouth of your vinegar crock to allow oxygen to enter but keep fruit flies and other critters out. Not all cheesecloth is created equal. The material that is sold as "cheesecloth" at the supermarket is not suitable for

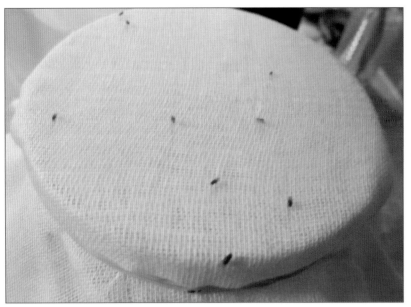

⊗ Use a doubled piece of high-quality fine cheesecloth to cover your vinegar urn. Otherwise, fruit flies will get into your vinegar.

Miscellaneous Supplies

A vinegar raft is a small, thin piece of oak that floats on top of your wine. It's purpose is to keep the vinegar mother from sinking because if the vinegar mother sinks, it will stop making vinegar. These are available in vinegar kits or individually from many Internet sites. Just type "vinegar raft" into a search engine.

Some people prefer the taste of vinegar that has been aged in oak, or the astringency contributed by the tannins leached from the oak. Oak barrels are expensive and time-intensive to maintain. An alternative is adding oak chips or oak cubes to the vinegar. Add a quarter cup per gallon, enclosed in a tied spice bag for easy removal later. The chips or cubes are added during the aging process and left in the vinegar for four to six weeks. For these purposes, you don't want to use oak from your building supply store. Instead, order it from a wine making supplier.

making cheese, and even doubled or tripled it won't keep fruit flies out of your vinegar.

Unless you have a good gourmet shop nearby that sells real cheesecloth, you may have to order it from a supplier of cheese making supplies over the Internet. Even though it is a bit expensive when you include shipping, I'd recommend saving on shipping by ordering a couple of packages. They won't go to waste because you'll need the cheesecloth for making cheese in the next chapter.

The size of the needed rubber bands will be different depending upon the size of the mouth of your vinegar crock. The only caution worth mentioning is that light and vinegar fumes will degrade the rubber, so check the rubber bands weekly and replace if you see signs of deterioration. Otherwise you'll look at your crock one day and find more flies in it than vinegar.

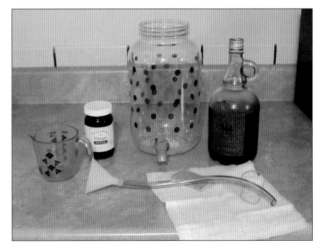

⊗ The materials for making vinegar are simple and inexpensive.

Wine making suppliers can offer a range of oaks with different taste characteristics that you know aren't contaminated with anything nasty.

Canning jars are a good choice for aging and storing vinegars. They seal tightly, which will cause the vinegar mother to go dormant during aging, and they can be used repeatedly which makes them a good bargain.

One other thing you may find helpful is a funnel that you have attached to a piece of plastic hose such as the hose used for racking wine. As vinegar is being made, you need to add more wine. The easy way to do this without risk of disturbing the vinegar mother is to insert the hose into the liquid in the vinegar crock, and add the wine through the funnel.

A candy thermometer will be needed for pasteurizing vinegar, unless you plan to can it using a boiling water bath canner for long-term storage.

Consolidated Equipment and Ingredient List

- Vinegar crock
- Vinegar mother
- Cheesecloth
- Rubber bands
- Vinegar raft
- Canning jars
- Candy thermometer
- Oak chips or cubes (optional)

Making Your Vinegar

1. Clean your vinegar crock thoroughly and sanitize it using sulfite solution. (The prior chapter explains how to make sulfite solution.)

2. Check the capacity of the container of vinegar mother you ordered. Usually it is eight ounces.

3. Add wine to the vinegar crock. The amount added should be twice the volume of the vinegar mother. So if you have eight ounces of vinegar mother, put sixteen ounces of wine in your crock.

4. Add good non-chlorinated water to the vinegar crock. The amount added should be the same as the volume of the vinegar mother. So if your vinegar mother is eight ounces, add eight ounces of water to the wine.

5. Open your vinegar mother. If it is gelatinous, place your vinegar raft on top of the water/wine solution in the vinegar crock.

6. Add the vinegar mother. If it is all liquid, just gently pour it into the crock. If it is gelatinous, add it on top of the vinegar raft.

7. Cover the mouth of the container with cheesecloth and hold it in place with a rubber band.

8. Set the container in a dark place or at least someplace well out of the sun. The ideal temperature range is 80 to 90 degrees, but it will progress fine at 70 to 100.

9. Depending on temperature and other factors, the complete conversion of wine to vinegar can take anywhere from six weeks to three months. Check your vinegar weekly by sniffing it through the cheesecloth. It should smell like vinegar is forming.

10. Starting at the fourth week and every fourth week thereafter, if you want to increase the volume of the vinegar being made, you can add more diluted wine. Dilute the wine with two parts wine to one part non-chlorinated water, and add by using the funnel and tubing.

11. Six weeks after the final addition of wine, start tasting small (less than ¼ teaspoon) samples of the vinegar to see if it is done. It's done when all the alcohol flavor has been replaced with vinegar flavor. Your tongue and nose are amazingly sensitive and able to detect many substances in very low concentrations of parts-per-million and will be as accurate as any easily performed test in determining if the wine is done.

12. Once vinegar is done, it is important to remove it from the vinegar crock because with all the alcohol gone, the vinegar mother will start consuming the acetic acid, and thereby destroy the vinegar. Take out as much vinegar as you can through the spigot and then start your next batch using the same vinegar mother in that container.

Aging Vinegar

Just like wine, vinegar made from wine will mellow with age. Freshly made vinegar is very sharp with a lot of pointed edges. When it is allowed to age, the compounds within the vinegar combine in various ways that make the wine more mellow and to bring out other flavor components.

Even though it is easy to visualize the vinegar mother as sitting on top of the wine, many of its bacteria are spread throughout the vinegar. When you draw off a sample, even if it looks clear, it is filled with acetic acid bacteria. (These bacteria, incidentally, are totally harmless to humans.) Freshly made vinegar is teeming with life.

When vinegar is aged, it is aged with that life intact. The vinegar is drawn from the crock via the spigot and placed in a container sealed so as to exclude air. This renders the acetic acid bacteria dormant. Vinegar can be kept in a sealed container for an indefinite period of time. In fact, genuine balsamic vinegar is aged for at least twelve years, and often for as long as twenty-five years. The minimum period of aging I would recommend is six weeks.

Vinegar can be aged in porcelain, glass, impervious plastic or wooden barrels. A lot of the better traditionally made vinegars feature oak aging. The oak aging serves to impart an astringent principle to the vinegar in the form of tannin. Tannin is not just one substance. The term "tannin" refers to literally dozens if not hundreds of related compounds formed around either a gallic acid or a flavone core. Tannins have in common not only their astringency, but also their ability to bind and precipitate proteins. This means that tannins introduced into vinegar will scavenge stray proteins left over from fermentation by combining with them to form an insoluble substance that will sink to the bottom of the container.

So over time, an initially high level of tannins is reduced and a number of protein or amino acid based substances are removed. This serves to alter the flavor in more ways than merely introducing astringency. In fact, the addition of tannin, through its ability to remove other substances, can paradoxically decrease the astringency of vinegar over a period of aging by removing other substances. Tannins also combine with metals in a process known as chelation. Chelation forms soluble compounds that include the metal but render it unavailable to combine with other substances. This likewise affects the flavor.

You can use oak in the aging of your wine by placing a quarter cup of the cubes or chips in a tied spice bag in your aging wine. Leave it in the

⊗ The materials needed to age vinegar for professional results are readily available.

container for six weeks, and then remove it using sterilized tongs and reseal the container. The rest of the vinegar's aging will continue to be affected by the tannins imparted by the oak.

Keeping Vinegar

Eventually, the aging process should end and the vinegar should be made ready for use. In order to make it ready for use, it is usually filtered and pasteurized. Perfectly adequate filtration is achieved by pouring the vinegar from the jar in which it is aging through a funnel lined with a coffee filter into a clean canning jar.

The jar containing the filtered vinegar is filled to within a quarter inch of the top, and the two piece canning lid is installed. Process for ten min-

utes in a boiling water bath or steam canner and pasteurization has been achieved.

Making Herbal Vinegars

I'll confess that I have never purchased an herbal vinegar. Anytime I have seen herbal vinegar, it is usually in some sort of craft shop. The vinegar is in an ornate bottle with a sprig of some herb and a fancy label. It also has an obscenely fancy price. The price seems crazy to me because I'm pretty certain that the vinegar they used was $1/gallon commodity vinegar and the sprig of herb cost about a penny, and they are wanting $12 for six ounces. No thanks!

Herbal vinegars can be quite nice, though, and making your own is easy enough. You can make it using commodity vinegar from the supermarket or your own handcrafted vinegar. I don't recommend using cider vinegars for herbs.

As you know from an earlier chapter, growing your own herbs is easy, but if you haven't made herbal vinegar before, choosing which herbs to use (and how much) is a hit or miss proposition. To help you get started, I suggest the following single herbs: borage, thyme, rosemary, dill, basil, tarragon and oregano.

I recommend making your herbal vinegars from fresh herbs when possible. When using fresh herbs, I recommend using ½ ounce of fresh herb per cup (eight ounces) of vinegar as a starting proportion. Because the vinegar is a preservative, the herbs won't rot. When using dried herbs, use two tablespoons of dried herb per cup of vinegar.

The procedure is straightforward. Add the cleaned herbs to the container that will hold the herbal vinegar. Heat up the vinegar to a simmer

(NOT a boil!), and then pour the vinegar into the container containing the herb. Seal the container. Allow the flavors to meld for three or four weeks to develop the full flavor before using.

If you want something really impressive for making an oil and vinegar dressing for salad, I would suggest making vinegar from pear wine, and then using the pear vinegar to make a borage herbal vinegar.

The purpose of the xanthan gum or purslane in this recipe is to keep the mixture from separating too quickly for practical use because oil/vinegar and oil/water don't normally mix. The xanthan gum or purslane helps to keep it in suspension. If you use xanthan gum, don't use more than the recommended amount or you'll end up with a jelly-like substance rather than dressing.

Oil and Vinegar Dressing

Ingredients:

11 ounces virgin olive oil
5 ounces handcrafted wine vinegar
2 ounces water
1 Tbsp pulverized dehydrated sweet red pepper
1 Tbsp pulverized dehydrated onion
1 tsp sea salt
1 tsp garlic powder
1 tsp dried oregano
1 tsp dried basil
⅛ tsp xanthan gum OR ½ tsp dried powdered purslane or okra

Procedure:

Add ¼ cup of water and ½ cup plus 2 Tbsp vinegar to your container. Add the remaining solid ingredients except for the xanthan gum/purslane. Shake and allow to sit for a few minutes. Add the xanthan gum/purslane and shake thoroughly. Add 1¼ cup plus 2 Tbsp of olive oil. Shake thoroughly.

25

Making Cheese at Home

Protein is an essential part of the human diet. Though vegetable sources can provide protein, in most cases the protein lacks crucial amino acids. The most readily available complete proteins are meats, eggs and dairy, of which the latter two are the least expensive. Continuing the theme of preserving nutritive content through fermentation, we arrive at cheese. Milk contains a lot of complete protein, but it is also highly perishable.

In the ages before refrigeration was reliably available, one of the few ways to make the nutritional value of milk last longer while also making it quite portable was turning it into cheese. Hard cheeses in particular, if waxed, can last for years.

Another advantage of cheese is that many hard cheeses lack lactose. Lactose is a sugar in milk that a substantial portion of the human population has not yet evolved the genetics to be able to digest. As a result, if they consume most milk products they will suffer severe gastrointestinal distress—sometimes for days. When the whey and curd are separated in the first phases of making cheese, 94 percent of the lactose stays in the whey. Most aged cheeses lack lactose and as a result provide lactose-intolerant people with a delicious way of obtaining the nutritional benefits of milk.

Cheese also has its own health benefits. It is rich in cancer-preventing conjugated linoleic acid and sphingolipids, fights tooth decay and helps maintain bone strength.

Like wine making, cheese making is both art and science. If anything, there is even more art to making cheese because it requires practice to master the various steps. So this chapter is enough to get you started, but you'll likely want to branch out once you've mastered the techniques covered here.

What Is Cheese?

Cheese is the coagulated fat and protein from the milk of domesticated dairy animals. The fats and proteins of milk are coagulated in various ways for the manufacture of different types of cheese. In some cases, a bacterial culture is added. The bacterial culture consumes lactose to make lactic acid, and this lactic acid causes the coagulation.

In other cases, rennet is added. Rennet is a complex mixture of enzymes that likewise coagulates milk. In yet other cases, an acid such as citric acid, tartaric acid or even vinegar is used to cause coagulation. Though the products of these various methods of coagulation are markedly different, they are all cheese because they have in common the coagulation of milk.

Milk: Where It All Begins

In the United States, cows are the usual source for milk, though goats are utilized to a lesser extent. In other countries, the milk of bison, buffalo, sheep, horses, yaks and other animals are also used. The nature of the milk of different species varies appreciably and this is reflected in the character of the cheese produced. Theoretically, you could make cheese using the milk of any mammal, though I wouldn't attempt this until you get good at making cheese from well-characterized herbivores such as cows and goats. Not only that, trying to milk a tiger or a bear is probably more dangerous than warranted.

Likewise, the components of the milk will vary between different breeds of dairy cattle and even the milk of a particular cow will vary with season and diet. Probably the most striking example of this was in the cream cheese my grandmother would make from cows that had been eating wild onions. The smell and taste of the wild onions was transferred to the milk and hence to the cheese. In the case of cream cheese, the results were delicious!

But for the purposes of this chapter we are going to work exclusively with pasteurized and homogenized cow's milk like you buy at the grocery store.

It is important to know that though pasteurized milk is fine, the *ultra*-pasteurized milk that you find in the store is unsuitable. This is too bad, because it is the organic brands that tend to be ultra-pasteurized. Ultra-pasteurization is used to extend the shelf life of expensive milk that wouldn't turn over very quickly. Unfortunately, that process damages the protein in milk so extensively that it is unsuitable for making cheese.

Milk from other animals can certainly be made into cheese, but doing so would require changes in timing, temperature, quantities of ingredients and so forth that are simply too extensive to be treated in a single chapter.

⊗ Most organic milk is ultra-pasteurized, making it unsuitable for cheese.

So we are going to use pasteurized, homogenized cow's milk from the grocery store as the learning medium for your first forays into cheese making. After you have mastered these skills, you can branch out from there. You can find specific types of milk suitable for your needs by finding a local dairy at www.smalldairy.com.

About Raw Milk

Cheese connoisseurs insist that the best cheeses are made from raw milk that has been neither pasteurized nor homogenized. The trouble is that raw milk is not readily available and quite often there are legal impediments to getting it directly from farmers. The basis for these legal impediments is widespread recognition of the likelihood of the presence of pathogens in raw milk.

Though in former times the largest risks were brucellosis and tuberculosis, today the risks are e. coli, salmonella and listeria. Testing of vats of milk in modern times shows that even from healthy cows, anywhere from 0.87 percent to 12.6 percent of raw milk harbors dangerous pathogens.[9] How do healthy cows give pathogen infested milk? They don't. Inadequate sanitation and cleaning of equipment introduces fecal bacteria into the milk. The reason pasteurization became a requirement in the first place was that farmers were actively falsifying their records so that tuberculosis-infected cows wouldn't have to be removed from milk production.[10]

The reason it continues to be required is because human nature hasn't changed, and that maintaining sanitation on an industrial scale of a biological product created by an animal that excretes feces requires extreme levels of conscientiousness that cannot be guaranteed. In essence, because the healthiness of cows and their milk can be tested to assure a safe product without pasteurization, it is possible to sell perfectly healthy raw milk. But pasteurization is required anyway to compensate for the existence of lazy or dishonest people that will prioritize the production of a single infected cow over the health and well-being of their customers. Most people I'm quite sure would do the right thing, but in an industrial system where the outputs of various farms are mixed together, it only requires one feces-contaminated vat to sicken thousands of people.

Obviously, raw milk that does not contain pathogens can be made. Humans have consumed raw milk for thousands of years before pasteurization was invented; it's just that such

---

9   Position Statement on Raw Milk Sales and Consumption, Cornell University Food Science Department.

10   "Not on My Farm!: Resistance to Bovine Tuberculosis Eradication in the United States, Alan L. Olmstead and Paul W. Rhode," January 2005, *The Journal of Economic History* (2007), 67 : 768-809 Cambridge University Press, Copyright © 2007 The Economic History Association, doi:10.1017/S0022050707000307.

milk was collected at home by the end users, so there was a direct correlation between shoddiness and adverse consequences that would result from collecting milk in a bucket that wasn't clean. The milk was used immediately rather than transported thousands of miles, and so any pathogens present had less opportunity to multiply to dangerous or infective levels. It is therefore possible to obtain raw milk that will not make you sick, provided it is supplied by an honest and conscientious farmer.

How to determine if someone is honest and conscientious, I can't say. If I could write a book describing a sure-fire technique of that sort, personnel managers across the world would rejoice. In the absence of that, I would instead look at the idea of mutual self-interest. If a farmer were to sell you raw milk that made you sick, your family could sue him into oblivion. So it is in his best interests, if he sells raw milk at all, to make sure it is pristine. Many such farmers use small-scale low temperature vat pasteurization just to be sure, and this process is less damaging to the milk proteins than standard pasteurization processes.

One other layer of protection is to only use raw milk to make hard cheeses that are aged for longer than two months. The process of cheesemaking, when combined with the conditions of aging in cheese serve to eliminate potential pathogens and render the cheese safe. This only applies to aged hard cheeses! Soft cheeses and those eaten less than two months from manufacture should be considered as risky as raw milk, and I would personally avoid making them from raw milk, though that's an individual choice.

If you use raw milk in cheese making, there are only two procedural changes you'll need to adopt. The first is that you can avoid using calcium chloride (described later), and the other is that when heating the milk, especially for thermophilic cheeses, you will need to top stir the milk. Top stirring is just slowly dragging a utensil across the top quarter-inch of milk in order to keep the milk fats from separating out.

To find raw milk, I recommend the following Internet resources:

* A Campaign for Real Milk: www.realmilk.com
* The Weston A. Price Foundation: www.westonaprice.org
* Farm-to-Consumer Legal Defense Fund: www.farmtoconsumer.org

Categories of Cheese

Cheese can be categorized in various ways depending upon the substances from which it is made, its appearance or consistency, whether it is aged or eaten fresh and the procedures used to produce it. For our purposes, we will use fresh and aged cheeses as categories, as well as soft and hard cheeses, as these categories have the greatest differentiation.

Equipment

When it comes to the equipment needed to make cheese, quality matters. The good news is that most of this equipment is a once-in-a-lifetime purchase that can be passed along to kids or others. You will likely end up ordering most of these items over the Internet because you may have difficulty finding them locally.

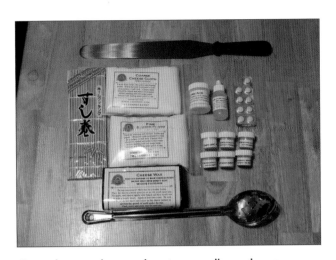

⊗ Quality ingredients and equipment will contribute to a quality product.

Measuring Cups and Spoons

You want both a large (2+ cup) and small (1 cup) Pyrex™ glass liquid measuring cups. You should be able to find these nearby if you don't already have them. You will also need measuring spoons, but not the ordinary cheap ones you get at the dollar store. You want high quality stainless steel measuring spoons that measure in ¹⁄₃₂, ¹⁄₁₆, ⅛ and ¼ teaspoon increments, as well as the traditional sizes.

I have noted by comparing volumes to my laboratory standards that cheap measuring spoons are often undersized or over-sized. This is not a critical matter when making a cake, but when making cheese it can spell the difference between success and failure.

Large Double-Boiler

With batches of cheese starting with a gallon of milk or less and that use a mesophilic starter culture (more on starter cultures later), you can get by with a standard large pot that you set in a sink of hot water. But for batches of cheese requiring more than a gallon of milk or using a thermophilic starter culture, you will need a double-boiler. In cheese making, this double-boiler is also called a "cheese pot." For very small batches of cheese starting with a quart of milk, you can improvise by setting a smaller pot into a larger one as long as the handles on the smaller pot will sit on the lip of the larger pot so the smaller one is surrounded by water.

Again, depending on the size of your largest intended batch of cheese, you may be able to use a double-boiler as small as eight quarts. But because it takes a large amount of milk to make enough curd to yield very much hard cheese after pressing, you wouldn't go wrong with one as large as twenty quarts. No matter what size you use, make sure it is stainless steel because acidified milk will leach aluminum or iron into your curd and impart metallic flavors.

If you don't already have a double-boiler, this is probably the most expensive item you'll need to get. Searching the Internet, I found prices ranging from $88 to $130 for a twenty-quart model. It won't come cheaply, but you'll be thankful that you got it. You can use it for batches of cheese starting with anywhere from one gallon to four gallons of milk, and its configuration will help to hold temperatures steady while preventing scorching. The results of your efforts will reflect the benefits of this device.

Colander

You'll need a large eight-quart colander that will fit into the cheese pot with the handles resting on the edges of the pot. You'll use this to separate the curds from the whey, with the whey going back into the pot.

Special Utensils

You need a large stainless steel slotted spoon, a stainless steel skimming ladle and a stainless steel curd knife. This latter utensil is pretty specialized so you will probably have to get it via an Internet source.

Cheesecloth

You want high-quality coarse (twenty thread count) and fine (sixty thread count) cheesecloth. The fine cheesecloth is used for making soft cheese such as cream cheese whereas the coarse cheesecloth is used to hold harder cheeses during the pressing or curing process.

Cheesecloth is packaged in two-yard increments, so you get a piece that is three feet wide and six feet long. Cut off pieces as needed with good scissors. Before use, cheesecloth must be sterilized. Put it in a pan of water, boil for five minutes and then dump the cheesecloth and water into a colander in the sink. Cheesecloth can be reused. Rinse it under cool running water, and then work a few drops of dish liquid into it. Then rinse it thoroughly, and boil it for five minutes. After boiling, hang it up to dry then store the dried cheesecloth in an airtight bag. Don't forget to sterilize it before using it again.

Bamboo Sushi Mats

These allow good air circulation for cheese that is either draining or aging, and so are essential if hard cheeses will be made. Luckily, they are inexpensive at $4 each or less, because they can't be sanitized after use and hence should be discarded.

Cheese Wax or a Vacuum Sealer

Cheese wax is used to protect the cheese from air while it ages. This is a special kind of wax that melts at a low enough temperature that it won't hurt the cheese when you brush it on. Don't try to substitute canning wax for this! Another alternative is to use a vacuum sealer to seal the wax in an airtight bag from which all air has been evacuated. That's what I do because it is more convenient than waxing.

Cheese Press and Mold

A cheese press is used to knit the curds together into a solid mass while expelling excess whey. There are a variety of designs of varying expense and complexity. A search on the Internet will even reveal many free plans for making your own.

For the batches of cheese in this chapter, I am using a simple plastic press and mold that only cost $21. The downside is that you have to use external weights with it. Still, you can't beat it for the price and ease of use.

Instant-Read Digital Thermometer

Temperatures are critical when making cheese. Some types of cheese require gradually raising the temperature or holding at a certain temperature for a specified time. The best thermometer for such purposes is one that give you an instant and accurate reading. A good digital thermometer is not expensive.

I have a Norpro electronic digital read thermometer/timer that only cost $16. It has programmed cooking temperatures for meat that make it a bit inconvenient, but you can set it for temperature-only so it doesn't beep. The reason I chose that model is because it has a stainless steel probe that makes it easy to clean and it was the only model I could find locally that suited my purpose. You could undoubtedly find other suitable digital thermometers at a nice cookware store.

Dedicated Small Refrigerator

Traditionally, many styles of cheese were quite literally aged in caves. Caves maintain a constant temperature and humidity throughout the year. Most of us don't have access to a suitable cave, and we don't have an area in the house that will reliably maintain a certain temperature for months on end.

If you decide to make cheeses requiring aging, you will find a dedicated refrigerator indispensable. A secondhand dormitory-sized refrigerator and an external thermometer set up to turn it on and off as needed will work perfectly for such an endeavor. A refrigerator dedicated to cheese making is called a "cheese cave."

Ingredients

Not all of these ingredients are needed for all cheeses, but you'll want them on hand. Some of these you likely already have from your excursions into wine and vinegar making.

Vinegar, lemons and tartaric acid

These common acids are used to make soft cheeses via the direct acidification method. In this method, the milk is heated to a certain temperature, a measured amount of acid is added and stirred into the milk, and then the milk clots after a period of time. This clotted milk is poured into a colander lined with cheesecloth, then the cheesecloth is tied into a bag. The bag is hung in a warm place for the whey to drain out of the soft curds. These are among the easiest cheeses to make, and they work especially well as dips and spreads.

Calcium chloride, 30 percent solution

When milk is pasteurized, the calcium ion balance is upset in the milk, and this can impede proper curd formation. A small amount of calcium chloride solution diluted further in distilled water and mixed into the milk can correct this imbalance.

You can order food-grade calcium chloride and make the solution yourself (percentages are by weight!), or you can order the pre-mixed solution from various Internet stores specializing in cheese making supplies.

Calcium chloride, incidentally, is also an ingredient in some ice-melting pellets used on sidewalks and driveways. This is a very crude product that isn't suitable for human consumption, so make sure you get food-grade calcium chloride.

Flaked or canning salt

Salt is used as a flavor enhancer, a bacteriostatic preservative, a modulator for enzymatic action and to help expel water from cheese curds through osmotic pressure. Special "flaked" cheese salt is sold, and you can get that, but canning salt will do as well.

The important thing is to avoid the ordinary salts in the grocery store because not only do many of them contain iodine, they often contain anti-caking agents and other chemicals that could interfere with cheese making. So anything you use should be purely salt.

Starter culture

Starter culture is an inoculant containing a mix of bacteria that eat the lactose in milk and excrete lactic acid. The first purpose of these bacteria is to lower the pH of the milk in order to encourage curd formation. The second purpose is the continuing development of flavor characteristics during the making and aging of the cheese. The nature of the starter culture strongly influences the flavor of the cheese.

Starter cultures are either mesophilic (meaning "medium heat loving") or thermophilic (meaning "high heat loving").

Mesophilic starter cultures work best at room temperature—around 72 degrees. They usually contain at least *Streptococcus lactis*, and many also contain *Streptococcus lactis var. cremoris* along with other lactic acid bacteria such as *L. delbrueckii* subsp. *Lactis, L. lactis* subsp. *lactis* biovar *diacetylactis and Leuconostoc mesenteroides* subsp. *cremoris* .

Streptococcus lactis is used to make buttermilk, so fresh buttermilk with active live cultures can be used to make a mesophilic starter culture for cheese making. Cheeses that begin with a mesophilic starter include farmhouse cheddar, edam, stilton and Monterey Jack, among others.

Thermophilic starter cultures work best at temperatures above 80 degrees and below 130 degrees. A specific recipe will dictate the best temperature within this range for the particular cheese being produced, but the culture works best at 110 degrees. Exceeding 130 degrees may kill a thermophilic culture. It may like heat, but it doesn't want to be scalded or boiled. Thermophilic starters are used to create Swiss and Parmesan cheeses among others. *Streptococcus thermophilus* is a common bacteria in thermophilic starter cultures, but *Lactobacillus delbrueckii* subsp. b*ulgaricus, L. delbrueckii* subsp. l*actis, L. casei* and *L. plantarum* are all used.

Yogurt is made with thermophilic bacteria. One prominent brand of organic yogurt uses six live cultures that include *Streptococcus thermophilus, Lactobacillus delbrueckii subsp. Bulgaricus* and *L. casei*, so not only can plain yogurt be used to make more yogurt, it can also be used to make a thermophilic starter culture for cheese.

So you can buy starter culture in packets from a supplier, or you can make your own from buttermilk and yogurt.

If you opt to buy starter cultures from a cheese making supply store, there are only two important things you need to know: you want the sort of culture called a "direct vat" culture, and you should put it in the coldest part of your freezer the very second you get it. Keep it in the freezer until ready for use.

Rennet

Rennet is an enzyme that was originally derived from the stomachs of suckling animals. It is a proteolytic enzyme that breaks protein bonds in such a way as to turn liquid milk into solid curds. All infant mammals produce rennet. This turns milk into a solid form that stays in the digestive tract longer. That's why, when a baby spits up milk, it has mysteriously turned into a clumpy solid. Babies of all mammals have miniature internal cheese factories.

In practice, animal rennet is a byproduct of veal production. Animal rennet of this sort is extremely perishable and has to be kept refrigerated. It's also pretty expensive.

Rennet can also be made from certain fungi and plants. The sort made from plants has to be made fresh on the spot, which may not be feasible during winter or if you can't find the plants, so for our purposes I am recommending vegetable rennet, which is actually made from fungi. It is inexpensive and if you put it in the freezer it will stay good for at least a year. It comes in tablets that can be divided into halves and quarters, though this must be done carefully as it has a tendency to disintegrate.

Rennet is an extremely powerful enzyme. Tiny quantities will clot gallons of milk. When adding rennet, dissolve the required amount into a quarter cup of distilled water over a period of twenty minutes and then sprinkle it over the surface of the milk. Mix it into the milk using up-down and back-and-forth motions rather than swirling because swirling doesn't mix as efficiently. It's important that rennet be mixed efficiently because otherwise the curd it forms will be of uneven consistency.

Other cultures and enzymes

As your cheese making expertise increases, you'll want to try to make specific types of cheese. Toward that end, you will need different cultures and enzymes.

Lipase is an enzyme that splits milkfat into free fatty acids. It is used in manufacturing feta, blue, mozzarella and provolone cheeses, and develops a characteristic picante flavor in those cheeses. Like rennet, it is extremely powerful. Unless a recipe directs otherwise, use between $\frac{1}{16}$ and $\frac{1}{8}$ teaspoon of the powder per gallon of milk. Dissolve the powder in a half cup of cool water for thirty minutes prior to use. Lipase is added immediately before rennet by sprinkling it on top of the milk and mixing it in using an up-down and back-and-forth motion.

Propionic Shermanii culture is used to create the characteristic holes and flavor of Swiss cheeses. As it ferments, it creates carbon dioxide that expands to create the holes. This is added to thermophilic starter culture at the rate of $\frac{1}{16}$ teaspoon per gallon of milk.

Not all mesophilic or thermophilic starter cultures are created equal. The specific varieties of bacteria make a difference in the ultimate flavor of your cheese. As you learn more about cheese, you will want to try other starter cultures.

How to Have a Lifetime Supply of Buttermilk and Mesophilic Cheese Starter

I have always loved buttermilk. Its thick consistency with sweet tartness is irresistibly delicious, and it makes wonderful pancakes as well! Buttermilk costs 70 percent more than regular milk, so if you like it, you can save money by making your own.

Start with buttermilk from the store that uses live cultures. You can make any amount of buttermilk you'd like from this by re-culturing. To re-culture, put the amount of milk you would like to turn into buttermilk into a stainless steel container. Using a double-boiler or putting the container of milk into a sink of hot water, raise the temperature to 86 degrees.

Hold at 86 degrees for ten minutes, then add ¾ cup of buttermilk per quart of milk. (So that would be one and half cups of buttermilk for a half gallon and three cups of buttermilk for a gallon.) Remove the milk from the heat, cover with cheesecloth to keep out bugs but allow oxygen, and allow it to sit at room temperature undisturbed for twelve hours.

That's it. Really. Just refrigerate it after the twelve hours are up, and it will keep in the refrigerator for up to two weeks. Anytime you want more buttermilk, just repeat this procedure using a bit of the buttermilk you already made and you can have buttermilk forever unless your supply becomes contaminated.

Anytime a cheese recipe calls for "mesophilic starter" you can use your buttermilk at the rate of four ounces of buttermilk per one gallon of milk that you'll be turning into cheese. Though you can freeze this buttermilk for use later to make cheese, I don't recommend that as viability of the culture becomes spotty. I would only recommend using unfrozen buttermilk to make cheese.

How to Have a Lifetime Supply of Yogurt and Thermophilic Starter Culture

Yogurt is a bit more difficult to make than buttermilk because it requires the yogurt-in-progress to be held at a higher temperature for a long time. Though yogurt making machines are sold, this can also be accomplished by arranging to make yogurt on a weekend so you can keep an eye on it. Still, if you find that your family uses a lot of yogurt, you can find some pretty good machines out there for less than $100. Given that yogurt costs anywhere from 300 percent to 400 percent more than milk, if you eat a lot of yogurt you can save a lot of money by making your own.

You can make yogurt successfully from plain yogurt from the store, or you can buy a starter culture for the specific type of yogurt you wish to make. Viili culture produces a thick but mild yogurt similar to what you you mostly see in stores, whereas Piimä culture makes a thinner drinkable yogurt. There are many other cultures available, but no matter how you start your first batch, yogurt cultures are *serial cultures*, meaning that you can continue to propagate them indefinitely simply by using a quantity from the last batch to make the next.

If you decide to use plain yogurt from the store to make more yogurt, please read the ingredient label carefully to make sure you are buying a product made only from milk and cultures. There are some yogurt brands whose "plain" yogurt contains adulterants and other ingredients that won't be helpful. Pectin is often used as a thickener and this is okay.

First, heat your milk to 185 degrees in a double-boiler while stirring often. This is to kill off competing organisms. Then, remove the milk from the heat and allow it to cool to between 105 and 122 degrees. Once it is between these two temperatures, add either your starter culture or the live yogurt. Pour the mixture into cleaned and sterilized quart canning jars, and adjust the two-piece caps for a seal. Keep the temperature of these containers at 105 to 122 degrees for the next eight hours. Then, put your jars in the refrigerator where the yogurt will keep for two weeks.

Maintaining this temperature for so long will be difficult, but the bacteria have a better sense of humor than most regulatory agencies, and as long as you keep the temperature above 98 but below 130, your yogurt will still be fine. There are a lot of things that could work. A mattress heating pad or wrapping the jars in an electric blanket will likely work well; just be sure you keep an eye on things and check frequently so it doesn't overheat. Some ovens will maintain temperatures under 120. A slow-cooker with water on the lowest setting may work. You could set the jars in water in the slow-cooker and keep an eye on the temperature. You could also set them in a sink of water at 115 degrees and as the water cools add a bit of simmering water from a pan on the stove. The key is you'll need to improvise creatively.

The yogurt you create is plain yogurt. You can mix anything with it you'd like—fruit, nuts, granola, sweeteners, etc. If you decide to use it as a thermophilic cheese starter, use four ounces of your fresh plain yogurt per gallon of milk that you will be turning into cheese.

Okay, Let's Make Some Cheese!

Cheese is a pretty involved subject so there were a lot of preliminaries. And even with all of that, a single chapter in a single book can hardly scratch the surface. There are literally hundreds of types of cheese, all of which require differences in procedure, technique or ingredients. Rather than try to cover all of it, I am going to illustrate how to make three representative cheeses that are easily made at home using the ingredients and equipment described. Between these three cheeses, all of the basic techniques will be covered, and you will gain enough experience to experiment and branch out.

I am going to cover a direct acidification soft cheese. Using the same principle, you could make a soft cheese using a different acid. Then, I will demonstrate a soft cheese using a starter culture. Finally, I will demonstrate a minimally aged hard cheese using both starter culture and rennet.

Soft Cheese by Direct Acidification: Queso Blanco

Using a double-boiler, raise the temperature of 1 gallon of milk to 180 degrees while stirring so the milk doesn't precipitate protein. Add ¼ cup of vinegar by slowly dribbling it into the milk while stirring. (You can use distilled vinegar or some of your homemade vinegar from the prior chap-

⊗ Raising the temperature to 180 degrees before adding the vinegar. Notice the cheesecloth boiling on the right.

ter. For a different taste, you can use the juice of three to five lemons.) Continue to stir for ten to fifteen minutes until the milk is completely clotted. If the milk doesn't clot, add up to four more tablespoons of vinegar while mixing for another ten to fifteen minutes.

Meanwhile, prepare the cheesecloth by boiling in a pan of clean water. After boiling, use the cheesecloth to line a colander. Pour the clotted milk into the cheesecloth lined colander, allowing the liquid to go down the sink. After the cheese has cooled, form the cheesecloth

⊗ The clotted milk draining in the colander.

into a bag and hang it over a bowl until liquid no longer drains out of the bag. (This works best at standard room temperature. If the temperature is too cold, the cheese won't drain well. This process should complete within five to seven hours.)

I have a hidden hook ⊗ under my cabinets for hanging cheese to drain.

Scrape the cheese out of the cheesecloth into a clean covered container. You can mix salt and dried herbs such as garlic powder, dill or basil into the cheese as desired. This is what is called a "fresh" cheese, and it should be refrigerated promptly after making and used within a week to avoid spoilage. Because of all the different things you can mix with this, it is a very versatile cheese that can be used for bagels, dips and dressings.

⊗ This easy cheese is great on bagels or mixed with herbs as a vegetable dip.

Soft Cheese using Yogurt Starter Culture: Farmer's Cheese

Add ½ teaspoon of 30 percent calcium chloride solution to ¼ cup of water, and mix this thoroughly with one gallon of milk in a double-boiler. Using the double-boiler, raise the temperature of the gallon of milk to 105 degrees. While the milk is heating, dissolve ¼ of a rennet tablet in ¼ cup of cool non-chlorinated water. Once the milk has reached 105 degrees, keep it

⊗ I'll add the yogurt once the milk reaches 105 degrees. You could also use commercial thermophilic starter culture for this step.

there for five minutes and then add one cup of plain yogurt, stirring it in thoroughly. Keep the temperature at 105 degrees for ten minutes, then turn off the heat.

Once the temperature has dropped to 95 degrees, add the rennet by sprinkling it over the milk and mixing using a gentle up-down and back-and-forth motion. Remove the pot and cover it with the lid. Allow the mixture to set for about an hour and then check for the development of

⊗ Here I am adding the dissolved rennet by pouring it slowly through a slotted spoon for better distribution.

the curd. Check the curd by inserting a clean and sterile blunt object (such as a glass candy thermometer). If it can be withdrawn cleanly without anything sticking to it and the hole it makes doesn't immediately fill with liquid, the curd is ready and you have what is called a *clean break*. If the curd isn't ready, allow the pot to set while covered for another thirty minutes and check again.

Now that you have a clean break, you need to cut the curd. The purpose of cutting the curd is to allow for uniform drainage of the milk liquid (known as whey) from the curd. (Yes, this is the famous "curds and whey"—a primitive predecessor to cottage cheese—likely eaten by Miss Muffet in the nursery rhyme.)

Your goal in cutting the curd is to cut uniform-sized curds for even drainage of whey. In general, the smaller you cut the curds initially, the harder the style of cheese you are making, though there are practical limits. In this case, you are cutting the curd into one-inch cubes. Do this by using your curd knife to first cut a grid at right-angles the entire depth of the curd so you end up with a one-inch checkerboard pattern. Then, you can make the horizontal cuts by positioning your curd knife at a 45-degree angle and cutting along one row of parallel lines in your grid. Though there are all sorts of other ways to do this and special gear you can buy, it is really that simple.

Once your curd is cut, cover the pot again and allow it to sit for another fifteen minutes so some whey can gather at the bottom of the pot. Then, put your pot back into the double-boiler and slowly, over a period of thirty minutes or so, raise the temperature of curds to 110 degrees. As the curds are heating, gently—very gently so you don't break them—use your slotted spoon to stir

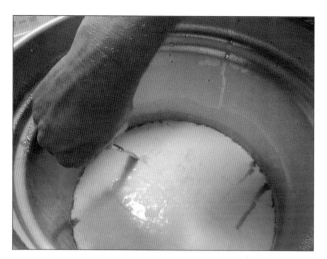

⊗ The horizontal cuts are being made by tracing the grid with the knife held at a 45-degree angle.

⊗ The curds will release whey and shrink. The metal device is the temperature probe.

the curds in such a way as to exchange those on the top with those on the bottom in order to promote even heating. Once the curds have reached 110 degrees, keep at that temperature for thirty minutes while gently mixing every five minutes or so. You will notice the curds getting smaller and the amount of whey increasing. While this process is ongoing, prepare a large piece of cheesecloth by boiling.

Line your colander with a double layer of cheesecloth, and gently pour the curds and whey into the colander. You can save the whey for baking later, add it to your compost pile or just let it go down the sink. (If the whey is greenish, do not be alarmed—this is normal!) Let the curds drain in the colander for an hour or so, and then put the curds into a bowl and salt to taste, turning the curds evenly for uniform distribution. I prefer sea salt for this, but you can also use cheese salt or canning salt. Do NOT use reg-

ular table salt (iodized or not) or you will be sorry because your cheese will be bitter.

Prepare some more coarse cheesecloth by boiling, and then use a double layer to line your clean cheese mold. Add the curds to the mold, fold the cheesecloth over top of the curds, and put the

⊗ The cheese is being mixed with flaked cheese salt.

top of your mold on top of the cheesecloth. Put your mold in a shallow pan (a disposable pie plate would be ideal) to catch whey that is expelled, put two pounds of weight on top of the mold, and place the whole works in the refrigerator.

Once the cheese and press have been allowed to work in the refrigerator for four or five hours, turn the cheese out of the mold, unwrap it, and place in a closed container in the refrigerator. Use within a week.

⌄ I used a 2.5 pound weight on the cheese press, and it worked fine.

⌄ The completed cheese before wrapping it in plastic and storing in the refrigerator.

Hard Aged Cheese Using Mesophilic Starter: New Ipswich Jack

Mix one teaspoon of 30 percent calcium chloride solution into a quarter cup of water, and mix this with two gallons of milk in a double-boiler. Bring the temperature of the milk up to 85-90 degrees, and add either ½ tsp of powdered mesophilic starter or one cup of fresh buttermilk", mixing thoroughly. Cover the mixture and allow it to ripen for thirty to forty minutes while maintaining the temperature between 85 and 90 degrees.

While the mixture is ripening, prepare your rennet solution by mixing ½ tablet of rennet with ¼ cup of cool non-chlorinated water. Once the mixture has ripened, add the rennet solution by dripping it around the milk and mixing it gently but thoroughly using up-down and back-and-forth motions. Continue to maintain a temperature of 85 to 90 degrees while allowing the mixture to sit covered for an hour. At this point, the curds should give you a clean break.

Use your curd cutting knife to cut the cubes into ¼-inch cubes. Continue holding the temperature at 85 to 90 degrees for another forty minutes while gently stirring the curds every five minutes or so. Keep the curds covered while not stirring or checking the temperature. You'll notice the curds shrinking and the volume of whey increasing.

Slowly increase the temperature to 100 degrees over a thirty-minute period while stirring every five minutes or so. This amounts to about two degrees every five minutes. Hold the temperature at 100 degrees for another thirty minutes while stirring every five minutes.

Now, very gently so as not to damage or lose curds, pour off as much of the whey are you can. This may be easier to do with a helper holding back the curds using the slotted spoon while someone else tips the pot over the sink.

Put the pot back into the double-boiler and continue to stir for another thirty minutes while maintaining the temperature at 100 degrees. Meanwhile, prepare a double layer of course cheesecloth by boiling, and use it to line a colander. Pour the curds into the cheesecloth-lined colander. Add two tablespoons of cheese salt and mix the curds gently.

Line your cheese mold with cheesecloth, and then pack the mold closely with the curds. Fold your cheesecloth over top of the curds, install the top of your mold, and put your mold in a shallow pan to catch the whey that will be expelled.

Put a ten pound weight on top of the mold to press the cheese for fifteen minutes. Then, remove the cheese from the mold, take it out of the cheesecloth, flip it over in the cheesecloth, and put it back in the mold.

This time, press the cheese for thirty minutes with a thirty-pound weight. (I recommend just stacking three ten-pound dumbbell weights as ten-pound weights are easier to handle.) Then, take the cheese out of the press, take it out of the cheesecloth, flip it again in the cheesecloth, re-cover it, and put it back in the mold. Press it this time with forty pounds for twelve hours.

After this, take it out of the mold and cheese-cloth, and lay it on a bamboo sushi rolling mat. Flip it on the mat once a day so that it dries evenly. After three to five days, it should be dry to the touch. Once it is dry to the touch, it is ready for aging.

This cheese should be aged at temperatures of from 50 to 60 degrees for anywhere from one to three months. Maintaining such temperatures is a tall order in most homes, but any temperature range from 45 to 68 will do. Luckily (at least in this respect) my house is old and drafty, so I can age cheese in a kitchen cabinet anytime from November to April without need of maintaining a special environment.

If, however, you happen to either live in a warmer climate or have a more energy-efficient home, you will likely need to create a cheese cave from a dorm refrigerator as described earlier in this chapter.

Larger cheeses will form a natural rind that will protect them from invasion, but smaller cheeses (like the size that we have made in this example) will need to be protected by either wax or plastic.

If using plastic, first wash the cheese using vinegar on a clean paper towel to reduce bacterial counts, then seal it in plastic using a vacuum sealer.

If you are using cheese wax, melt it by putting a small stainless steel bowl in a pot of boiling water and adding wax to the bowl. (This bowl will be almost impossible to clean after, so you might want to get a cheap bowl at a department store for this purpose.) After you have washed the cheese with vinegar, use a natural bristle brush to dip in the melted wax and then paint it onto the cheese. Once the wax has hardened on one side of the cheese, turn the cheese over and coat the other side. Check the cheese over thoroughly to make sure you haven't missed any spots and that the cheese is coated uniformly, and then set the cheese aside to age.

⊗ Despite a couple of imperfections in uniformity of coating, this waxed cheese is aging nicely.

After this cheese has aged for a month, it is safe for people who are lactose-intolerant; and after it has aged for two months, it is safe even if made from raw milk.

Experiment and Keep a Log

A lot of times people want to make cheeses like those they buy. If you want to do that, there are a host of sites on the Internet that give specific recipes. But what I would like you to do, instead, is experiment and keep a log. I have covered all the fundamental principles you need to know in order to make your own unique cheeses so long as a few basics are understood. Fresh cheeses have to be refrigerated to be safe and should be used in less than a week. Cheeses made from raw milk have to be aged for at least two months to be safe. Hard cheeses need to be pressed with increasing

amounts of weight. But now, from just the three cheeses I have given in this chapter, I'd like you to think about the variations.

The Queso Blanco recipe was a direct acidification cheese made with vinegar. What would happen if, instead of adding vinegar, you added a mesophilic starter and held it at 88 degrees for an hour before pouring into the cheesecloth? It would certainly taste different!

The soft Farmer's Cheese described earlier used a yogurt (thermophilic) starter culture. What if you used the same technique, but instead used a buttermilk (mesophilic) starter and varied the temperature accordingly?

The Jack cheese recipe is pretty interesting. Don't you wonder what would happen if you used a thermophilic starter and some lipase instead of a mesophilic starter? How would it come out? What would it taste like? What would happen if you added a pint of heavy cream and a tablespoon of wine vinegar to one of the recipes?

So rather than copying other recipes, what I am encouraging you to do is follow the general principles I have described here to make your own and keep notes. I think you will be very pleasantly surprised at how easy it is to make astonishingly good cheese that is uniquely your own and can't be bought anywhere at any price, and that is ultimately what will make cheese making a worthwhile thing for a mini-farmer.

26

Ten Further Secrets of Food Self-Sufficiency

Because I'm interested in helping people take charge of the food portion of their budgets, it's only natural that I'd pay close attention to studies and statistics pertaining to family food budgets. One thing I learned is that over 40 percent of the average household food budget for Americans is spent on eating out.[11]

It stands to reason that if 40 percent of a family's food dollars are spent on food prepared by others, even the most comprehensive approach to producing food at home will have a limited effect. Maximizing the positive economic role of mini-farming requires that a dent be made in the budget spent eating out.

Why do people eat out? Obviously, there are those special celebratory occasions or dates. But most often Americans eat out because they lack the time or energy to prepare food at home. It's a simple mathematical equation. If you get out of work at half-past five, pick up your son at daycare at half-past six and get home at half-past seven with junior's bedtime only a scant ninety minutes away, you simply do not have time to make a meal and clean up after.

11 Duquesne, B., Matendo, S. Lebailley, Ph. (2011), "Profiling Food Consumption: Comparison between USA and EU," Gembloux Agricultural University.

A lot of times this is a chicken-and-egg problem. You go to the grocery store in good faith and buy food you plan to prepare, but you end up working late or there is a last-minute project one of your kids forgot to mention, and you literally end up throwing food away. Why waste money? So eventually you stop buying it because you don't want to take the risk of waste. So not only do you not have the time to cook, but if you did have the time, you wouldn't have the ingredients.

Mini farming takes you a step closer to having the ingredients because of the vast quantities of food you will be putting in the freezer or cans. Almost all of it can be prepared in the microwave in five minutes.

And there is another insidious aspect to the amount of money we spend at the grocery store. Most of that money is spent on pre-made foods and meals, rather than on raw ingredients. Breakfast cereals that you can just pour into a bowl and top with milk have an entire aisle dedicated to them. The same applies to cookies and crackers. There is a pretty large selection of pre-made soups, stews, pastas and more. And then, in the freezer section, the amount of freezer space dedicated to what used to be called "TV dinners" is several times larger than the space devoted to frozen vegetables.

So even the portion of the food budget that isn't spent on eating out is largely dedicated to pre-made foods. Again, the primary reason for this is speed and convenience. Frying up some bacon and eggs in the morning takes more time than pouring some cereal in a bowl, and every minute seems to matter.

I am not a nutritionist or dietitian, but I can certainly see the obvious correlation between what we eat and how healthy (or unhealthy) we

are. All of these convenience foods are not helping our waistlines or health. Though I disagree with the official guidelines of what constitutes "overweight" or "obese," I think most of us realize that as Americans have moved from home-cooked meals to eating out and eating pre-made meals, we have become heavier. I was just reading the label on a canned lasagna marketed by a famous national brand. The ingredients include glyceryl monostearate, modified food starch and high fructose corn syrup. None of these is a deadly poison, but I think it is safe to say that they contribute nothing to the nutritional value of food and you are unlikely to add them to your own cooking.

This seems like an inescapable cycle, but it isn't. There are ways to take charge of this aspect of your food budget so you can become more economically self-sufficient while reserving trips to a restaurant for those truly special occasions. Here are the closely guarded secrets of the thirty-second degree of the inner-sanctum of food self-sufficiency.

Secret #1: Preparing Two Meals Takes the Same Amount of Time as Preparing One

To be 100 percent honest, it doesn't take exactly the same amount of time, but the difference in required time is only marginal. I've done this a lot, and I have concluded that with only a 10 percent increase in the amount of time, you can double the amount of food you prepare when you make a meal.

The reason for this is because most of the time involved in making a meal is spent in getting all the ingredients together, waiting for the stove and cleaning up the mess. The actual time spent chopping and mixing is quite small.

⊗ If you are already cooking, the marginal increase in time to cook other items simultaneously is inconsequential.

When I make London Broil steaks in the oven, I don't put in just enough for the current meal. Instead, I put in enough for two or three meals. It takes the same amount of time. I just put the extra steaks in containers and pop them first in the refrigerator, and then the freezer. Now, in addition to having made the main course for the current meal, I have also made the main course for two other meals. Even better, those main courses only require being zapped in the microwave for five minutes on an evening when I am too time-pressed to cook.

I do the same thing when I make salad. If I make salad for dinner, I get out some containers and just go ahead and put salads in those too and put them in the refrigerator for the next day.

Over time, this builds up. If I do this four days a week—say, Saturday, Sunday, Tuesday and Thursday—I will start building a reserve stash of ready-made main courses. Let me trace this through the week.

On Saturday I make three meals of London Broil steak. I eat one of them and put two in the freezer. On Sunday I make three meals of baked chicken thighs and drumsticks. I eat one of them and put two in the freezer. On Tuesday I make three meals of swordfish steak. I eat one and put two in the freezer. On Thursday I make three meals of pork chops. I eat one and put two in the freezer.

Let's say that on Monday I eat London Broil from the freezer, on Wednesday I eat chicken and on Friday I eat swordfish. At the end of the week, I still have one London Broil, one chicken, one swordfish and two pork chop main courses in the freezer.

This same holds true for practically anything. Mashed turnips, squash, beef bourguignon, stir-fried broccoli and even spaghetti with sauce all freeze fine. They can all be cooked in just five minutes in the microwave.

Secret #2: Freeze Main Courses and Side Dishes Separately

Except for one-dish meals, freezing side dishes separately from main courses will make it easier to maintain dietary variety. If roast beef is served with broccoli one night, it can be served with squash on another night and carrots the next time.

When you do this, you can even customize meals. Would you like salmon or turkey this evening? Would you prefer parsnips, Swiss chard or braised squash as your side?

Secret #3: Use the Weekend to Get a Head Start

You don't have to work and slave all weekend. All you need to do is spend a couple of hours on a weekend day doing something else while a big beef roast or a couple of broiler chickens cook in the oven. While those are cooling, steam a large batch of carrots and fry up some summer squash.

These are the sorts of dishes you simply won't have time to make during the week, but you can often put away more than eight servings of each food cooked, and these will serve as a sort of "go-to" base in your freezer for times where you may be tied up and home too late to cook for an entire week.

⊗ The weekend gives a head start in prepared meals.

Secret #4: Aluminum Baking Pans

I know that using anything disposable is politically incorrect, and with good reason. But at the same time, one major hurdle to cooking is the time required for cleanup, and scrubbing baked-on grease splatters from the edges of a baking pan is pretty time-consuming. And anyone who has ever tried to use a dishwasher to clean baking pans knows it is a futile endeavor.

Recycling aluminum saves 95 percent of the energy of making new aluminum, and every pound of aluminum recycled prevents the mining of four pounds of bauxite. So even though I am encouraging you to use a disposable product, I encourage you to give the pans a quick rinse with soapy water and take them to your local recycling center. This way, most of the harm resulting from using a disposable product is averted.

Using disposable baking pans makes a tremendous difference in terms of efficiency because it eliminates the most time consuming cleanup chore associated with baking. This has a worthwhile psychological effect on your willingness to bake things in the first place. Furthermore, you can often fit several of these in the oven at once, and this serves to get the most out of your baking time.

Secret #5: Use the Cooking Methods Requiring the Least Active Intervention

You've likely noticed that I have mentioned baking a lot. The reason is because baking and broiling are the sorts of cooking methods that allow me to get the food ready, put it in the oven, and then go about other important tasks. The stove has a timer, so it will get my attention when it is needed, but otherwise I am free.

Unless I am making an artisan bread as a special treat, when I make bread, I use a bread machine. My bread machine has a custom cycle that I have programmed, and all I have to do is pour in my ingredients and press two buttons. When the beeper goes off, the bread is ready. To make this even easier, whenever I make bread, I leverage my time by packaging all the solid ingredients (except the yeast) together in a vacuum-sealed bag.

I make three or four bags like this, because the time consuming part is just gathering the ingredients. Now, to bake bread, all I have to do is put water in the bread pan, dump in my mix, put a tablespoon of yeast in the center, and add a tablespoon of butter cut into chunks. Then I push two buttons. Making bread literally takes me less than five minutes. Anytime I have made bread this way, nobody in the family has ever complained of the lack of mono- and di-glycerides either.

Cooking methods such as pan frying and boiling require your active presence, whereas baking and steaming do not. That is not to say you should never pan fry or boil your food. Some food simply tastes better when prepared using those methods. Rather, I am saying you should consider broiling a London Broil steak instead of frying it in a pan, because you can broil a lot of steaks at once while you are busy doing something else.

Secret #6: Disposable Plastic Containers

One of my personal hurdles is that I tend to be forgetful about food containers. Maybe I'll eat my peas and leave the container in the back seat for a couple of days because I forgot to bring it in. At that point, it is unusable for food again. The durable name-brand plastic food containers are expensive, sometimes costing more than $4 each. At that price, being forgetful about three containers can make bringing my own food as expensive as eating out.

The solution is reusable but disposable plastic containers. These cost in the neighborhood of 50 to 70 cents each, so even forgetting three of them is less expensive than buying a burger. If I am not forgetful, they can be reused several times. Likewise, if used for something like fish or spaghetti sauce that often ruins containers, I am still way ahead financially.

The fact a container can't be reused because I allowed food to rot in it or it was used for baked tuna doesn't mean that it has to be thrown away. Disposable plastic containers are made of polypropylene, with recycling resin identification code "5." Recycling these containers will save both energy and fossil fuels while saving space in landfills.

So whenever I've cooked extra, that additional food goes into a container and is placed in either the refrigerator or the freezer. It is simple, fast, inexpensive and most importantly makes it *easy*.

Secret #7: Use Insulated Bags and Cold Packs to Pack Meals

There are three major impediments to packing lunch. The first is that the commute is so long that the food could go bad on the way. The second is the lack of a refrigerator at work. The third is the lack of time to pack the lunch.

The third impediment has already been addressed. Just grab some containers out of the freezer. Packing lunch takes thirty seconds. It could take a bit longer if you also take some time to throw in an apple and a banana; but even so, that's less time than the drive-thru window, so you are going to be saving time too.

The first and second impediments are answered with insulated bags and cold packs. Insulated bags are the new "lunch box" and they work far better than their ancestors. The reusable cold packs available in stores for as little as $1 apiece, when enclosed in your insulated bag, will keep your food cold and fresh for a long time.

Secret #8: Adopt Time-Saving Cooking Methods

Other than baking, I should also mention pressure cooking, crock pots, outdoor grilling and thermos cookery.

Very often, people forget their outdoor grills except for the occasional burger or family event, but grills offer the advantage of reducing cleanup of bakeware. Most meats and vegetables can be grilled; if not directly then wrapped in aluminum foil. Cleanup time is reduced.

A good stainless steel pressure cooker is not cheap, but it is a wise long-term investment because it can dramatically compress cooking times for roasts, stews, beans and other foods that can often require hours to cook. I have a Fagor™ pressure cooker, and using the included recipe book I've cooked dried bean and meat stew dishes in less than an hour that would otherwise take practically all day. You can cook a two pound beef roast, including prep time, in thirty-five minutes.

Crock pots have been around for a long time, but seem to have fallen off the radar for most people. If you get a crock pot with an insert (something I highly recommend), you can get the food ready the night before and leave the insert in the refrigerator. In the morning, just put the insert in the device and turn it on. You'll come home to the aroma of a delightful slow-cooked meal. Crock pots come with recipe books and there are a good many recipes on the Internet. I use mine for thickening homemade ketchup and spaghetti sauce as well.

Very few people have heard of thermos cookery, and that's too bad. Cooking with a thermos is one of the most time and energy saving methods of cooking imaginable—especially for whole grains such as wheat, dried beans and other foods that would require overnight soaking and long periods of cooking on the stove. If filled with food heated to boiling, a good thermos will still maintain a temperature exceeding 160 degrees (the internal temperature to which meats need to be cooked in order to be safe) twelve hours later, and a temperature exceeding 140 degrees (hot enough to kill pathogens) twenty-four hours later.

You can't use just any old thermos. You want one that is lined with stainless steel rather than glass or plastic, and with a wide mouth. I use a Stanley Aladdin, but have also used a good Thermos brand stainless steel bottle for many years. You can find hundreds of recipes on the Internet and once you get the hang of the underlying principles, you'll soon be adapting. I mainly used mine to get my whole wheatberry and oatmeal with strawberry and banana ready. A hot, delicious breakfast was ready for me the moment I was ready!

Secret #9: Make Your Own Drinks

It adds up over time. Coffee with breakfast ($2.50), a soda with lunch ($1.74) and some bottled water on the way home ($1.29). It adds up to $110/month. You can make a large dent in that by getting an iced tea maker, a coffee maker, some coffee and tea or herbal teas and a couple of stainless steel beverage bottles.

Like a coffee maker, an iced tea maker offers the advantage of making the iced tea in one step. Mine only cost $22, so it paid for itself in short order.

Stainless steel beverage bottles are durable, easily cleaned, and are unlikely to accumulate crud that would make drinks stored in them unpalatable. Their chemical makeup renders them impervious to acidic drinks, so that the metal isn't leached into the beverage. I got mine for $1 each at an end-of-season sale.

⊗ This iced tea maker has paid for itself many times over by reducing the purchase of bottled products.

Secret #10: Meals in a Jar

My local supermarkets have large sections dedicated to what could be called "meals in a jar." These include canned soups, pastas, stews and similar items. But when you look at the ingredients and nutritional content, most of these are little more than caloric energy—mostly from **sugar** or carbohydrate.

All editions of the *Ball Blue Book of Preserving* that were printed in the past couple of decades include sections on canning your own stocks, soups, stews and even baby foods. Likewise, in *Mini Farming: Self Sufficiency on ¼ Acre*, I give guidelines that will allow you to can practically any prepared food made of mixed ingredients. This way, you need not rely on a particular recipe in a cookbook. If your family is used to meals in a jar, you can easily make your own. And those that you make yourself will be far superior to anything you purchase in terms of the quality of ingredients.

Of course, making and canning food can be time-consuming, which sort of defeats the purpose. I use two methods for dealing with this. The first is that I keep a stash of cleaned jars handy. If I make a good stew, I can dump it in the jars, heat up the canner, and can a few jars right away. I have both a large and a small pressure canner, and the smaller one is no larger than the pot in which I cook pasta.

The second is that I freeze rather than can. If I just made a delicious bowl of glop but don't have the time to even heat up the canner, I dump my glop into a disposable plastic container destined for the freezer.

Canned foods can be eaten right out of the can or require only sixty seconds to heat up in the microwave, whereas frozen foods take five minutes or more to be properly heated in a microwave. So in aggregate, you will tend to save time overall by canning instead of freezing, but you have to grab your time where you can and no matter the means used, anything made at home contributes to your food self-sufficiency.

The Secret That Is Not a Secret

Before I finish this book and drop you into a seemingly endless alphabetical index, I want to share one other thing I consider to be important. As an engineer, you could say that my daily task is to accomplish things that others would consider impossible. Because of this, I'm likely to have an almost naively positive attitude about what is or isn't possible. Even so, I believe that too often people invent their own limitations from their own untested assumptions about things they "can't" or "could never" do.

One of my goals in writing about mini-farming and self-sufficiency topics is to show people just how easy it really is for you to achieve levels of self-sufficiency that most people would deem "impossible." And I hope that within these pages I've also imparted some ideas that will help make things easy.

The last secret I wish to divulge in this book isn't a secret at all: you *can*. You *can* grow a substantial portion of your own food, you *can* make your own wine or cheese, you *can* reduce your dependence on eating out and quite frankly if you are willing to work at it, you *can* achieve nearly anything you believe is within your capacity.

From Markham Farm to your home: best wishes to you and yours!

Index of Recipes

Alphabetical Index

Lettuce, 52, 60, 67-68, 70, 72-73, 133, 163
Lime, 5-8, 14-15, 36-37, 51, 90, 97, 100, 122, 135
Lipase, 227, 235
Lipid supply, 191
Liquid fish fertilizer, 8-9
Listeria, 221
Lodging, 53
Long-day, 94
Lovage, 75, 79
Lutein, 27
Lycopene, 85, 141

M

Macronutrients, 6-7, 96, 113, 122, 153
Magnesium, 5-8, 10, 113, 27, 192
Malic acid, 189, 195, 202
Malt, 209
Manganese, 10, 27, 41, 131, 151
Manual rotary cultivator, 176
Marjoram, 79-80
Melomel, 196
Melons, 59, 85-92, 147, 214
Mesclun, 68, 71-72, 161
Mesophilic, 223, 226-228, 233, 235
Metheglin, 196
Methyl bromide, 124
Micronutrients, 9-10, 42, 51, 104, 122
Microorganisms, 4, 7-8, 35, 78
Milk , 23, 52, 54-55, 116, 134, 219-223, 225-230

Milky spore disease, 23, 52
Miner's lettuce, 70
Minerals, 9-11, 13-14, 27, 33, 60, 68, 70, 72, 100, 131, 141, 151, 153, 196
Mini farming self sufficiency, x-xi, 3, 9, 11, 243
Mini farming, v, x-xii, 10-11, 14, 25, 52, 90, 99, 175, 238, 243
Mini-seedmaster, 165
Mint, 75-76, 79-80
Molasses, 195-196
Molybdenum, 10, 59
Moon and stars, 86
Mosaic, 37, 86, 115, 134-135, 145
Mosaic virus, 37, 86, 115, 134-135, 145
Moth, 36, 41, 52 135-136, 141
Mulch, 4, 15, 30, 44, 62, 78, 86-87, 98-99, 133-135, 155
Mulching, 15, 87, 98
Muskmelon, 86-87, 89-90
Must, 184, 186, 189-99, 201-02, 205-06, 211, 212
Mustard, 17-18, 35, 67-68, 70, 80, 82, 84, 124, 144, 149, 155, 160, 175

N

Nantes, 42
Nectar, 196, 200, 211
Neem, 24, 29, 36, 87, 134
New potatoes, 121, 126, 128
Niacin, 131, 151
Nickel, 10

Nitric oxide synthesis, 85
Nitrogen, 4, 7, 9-10, 21, 23, 25, 35, 42, 51, 68, 86-87, 96-97, 100, 103-04, 143, 191-92
Normal sugary, 50
Npk, 60, 86
Nuclear polyhedrosis virus, 36
Nylon straining bags, 187-88

O

Oak casks, 184
Oak chips, 206, 213-14
Oak cubes, 212-13
Ocean minerals, 11
Old-fashioned green beans, 245
Omega-3 fatty acids, 69, 131
Omega-6, 151
Onion maggots, 100
Onions, 31, 39, 78, 82, 93-98 100-101, 103, 108, 124, 133, 144, 149, 163, 177, 220
Orach, 250
Oregano, 75, 79-80, 216-17
Outbreeding, 55, 127, 154
Oxalic acid, 30, 70
Oxygen, 3, 7, 55, 78, 184-85, 194, 202, 204, 211-12, 228

P

Pantothenic acid, 27, 131
Paper clip, 186
Parsley, 42, 72, 75, 80-81
Parsnip, 123, 239, 245